The Family and the Nation

THE FAMILY AND THE NATION

Gender and Citizenship in Revolutionary France, 1789–1830

JENNIFER NGAIRE HEUER

Cornell University Press

ITHACA AND LONDON

First printing, Cornell Paperbacks, 2007
First published 2005 by Cornell University Press

Printed in the United States of America

Library of Congress Cataloging-in-Publication Data

Heuer, Jennifer, 1969–
    The family and the nation : gender and citizenship in revolutionary
France, 1789–1830 / Jennifer Heuer.
        p. cm.
    Includes bibliographical references and index.
    ISBN-13: 978-0-8014-4286-5 (cloth : alk. paper)
    ISBN-13: 978-0-8014-7408-8 (pbk. : alk. paper)

    1. France—History—1789–1815. 2. France—History—Restoration,
1814–1830. 3. France—Social conditions—18th century. 4. France—
Social conditions—19th century. I. Title.
    DC158.8.H48 2005
    342.4408'3—dc22   2004030166

Cornell University Press strives to use environmentally
responsible suppliers and materials to the fullest extent
possible in the publishing of its books. Such materials include
vegetable-based, low-VOC inks and acid-free papers that are
recycled, totally chlorine-free, or partly composed of nonwood
fibers. For further information, visit our website at
www.cornellpress.cornell.edu.

Cloth printing   10 9 8 7 6 5 4 3 2 1
Paperback printing   10 9 8 7 6 5 4 3 2 1

Contents

v

Conclusion: Reversals and Lasting Contradictions   *192*

Acknowledgments

Acknowledgments are simultaneously the easiest and the hardest part of this book to complete: they are easiest in the pleasure of recognizing friends and colleagues who helped this work come into being; hardest in adequately thanking all those whose help has been essential.

I have been inspired by many who have read the manuscript, or key parts of it, at various stages. William Sewell has shown remarkable confidence in this project since its earliest incarnations. Suzanne Desan and Peter Sahlins have offered intensely knowledgeable and thoughtful comments on various aspects of the work. David Bell's feedback was particularly useful in thinking about constructions of the nation during the Terror, while Judith Miller and Howard Brown's suggestions helped refine my work on the late 1790s. I have deeply welcomed Anne Verjus' enthusiasm and keen intellectual engagement in conversations both literal and electronic. Alyssa Sepinwall showed a generous willingness to read large chunks of writing on short notice. Conversations with Elisa Camiscioli helped clarify my understanding of the long-term stakes of women's citizenship and immigration. Ian Barrow and Louisa Burnham also gave insightful suggestions. The comments of the anonymous reviewers for Cornell University Press were deeply helpful in the later stages of the project.

I also want to thank those who offered probing questions and astute comments in various forums, including meetings of the Society for French Historical Studies, the Western Society for French History, and the Berkshire Conference of Women's Historians, and talks sponsored by the Minda de Gunzburg Center for European Studies, the Workshop on Modern France at the University of Chicago, and Middlebury College.

Generous financial support for the book at different stages came from the American Philosophical Society, the American Historical Association, the Five College Women's Studies Research Center, the French Ministry of

Foreign Affairs, the Société des Professeurs Français et Francophones d'Amérique, the University of Chicago, and Middlebury College.

Earlier versions of some parts of this book were published in articles and essays. Parts of chapter 3 appeared in *French Politics, Culture, and Society* 17, nos. 3–4 (1999); while a segment of chapter 4 first saw light in *Taking Liberties: Problems of a New Order from the French Revolution to Napoleon,* edited by Howard Brown and Judith Miller (Manchester University Press, 2002). The latter appears here by permission of Manchester University Press. Some of chapter 7 was published in French in *Clio: Histoire, femmes et sociétés* 12 (2000). An article in French cowritten with Anne Verjus and published in *Annales historiques de la révolution française,* no. 327 (2002), represents an early attempt to work through some of the themes of the book.

There is another level of support, harder to quantify but equally crucial: those who made research and writing a joy. I owe a tremendous debt to the entire Garry family, especially Jean-Marc. Not only did their hospitality make it logistically possible for me to pursue research, but their warmth and enthusiasm made doing so a delight. Closer to home, my family has given me constant support and sustenance throughout this venture. My parents, Earl and Berys Heuer, instilled in me a love of learning and the confidence to do what interested me, both intellectually and professionally. Although my work must often have appeared as mysterious to her as monkeys' brains have to me, my sister Hilary's phone calls have kept me cheered during the seemingly endless process of researching and writing.

My husband, Brian Ogilvie, has lived with this project from its inception to its final form, tolerated frequent interruptions of his own work, and read innumerable drafts with patience, humor, and interest. I can only begin to express my profound appreciation for his love and companionship.

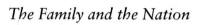

The Family and the Nation

Introduction

In 1794, at the height of the French Revolution, one young woman found herself writing to the National Convention. Five years earlier, she would undoubtedly have had little reason to petition the government. But now, in the midst of the Terror, she stood accused of leaving the Republican nation without permission. One of thousands charged with the crime of emigration, she argued that she was still a loyal French woman who "could not have lost the quality of a French citizen by a momentary sojourn." Though writing under the protective guise of anonymity, the young woman used her personal circumstances to excuse her absence from French territory. She focused first on her familial situation, contending that her father and husband had acted together to force her to leave home against her will and had prevented her from returning to her beloved land of liberty. Almost as an afterthought, she also referred to her gender, claiming that girls and young women were unlikely to harm the "sovereignty of the people" and that she should be treated leniently because of her age and sex.[1]

The young émigrée's plea provides one window onto a set of cases concerning nationality and citizenship in late eighteenth- and early nineteenth-century France. If we turn from the tribunals of the Terror to the Parisian civil courts of 1796, we find a businessman from Hamburg and a famous French actress battling for custody of their illegitimate child. M. Hoppé, the businessman, contended that although he was a foreigner, he was a father and thus capable of exercising all the legal rights of a father in France. His opponents countered that the child's inherent Frenchness trumped paternal authority: "The girl whose upbringing is being disputed is born French, of a French mother; our laws owe her protection; she cannot be abandoned to a foreigner without running the risk of being torn from her country [*patrie*] and all the advantages that her country guarantees her."[2]

I

Now let us jump ahead in time to the early days of the Bourbon Restoration in Strasbourg's city hall, where the recently appointed mayor was writing to his superiors. Unlike the young woman accused of emigration and the father eager to bring up his illegitimate child, the mayor was not concerned—at least not overtly—with his own status. Instead, he wanted to stop indigent German tailors, shoemakers, and weavers from settling in Strasbourg, opening up shop, and petitioning for French citizenship. But to date, he had been unable to do so, primarily because the laws of citizenship appeared to be malfunctioning. While the Napoleonic Civil Code mandated that French women who wed foreigners became foreign themselves, the mayor contended that immigrant men were actually using their marriages to French women to establish themselves in France: "contrary to the jurisprudence of all peoples, it has been the woman who established the residence or domicile of her husband, since it seemed to suffice here that he [an immigrant man] marry a Strasbourgoise or French woman in order to receive all the rights of citizenship [*droits de la cité*]."[3]

What do these cases have in common? They suggest, first of all, that family and citizenship rights were deeply entangled in the revolutionary era and early nineteenth century, and that membership in the nation had potentially different significance for men and women. In itself, this entanglement should scarcely surprise us. Family and citizenship are almost inevitably overlapping domains. From the Greek city-states of classical antiquity to the colonial Dutch West Indies to twenty-first century America, membership in a national community has involved genealogical principles. Even systems based on *jus soli* (law that privileges birthplace in determining national status) must take into account the effects of both birth and marriage on an individual's status. Moreover, metaphors of authority and solidarity are often transported from the family to the state, and vice versa.

But the three cases above, like many others revealed in the legislative debates, court cases, political pamphlets, naturalization records, and police records of the era, are not about a neatly balanced set of interrelationships. Instead, they reveal explicit conflicts between the rights and duties associated with the personal status of "French citizen" and those associated with men and women's legal position within the family. French revolutionaries dramatically transformed the significance of both family and citizenship rights, often in ways that their predecessors would have had difficulty even imagining. But because they did not address these domains together, they created fundamental contradictions. Women and, to a lesser extent, children had a set of rights and duties because of their individual status as members of the French nation. However, despite important changes in family law, women remained, both socially and legally, dependents within the household. This contradiction between independent citizenship status and dependence within the home fueled unprecedented conflicts between familial and national bonds. As representatives of the state and ordinary men and women sought to negotiate these conflicts during the tumultuous decades of the Revolution and early nineteenth century, they not only exposed these contradictions but also repeatedly challenged the significance of new institutions and laws in both domains.

Yet these recurrent challenges took different forms from 1789 to 1830. The accused émigrée, the competing parents of an illegitimate daughter, and the beleaguered Strasbourg mayor all struggled to understand the relationship between family and citizenship and to define it to their advantage. But they also had very different conceptions of the family and the state, the benefits and obligations of national citizenship, and its relevance to men and women. As revolutionaries and their successors attempted to exploit or resolve tensions between family and national bonds, they both redefined these institutions for their own purposes and faced the legacies of their predecessors' actions. Their assumptions and choices in changing political climates would ultimately shape institutions of family, nationality, and citizenship far beyond French borders. Indeed, their influence would stretch across the world, affecting places as diverse as the Netherlands, Argentina, the United States, and colonial Africa.

Remaking Citizens

Revolutionaries dramatically redefined the nature and significance of membership in a nation-state. Indeed, one scholar, Rogers Brubaker, has claimed that revolutionaries invented "national citizenship."[4] The term is an anachronism, as are many other modern variants. Eighteenth-century legislators and administrators did not use the word "nationality" (*nationalité*); Madame de Staël first introduced it to France in 1807, and it became widespread only in the late 1820s or early 1830s.[5] Similarly, although the word "citizen" (*citoyen*) was ubiquitous during the Revolution, men and women rarely used the abstraction "citizenship" (*citoyenneté*).[6] National citizenship, however, serves as convenient shorthand for a series of new laws and institutions.

First of all, legislators changed the basis of legal membership in the state. "French citizen" was a personal marker of membership in a national community in both Old Regime and revolutionary France. Referred to as an individual "title" or "quality" (usage that I will follow in this book), it could apply irrespective of their age or sex. However, before the Revolution, "French citizen," or its formal juridical equivalent, *régnicole*, conferred only a limited number of rights, primarily the right to bequeath and inherit property. These rights were visible not because they were perceived to be common to French subjects, but because they were denied to foreigners.[7] Apart from a few royal edicts, there was no common law in prerevolutionary France. Instead, the system of privilege or private law accorded status and rights to people on the basis of their membership in specific groups, such as artisanal guilds and professional organizations, towns and regional assemblies, and religious organizations. In the summer of 1789 the Constituent Assembly began to dismantle this system, issuing the famous Declaration of the Rights of Man and Citizen and formally abolishing privilege. These actions suddenly made the individual citizen, rather than the corporate group, the bearer of new and uniform rights.[8]

This legal transformation accompanied territorial and cultural redefinitions. Revolutionaries tried to replace a vision of sovereignty founded on royal jurisdiction with one of territorial belonging.[9] The territory of "France" itself had not been completely defined in the Old Regime. Internal customs barriers divided the kingdom, while towns and regions zealously guarded local privileges and rights. Foreign and ecclesiastical jurisdictions persisted inside France: Avignon still belonged to the pope, German princes controlled enclaves in Alsace, while the city of Mulhouse remained an independent city-state. The governments of the Revolution dismantled internal distinctions along with other privileges, annexed foreign territories inside France, and marked the new homogeneity of French territory by creating new geographic units, departments, to replace the older system of provinces.

As revolutionaries unified French territory, they also sought to create a new community, the nation.[10] Certainly, France had long existed as a powerful monarchical state with an elaborate apparatus of royal and national symbols. But the makers of a new social and political order transformed the meaning of the term "nation" to refer to a community of citizens who together formed a sovereign entity. They established a constitution and a uniform code of law for all and created a set of institutions, including schools, projects for language reform, theatrical performances, and festivals, designed to "regenerate" France and create a new collective culture. In the process, they turned the spotlight on membership in a national community as a whole, and on the distinction between citizens and outsiders. As Gérard Noiriel has suggested, the new unity of French territory combined with the abolition of legal differences among citizens within France to highlight potential distinctions between French and foreign.[11]

Finally, revolutionaries transformed the political nature of citizenship. Beginning in 1789 inhabitants of France claimed the right to act as citizens and to participate directly in their government. Three years later, in 1792, they declared a republic, prosecuting and ultimately beheading their former king. The subsequent radicalization of the Revolution and the violence of the Terror in 1793 and 1794 expanded both the rights and obligations associated with membership in the nation. Citizenship was, at least in theory, an individual act of will, an expression of personal patriotism and allegiance to the nation.

These dramatic transformations, however, are difficult to relate to gender and family relations without considering many questions often left aside by scholars of national citizenship in France. What did different dimensions of "national citizenship" actually mean for men and women? How, specifically, did aspects of family law or concepts of the family support or conflict with these changes? Why? What happened to the gendered significance of membership in the nation through the tumultuous years of the Revolution and the institutionalization of a more conservative social and political order under Napoleon and the Bourbon Restoration?

Gender and Citizenship

To answer these questions, we need to combine approaches from several different domains. Work on gender and political citizenship gives us one set of useful tools. In disciplines ranging from political science to philosophy, history to anthropology, writers have explored different possible meanings of membership in the nation for men and women. Some have suggested that the "social contract" at the basis of modern nations often depended on hidden "sexual contracts" and familial relations between men and women.[12] Others have argued about how different kinds of social and governmental structures and definitions of citizenship have made it easier or harder for women to demand participation in the state.

The French Revolution is one of the flashpoints of such discussion. Feminist scholars have debated passionately the consequences of the Revolution, a debate usually framed in terms of whether it emancipated women or fundamentally excluded them from political rights. There is strong evidence for both interpretations. New concepts of citizenship in the Revolution made it possible for women to claim unprecedented rights and to participate in moments of dramatic political action. As William Sewell has noted, the category of *citoyenne*, the feminine form of "citizen," was not created as a means to enfranchise women. It appeared instead because *citoyen* was meant to be a universal designation and thus required a feminine counterpart. But it unintentionally created a space that legitimated women's claims to be vital members of the sovereign nation.[13] Olympe de Gouges's 1791 *Declaration of the Rights of Woman and Citizen* is one of the most famous articulations of this new vision, as is the founding of the Society of Revolutionary Republican Women in 1793. In many cases, women, particularly in the lower classes, acted politically even when they were not officially accorded political rights. They attended political assemblies, were involved in the direction of Parisian *sections* (key neighborhood-based organizations), and led specific political actions, from the October Days march of 1789 to the invasion of the National Assembly during Prairial Year III (May 1795).

Some scholars have lauded such unprecedented claims and actions and have traced their repercussions throughout the nineteenth and twentieth centuries.[14] However, the predominant trend in the historiography on women and the Revolution has been to look at the "limits of citizenship," to use Olwen Hufton's deft phrase.[15] In 1793, after a dramatic conflict between market women and the Society of Revolutionary Republican Women, the National Convention prohibited women's political associations. Following a series of popular uprisings in Prairial Year III, women were forbidden to enter political tribunals or to participate in any political assembly, while any public gathering of more than five women risked arrest. Although scholars have offered very different interpretations of the immediate causes and repercussions of these laws, most emphasize the lasting exclusion of women from the political sphere.[16] In prerevolutionary France, the legal rights of both men and women had been determined by their social position as well by their sex; after the Revolution, male citizens were to be considered legally equal, but women were not.

Both scholars who see the Revolution as emancipating for women and those who see it as disenfranchising, however, have focused on the political dimensions of citizenship, leaving aside legal, territorial, and civil aspects of national belonging. But this focus distorts the issue as it appeared to contemporaries, who were often forced to consider the multiple dimensions of men's and women's relationship to the nation. Even when thinking about seemingly apolitical issues—like custody rights or the obligation to remain on French territory—men and women often found themselves debating precisely what national citizenship meant for both sexes, and especially what obligations it entailed.[17] As we will see, they often lacked a rigorous vocabulary for distinguishing among legal membership in a national community, patriotic duty, and the exercise of political rights. Jurists in the Old Regime had often employed a specific vocabulary for referring to legal membership in the nation, including expressions such as *régnicole* or "reputed French" (*réputé français*). But in many cases, especially after the declaration of a republic in 1792, revolutionaries simply substituted "citizen" as an all-purpose word to connote both legal Frenchness and the exercise of political rights. I contend that such ambiguity opened the way for passionate contestation not only over entitlement to political rights but also over the rights, duties, and precise status of "French citizens."

Many historians have also focused specifically on the actions of women in the Revolution or on the ways in which the gendering of citizenship excluded women. Yet gender and family relations potentially affected *both* women's and men's legal and social identities as citizens. If the authority of the *paterfamilias* could influence or conflict with the rights and obligations of legally subordinate members of the household, the converse was also true: the acquisition or loss of citizenship status could affect a man's authority over his family as well as his claims to social and political rights. Sometimes governments recognized and even sanctioned such connections, as certain constitutions made marriage to a French woman a means for a foreign man to become French, or required that Frenchmen appointed to certain political offices or exercising certain political rights be married. However, as the frustration of the Strasbourg mayor suggests, although authorities often did not anticipate tensions between family and citizenship bonds for women *or* for men, they were forced to confront persistent and pervasive conflicts.

Scholars also tend to stop short with the dramatic events of the early Revolution and the Terror. This is particularly the case among historians concerned with the exclusion of women from citizenship, following on Joan Landes' influential proclamation that "by 1793 women were banned from active *and* passive participation in the political sphere."[18] With some important exceptions, even those scholars who insist that the Revolution created new rights and opportunities for women usually concentrate on the years 1789–1793.[19] Yet although contemporaries were often obsessed with "ending the Revolution," it was a goal that was easier to proclaim than to realize. This book will show that fixing the long-term significance of revolutionary innovations in national citizenship for both sexes was particularly difficult.

Nationality and Foreigners

Work specifically on "nationality," or on the legal identification of foreigners and citizens, provides some further tools for understanding various meanings of national citizenship and their potential long-term relevance for men and women. Social scientists have analyzed the formal mechanisms for becoming French and scrutinized potential distinctions between juridical and political forms of citizenship, as well as contemporary conflations of the two.[20] They have shown both how the contexts of revolution, war, and territorial expansion could make it imperative to identify members of the nation and the practical difficulties of doing so.[21] Many also give a longer narrative than historians of gender, often focusing on very different events and very different points of the revolutionary era: they often see the Napoleonic Civil Code—rather than the Terror of 1793–94—as the key turning point.[22]

However, most big theories about nationality and national citizenship— like those put forth by Charles Tilly, Rogers Brubaker, and Gérard Noiriel—have rarely taken into account the person as a gendered category.[23] As Lora Wildenthal has pointed out in a study of German colonialism, many such theories "assume families which share a homogeneous national origin, not individuals as the objects of citizenship law," and do not consider whether or how laws applied differently to men and women.[24] This assumption has not only obscured the relevance of new institutions of national citizenship for women; it has also concealed the ways in which these institutions affected men, making it difficult to understand both their full significance and their evolution from the start of the Revolution through the consolidation of a new regime.

With a few important exceptions, most studies devoted explicitly to nationality or national citizenship in France have also focused on high political and legal discourse, like the debates of the National Assembly or the relevant articles of the Napoleonic Civil Code.[25] This focus on the letter of the law without also looking at its application has both contributed to and reinforced a blindness to the gendered significance of new institutions. The most vital consequences of French citizenship status for ordinary men and women often became apparent only when laws were applied or challenged. This is the case for our opening stories; legislators concerned with transforming the foundations of France's political order rarely imagined that new categories of national citizenship would be used to decide the possibility of escaping the guillotine during the Terror, the custody of an illegitimate child, or the right to open up shop in a frontier town. Unlike many previous studies, this book will exploit archives rarely considered together to show that the gendered salience of new laws and categories depended on their application. Legislators often used the generic terms "French" or "citizen," clarifying whether laws applied to one or both sexes only when pushed to do so by those affected by the measures in question.

Family and Nation

Historians of gender thus tend to focus on women's political citizenship during the height of the Revolution and to set aside other possible elements of national citizenship; conversely, historians of national citizenship often neglect issues of gender and practice. Combining these various approaches promises to help us better understand both. But there is another critical piece of the puzzle: the family. In transforming the family, lawmakers consecrated many of the same principles that undergirded new institutions of national citizenship, especially the importance of individual rights and contracts that could be both freely made and freely dissolved. In the Old Regime, a married woman's civil, political, and national identity had been legally subordinated to her husband's, while rights even of adult children were similarly restricted. Legislators began to dismantle this system beginning in 1789. The different governments of the Revolution established unprecedented ways of changing familial ties, making it possible for couples to divorce, parents to adopt, and children born out of wedlock to demand a share of their parents' estate. But if the same principles often shaped new institutions of both citizenship and family relations, there were also crucial differences. Although revolutionary lawmakers limited marital and paternal authority, they did not destroy it as they destroyed the political order of the Old Regime. Indeed, governments also suggested that, once shorn of abuses, such domestic authority could be both legitimate and benevolent.

Like scholars interested in nationality, those who work on the family see the Napoleonic Civil Code as crucial. Yet their interpretation of the Code is radically different. Rather than seeing it as a landmark in codifying and perpetuating key revolutionary institutions, many historians of the family view the Code as a reversal of revolutionary freedoms and innovations. By the late 1790s, and especially by the Napoleonic era, writers, lawmakers, and politicians often not only accepted the legitimacy of paternal authority but actively sought to promote hierarchical family relations.[26]

Yet just as contemporary lawmakers did not systematically address family and citizenship together, historians have rarely considered these simultaneously interconnected and divergent developments together. Few look both at changes in the civil law of the family and at women's relationship to political rights, except to point out the apparent paradox of the recognition of women as civil agents and their exclusion from politics during the Revolution.[27] As Suzanne Desan has noted, historians of family law have seldom examined how changing legal structures affected the relationships between the sexes, while feminist historians have usually ignored the question of women's new legal status in the family.[28] But as this book will demonstrate, thinking about family, gender, and nation separately makes it hard to see the ways in which institutional and social changes in each domain reinforced or challenged one another—to understand, for example, apparently contradictory aspects of the Civil Code and the practical challenges of putting it into effect.

Family was also connected to nation on another critical level: that of metaphor. Revolutionaries often spoke of the nation as the "great family." Immigrants were "adopted" by the French nation; émigrés were punished in part because of their "parricidal" actions toward the family of their *patrie*. However, despite innovative and controversial work on the general uses of familial metaphors during the Revolution, few historians have contemplated the ways in which such conceptions influenced the way contemporaries thought about national citizenship.[29] Yet revolutionaries and their successors made particular uses of this metaphor, seeing the nation as a family writ large that potentially took priority over literal family bonds—or, alternatively, as a composite of individual families that served as intermediaries between women and children and their country.

Revolutionary Reverberations

But when and why did ideas about the appropriate relationships between family and nation or the relevance of national citizenship actually change? Historians of gender and political rights give us a series of intriguing answers, attributing developments to individual activism or misogyny, confrontations between different revolutionary groups, or the philosophical dynamics of republicanism. Others have traced how laws concerning nationality and citizenship or the family changed during the 1790s, reflecting both general political vicissitudes and the agendas and interactions of particular lawmakers. But these interpretations, though often suggestive, often leave us wondering what happened outside legal chambers and political assemblies, and what happened not only during the height of the Revolution itself, but also through Napoleon's empire and the return of a monarchy. Were skirmishes over the significance of national citizenship after 1794 simply codas or reactions to earlier developments?

Here this work contributes to a growing body of research on the consequences of the Revolution. Historians of the French Revolution in general, like those interested specifically in gender, have traditionally focused on the years from the storming of the Bastille to Robespierre's fall from power. Yet scholars have begun to turn more systematically to the late 1790s, as well as the Napoleonic era and the Bourbon Restoration. They argue that political and social developments after the Terror were often both innovative and influential.[30] Subsequent generations had to confront the legacies of their predecessors' ideas and actions, but they also profoundly reshaped these legacies. Neither the experiences of the Terror nor the Napoleonic Code—nor even the establishment of the Napoleonic empire or the Bourbon Restoration—completely consolidated or broke with previous developments.

Many interested in long-term change have focused on political institutions or the administration of the state, often following on Tocqueville's claim that revolutionary changes concealed continuous state centralization.[31] The practices surrounding national citizenship, however, provide us with a particularly useful lens for considering developments throughout this tumultuous era. All governments of the era had to define membership in the nation, and to do so as the territorial, social, and political meanings of the nation shifted repeatedly and dramatically. They also had confront the implications, both intended and unexpected, of their predecessors' actions and definitions, especially when they tried to put new laws into effect. Interpreting and applying these definitions—often in the wake of both the Terror and the Napoleonic Code—profoundly reshaped how men and women negotiated membership in the state, and what that membership implied for both sexes.

The Borders of Citizenship

The procedures by which men and women became French citizens or, conversely, forfeited their membership in the nation reveal these connections and conflicts between citizenship and family rights with particular clarity.

As men and women struggled to define who deserved to become a French citizen or to lose the *qualité de citoyen français,* they directly confronted the tensions and contradictions built into new institutions. In the process, they articulated ideas about national citizenship, gender, and family relations that were otherwise often implicit or inchoate.

The dividing lines between "French citizens" and men and women who were legally "foreigners" because of their birthplace, familial descent, or formal ties to another state were often particularly important in working out the relationships between family and citizenship. When revolutionaries and their successors in the nineteenth century struggled to define how foreigners became citizens of the new nation, and what rights newcomers deserved in France, they explicitly addressed the "national" component of national citizenship. They debated whether women could naturalize in France or lose citizenship rights for serving another sovereign, whether a married woman was necessarily subsumed under her husband's citizenship status, what rights foreign-born fathers had over children in France, and whether immigrant men could gain citizenship rights in France through their marriages.

Like "citizen," however, "foreigner" (*étranger*) was a potent term. It had a multitude of connotations, encompassing both those who were non-French and those who were simple outsiders to a specific locality, both men and women who were juridically foreign and those defined as political and social enemies of the revolutionary nation. Of the many groups branded as foreigners, two categories of people were legally assimilated to status as territorial outsiders and subject to formal procedures granting them or stripping them of membership in the French nation: nobles and those subject to the special category of "civil death," particularly émigrés and certain criminals. Few historians have considered these groups together. Yet the application of laws on national citizenship to ex-nobles and the civilly dead, like the parallel mechanisms regulating access to French citizenship for literal foreigners, forced contemporaries to define how the boundaries of citizenship applied to both men and women.

Although nobility was abolished in 1791, former nobles were not only treated as outsiders in the revolutionary nation but also legally grouped with foreigners. The most explicit of such measures, that of 9 Frimaire Year VI (November 29, 1797), assimilated "former nobles to foreigners for the exercise of political rights" and obligated them to undergo the same procedures for access to French citizenship as territorial foreigners. Determining the salience of nobility, or former nobility, for men and women also directly required assessing familial relations. Old Regime structures of nobility had been based partly on the family, often requiring several generations of ennoblement before granting full nobility. Moreover, ennoblement and *dérogation*—the loss of noble status—were the sites in which men and women before the Revolution had most explicitly considered whether or how individual legal membership in a community was changed by marriage, childbirth, or widowhood. When former nobles tried to emphasize their personal titles to citizenship in the revolutionary republic, they confronted this heritage of familial citizenship and the associated idea that their place in the nation—or exclusion from it—was determined by the status of family members.

Just as the nobles were often assimilated to foreigners during the Revolution, so too were men and women condemned to *mort civile,* or civil death, a legal fiction by which the perpetrators of certain crimes were deemed legally dead.[32] The status was adapted from the Romans, who had applied it to slaves and used it as a penalty for certain egregious crimes, political transgressions, and unauthorized flights to foreign countries. Old Regime French law had limited its uses to punishment for serious crimes and, in a more limited sense, as a status for monks and nuns who had renounced their worldly rights.[33] Revolutionaries revived it as a political penalty, particularly applying it to émigrés, who were considered to have abandoned their nation. In the process, they called attention to its importance for the loss of citizenship rights in France. As the deputy Jean-Denis Lanjuinais remarked in 1793, the word "citizen" was commonly defined by its opposites: those who were foreigners or civilly dead.[34] Those proclaimed to be "civilly dead" were stripped of all property, rights, and titles in France. Legislators and jurists of the Revolution and early nineteenth century declared that civil death, unlike lesser penalties, necessarily entailed the loss of the *qualité de citoyen français* as well as other rights in France.[35] But civil death potentially dissolved familial as well as national bonds. The makers of the new order were thus forced to consider whether civil death ended marriage in France, and whether heads of households who were declared to be civilly dead retained rights in France over their wives and children.

The presence or absence of the *qualité de citoyen français* in these various circumstances—literal foreignness, membership in the alien "caste of nobles" during the Revolution, and civil death—was a contentious issue not only during the fervor of the early Revolution but also well into the nineteenth century. Defining who was French and what rights and obligations followed those definitions both reflected and shaped policies that went far beyond particular groups and circumstances.

The following chapters trace revolutionary innovations in national citizenship and family relationships from their dramatic origins through the series of vastly different political, legal, territorial, and social structures that together marked the beginning of a "new regime" in Europe. Part I, "The Family of the Nation," examines why conflicts between family and citizenship rights surfaced unexpectedly in the wake of new revolutionary laws and practice. It shows the increasing tendency of both representatives of the state and ordinary men and women to resolve such unexpected conflicts by emphasizing the citizenship rights and obligations of dependents over their legal position within the family. Part II, "Toward a Nation of Families," turns to the later years of the Revolution. It examines how and why this situation was reversed as authorities began increasingly to subordinate national bonds to familial ones while still arguing that women had important duties as members of the nation. Part III looks at the attempts in the Napoleonic Civil Code to establish a new order in which women's rights and obligations were consistently subordinated to their position in the family, and in which national citizenship was clearly delineated by gender. But the solution instituted by the Code was quickly challenged in practice as administrators and jurists confronted the legacies of past decisions and struggled to implement new laws on national citizenship. Even this paternalistic new order would not be able to overcome contradictions between individual national citizenship and family status that revolutionaries had woven into the very fabric of a new order.

From the birth of the Revolution in 1789 to the consolidation of a new monarchy, family and citizenship rights were thus both deeply intertwined and frequently opposed. The model of a "great family" of the nation shaped early attempts to redefine both family and citizenship relations. This model would become difficult to sustain in the wake of the Terror, and would be replaced by an increasing emphasis on the qualitatively different nature of family and citizenship bonds. Revolutionaries initially emphasized duty to the nation-state above loyalty to, and legal subordination within, the family; they and their successors would increasingly emphasize the priority of family over nation. From an ambiguous and multivalent model of "French citizenship," which implied that both men and women were part of the sovereign nation, legislators would progressively identify the citizen explicitly with the *paterfamilias* and limit not only the application of measures on political rights, but also those affecting women's legal membership in the nation. Yet these changes took place over a period of many years; the reworking of these categories and practices during the late 1790s and Napoleonic era was sometimes as crucial as early revolutionary innovations in shaping the long-term legacies of the Revolution. Such changes would also be constantly challenged, especially as contemporaries sought to relate new laws and abstractions to the complexity of daily life. Expectations about gender roles and legal traditions of hierarchical family relations shaped and limited new institutions of national citizenship, but such concepts of national citizenship would also pose deep and lasting challenges to family and gender relations.

Figure 1. "Dévouement à la Patrie" by Pierre Antoine de Machy after Antoine Talamona. Reprinted with permission from the Bibliothèque Nationale de France. The print sometimes bears the caption "The country is in danger: all prepare to sacrifice to it what they hold most dear—husband, children, jewels." While this image particularly emphasizes sacrifice to La France (symbolized by the statue on the left) and to war (the soldier being sent off on the right), the theme of duty to the country over familial loyalties was widespread in the early revolution.

Part I

The Family of the Nation

In Old Regime France, the king was known as the "father of the country" (*père de la patrie*). The title was widespread; it appeared inscribed on public monuments, in the tracts of theorists of absolutism eager to justify the submission of French subjects to their monarch, and in the solicitous letters of men and women hoping for royal favors.[1] Official decrees even portrayed the crime of regicide as one of "parricide," as in the cases of Ravaillac, the assassin of Henri IV, and Damiens, the attempted murderer of Louis XV.

The vision of France as a family headed by a father-king shaped both the incorporation of foreigners into the nation and the loss of citizenship rights for rebellious French subjects. Kings often treated the legitimation of children born out of wedlock and the naturalization of foreigners together, as Louis XIV did in his landmark 1696 edict, *Déclaration concernant les lettres de naturalité et de légitimation.*[2] Jurists described the granting of citizenship to immigrants as a process of adoption. Petitions on behalf of applicants for naturalization, especially women, also frequently appealed to the king as a benevolent figure who could establish both literal and figurative familial bonds for them in France.[3]

Edicts penalizing French subjects for leaving their home country were similarly framed in terms of a father's right to chastise his children. In 1669 Louis XIV forbade his subjects to live in foreign countries and ordered those established outside France to return to the kingdom; if they did not do so, they risked imprisonment and the loss of French citizenship.[4] The law was aimed particularly at Huguenots, but was phrased to include all rebellious subjects. Subsequent edicts reiterated this principle, declaring that all who left the kingdom without the king's permission would be defined as foreigners and deprived of rights in the kingdom.[5] As one lawyer explained the logic behind these repeated measures in 1733:

> The bonds that attach a subject to his sovereign are as respectable and indissoluble as the bonds that attach a son to his father; paternal authority is the principle and the model of sovereignty; a father has the right to disinherit an ungrateful son who abandons his name and his home to take a new name and a permanent new home with another family. . . . The sovereign, following the same principles, has the right to remove forever from the number of his subjects a rebel who has gone over to a foreign power.[6]

This model also affected the legal differences between foreigners and French subjects within the kingdom. The biggest difference was the *droit d'aubaine,* which limited a non-naturalized foreigner's ability to inherit or pass on property and goods in France to non-French heirs.[7] The monarchy of the seventeenth and eighteenth centuries justified the institution with financial and diplomatic rationales: it brought funds, albeit often limited ones, into the state coffers and was a useful subject of international treaties. For similar reasons, there were also myriad exceptions granted on the basis of a foreigner's origin or profession, the region in which he or she settled, or the benefits that an exemption promised to the French economy.

Yet the *droit* was also justified by particular concepts of the family and the state. Jurists viewed the family as a legal institution that functioned to preserve familial patrimony. Children born out of wedlock were considered to have no legal family bonds; they thus had no right to demand a share of their parents' estate. Conversely, even if a father recognized his bastard children, he could exercise little formal power over them because such authority was based on the transmission of familial property.[8] Non-naturalized foreigners were similarly restricted by the legal fiction that they had no family relations in France. As Colette Danjou has analyzed the situation, in both early modern French law and its model, Roman law, "a foreigner had no civil relations. . . . No legal bond united a father and son, uncle and nephew."[9] They could thus neither inherit nor bequeath familial property to their non-French heirs, and unless they asked to be made members of the family of the nation, the king was fully entitled to take property in their place.

This model of the king as the head of a great family both incarnated and transcended the contemporary political and social structure of France as a series of overlapping groups or "corporations." France was governed by privilege or private law; individuals had different rights or obligations depending on the groups to which they belonged, including religious, professional, and regional communities. The family was one of many such groups, and served as a model for political power. The converse was also implicitly true; the power of the king bolstered that of the head of the household. Yet the authority of the sovereign also transcended that of the *paterfamilias.* In general, married women and children were legally subordinate to the head of household, unless they had a particular legal identity, like that of public merchant (*marchande publique*). But in the case of acquisition or loss of citizenship, the same laws applied to both sexes regardless of their familial position. Both men and women could naturalize in prerevolutionary France; indeed, between 10 and 15 percent of foreigners accorded *lettres de naturalité* during the seventeenth and eighteenth centuries were women.[10] In many circumstances, it was necessary for women to naturalize, particularly if they wanted to protect property rights in France. Some other early modern governments conferred subjectship on women, especially women who were single or heads of household; women regularly received denizen status and naturalization in early modern England and America.[11] Yet in both permitting and requiring naturalization for women, French law was also stronger than that of many other countries, particularly that of its neighbor Spain.[12]

If men and women could become French by similar mechanisms, both sexes could also lose citizenship status by the same means. Women were expected to stay in France when the king ordered them to do so, and risked being "reputed as foreigners" if they left their homeland. The royal edicts that followed the revocation of the Edict of Nantes and forbade subjects of the king to leave France applied to both men and women, although the penalties were sometimes reduced for women. The reach of the laws is clear both in the general framing of measures against expatriation and in their interpretation in contested inheritance cases; lawyers and judges regularly proclaimed that such measures affected both sexes.[13]

Revolutionaries would fundamentally challenge this political order. They attacked both the power of the king and symbolic underpinnings of that power. They destroyed the legal system that had defined the distinctions between French and foreigners in the Old Regime, as well as the rights and duties of men and women in the nation. Beginning in 1789, revolutionaries abolished all forms of legal privilege and proclaimed that all were equal before the law. They sought to eliminate groups that stood between the individual and the state, particularly those that had a distinctive legal status, and often described individuals who continued to identify themselves in relation to those groups as foreigners to the new revolutionary community. Legislators outlawed nobility in 1790, while welcoming individual nobles who were willing to accept the common law of the nation and to support the Revolution. Revolutionaries also banned guilds and artisanal corporations in 1791. They dissolved monasteries and nunneries, not only to curtail the power of the church and to seize its assets, but also to dismantle religious corporations, which they saw as keeping men and women apart from the nation as a whole. Even the extension of rights to members of previously disenfranchised groups could reflect hostility to separate communities within the nation. Some scholars have seen the emancipation of Jews in 1790 and 1791 as part of an implicit quid pro quo: in exchange for full citizenship rights, Jews were expected to abandon their cultural particularities and collective institutions, especially any separate legal status or identity as a distinctive "nation" within France.[14]

As revolutionaries redefined the role of groups within the nation, they also redefined the particular group of the family. They transformed marriage from a permanent, religious bond into a secular, dissoluble contract that functioned like any other civil contract. They also established a uniform age of majority that would emancipate adult children from paternal control. Indeed, revolutionary law potentially transformed families into small societies of individuals whose bonds of marriage or parentage were no different from other civil bonds.[15] As one deputy, Prugon, proclaimed during a discussion on inheritance in April 1791, "Can it be a question of these bizarre arrangements that held that a family existed in a single man? There are no longer any castes, no longer any families properly speaking."[16]

Yet even as men and women changed the basis of the nation and the family, they continued to view both as similar kinds of institutions and to celebrate the "great family" of the nation. They continued to expect little conflict between familial and citizenship bonds. But as sovereignty was increasingly vested in the people of France rather than in the person of the king, men and women would find themselves facing unanticipated questions about the ways in which both sexes obtained or lost national citizenship and the rights and duties associated with that citizenship status. They also confronted unexpected contradictions between duty to their immediate families and duty to the "great family."

The two chapters in this section focus on these contradictions and tensions in the early years of the Revolution. Chapter 1 explores new visions of national citizenship as an individual and voluntary contract, family relations as mutable, and the revolutionary state as the creator of new citizens and new "children." It examines the conflicts that emerged from these transformations, concentrating particularly on emigration, the crime of leaving French territory. Like the men and women who had left the Old Regime kingdom without royal sanction, those who left France after 1789 without official permission risked losing rights in their homeland. Indeed, by 1793 they faced even an even greater penalty than their predecessors: *mort civile,* or the loss of all rights and titles in France. Petitioners argued that imposing such a penalty implied that émigrés had been political members of the revolutionary nation and had betrayed that citizenship by leaving French territory. They contended that women could not exercise political rights or defend their country and were thus incapable of such a betrayal; because women were French but not full citizens, they should not lose their rights as French women for crimes that only citizens could commit. Champions of émigrés also argued that dependents within the family had not left France voluntarily, but had been forced to do so: women followed "natural duty" by accompanying their spouses or fathers and were not able, or should not be obliged, to choose between family and nation.

The French government, however, ultimately decreed that duty to the nation superseded gender differences and legal and physical subordination in the family.

Chapter 2 examines family and citizenship rights during the most controversial moment of the Revolution. The Jacobin Republic of 1793–94 instituted radical forms of equality. Pushed by the slave rebellion in Saint Domingue (now Haiti), it abolished slavery throughout the French empire. Legislators also began to mandate increasing civil equality between men and women in France and further emancipated children from their parents' control. But the Terror was also the most violent and repressive moment of the Revolution, killing thousands in the name of liberty and equality. Revolutionaries limited political rights, suspending their second constitution, that of June 1793, and closing women's political clubs in October 1793. Yet they also increased obligations to the state. In the climate of civil and foreign war, men and women were not only to remain on French territory. They were also to submit to the new institution of mass conscription or convince their eligible male relatives to do so, actively support the revolution, and denounce those who did not do so—whatever their personal relationships to alleged traitors might be. Indeed, the Jacobin Republic in many ways marked the apogee of the model of the "great family" of the nation, a family that took priority over all other loyalties and duties, including those to literal families. Some historians have argued that this national family was imagined as a band of brothers, especially after the king's execution in 1793, a family that increasingly excluded women.[17] Yet revolutionaries continued to imagine both men and women as "children of the *patrie*" who had important rights, and especially duties to the nation.

I New Contracts of Kinship and Citizenship, 1789–1793

In late 1792, a young woman petitioned the Committee on Legislation to treat her as a French citizen. The self-described "citoyenne," Vanhoutem (née Welter) had been convent-educated and married at age sixteen to a spouse chosen by her parents, a man whom she described as annoying, stupid, dirty, and lazy. The two of them went to France together. He then left the country; she refused to accompany him and sought a divorce. The French courts turned down her request on the grounds that she was a foreigner and hence not subject to French law.

Vanhoutem drew on the new 1791 Constitution to ask that she be considered a French citizen in her own right because she identified deeply with the republican nation and had fulfilled all the requirements to become a citizen. "The new Constitution declares that a foreigner domiciled in France for a year is a French citizen; the *citoyenne* Vanhoutem has been here for three years. But since her husband left this honorable domicile, will she be forced to renounce it despite herself?" She acknowledged that under normal circumstances, a married woman could have no other domicile than her husband's and could be judged only by the laws of the country where she was united with him. But the times were exceptional, and she had chosen the land of liberty while he had abandoned both her and it. Her status should not depend on his: "Is she not a citizen, and a citizen independent of the wretch who abandoned her?"[1]

Like the self-proclaimed *citoyenne* Vanhoutem, another immigrant, Joseph Marie François de Longin, petitioned the National Assembly in late 1792 to decide what the articles of the 1791 Constitution concerning national citizenship meant for him. But rather than worrying that his marriage would prevent him from becoming a French citizen entitled to the benefits of French law, he feared the opposite. The Constitution might make him into a citizen involuntarily, and thus subject to revolutionary measures on emigration that forbade citizens to leave the country without governmental permission. Born in the Austrian Netherlands, he had married a woman from the French city of Lille and owned a house there, which the French government threatened to seize because he had left France. De Longin reviewed the requirements that the 1791 Constitution stipulated for becoming a citizen; the only one that applied to him was the "circumstance of my marriage to a French woman—but can this unique circumstance, isolated from all others required by the law, can it, I ask, attribute the quality of a French citizen to me against my will?"[2]

Vanhoutem's and de Longin's questions could not be answered without considering a series of unprecedented institutions, including not only the new Constitution, but also divorce—freshly institutionalized in September 1792—and the laws on emigration, which were first decreed in 1791 and intensified in 1792. Their direct queries to the central government implied further questions: Could a woman, especially a married woman, be considered a citizen of the new nation in her own right? What rights and obligations did such citizenship entail? Did the same mechanisms for becoming or ceasing to be a citizen apply to both sexes in a transformed nation? Since, following the 1791 Constitution, marriage had become purely a secular contract, could it make or unmake citizens against their will or prevent foreigners from becoming French? More generally, was it possible to choose between family and citizenship bonds, and if so, how could the validity of that choice be established?

Such questions were scarcely resolved in the first years of the Revolution. Legislators rarely expected contradictions between citizenship bonds and familial ones; indeed, they had difficulty even conceiving of them. But when conflicts did appear, representatives of the state and ordinary men and women usually tried to resolve them by placing the citizenship status of dependents in the family over their legal position in the household. They often treated a woman torn between patriotic and marital bonds as indeed a "citizen independent" of her spouse—at least when it came to certain key obligations of citizenship.

Unexpected Contradictions

If revolutionaries did not anticipate conflicts, it was in part because such tensions had been rare in the Old Regime. The model of the "great family" of the nation meant that both men and women could become or cease to be French by the same mechanisms, and that marriage did not directly affect citizenship. For those who were not directly affected by the edicts that forbade Huguenots to leave France, the principle of the "spirit of return" ruled; if emigrants had not shown definitively that they had renounced their desire to return to their native country, they remained legally French and subjects of the king. Marriage to a foreigner did not prove renunciation for either sex, even though women were otherwise legally subordinated to their husbands. Indeed, jurists often ruled that a married woman had not given up her rights in her homeland if she left it with a foreign husband because she could not prevent her spouse from moving the household.[3]

Individuals sometimes contested such judgments, arguing that marrying a non-French spouse, especially a husband, indicated a personal desire to renounce rights in France. The opponents of Françoise de Lescalle, a woman seeking an inheritance in France, thus argued in 1728 that Lescalle's marriage to a Germanic man should be regarded as a renunciation of her rights in the kingdom because she had made it as an adult: "It was by her own choice that she preferred Germany to France, since she was in full power of her rights when she married the Sieur de Belleny. Her parents were dead, as her marriage contract shows . . . her choice and will made her a wife of a German."[4] But such arguments were unusual; the more common assumption was that regardless of their motives or independence in choosing a spouse, women remained French and could resume their original status, especially if they returned to their homeland. Most women also still had living parents at the time of their marriages, and the need for parental consent clouded any discussion of individual intent to make oneself into a foreigner.

More generally, becoming or ceasing to be French was often an issue separate from marriage. With a few exceptions, neither a man nor a woman could become a French citizen simply by marrying a French native. Certainly, marriage played an important role in procuring foreigners privileges in specific localities in France. Many towns and cities granted rights to those who were or became "bourgeois" of such localities, and marriage to a native often expedited becoming a bourgeois. In Metz and Strasbourg, for example, marriage was a stepping-stone to obtaining rights and privileges during the Old Regime, though not a guarantee of it. Spouses of bourgeois in the city were likely, but not guaranteed, to become bourgeois themselves.[5] In more rural areas, strangers—both those from outside the kingdom and those from other parts of France—often obtained a share in *avantages communaux,* such as the right to gather firewood or to graze their animals on the town commons, through marriage. For immigrants from outside France's boundaries, marriages to native French subjects could occasionally suffice to make them legally French; for example, a 1669 royal edict proclaimed that a foreign man who settled in Marseilles and married a woman from the area would be considered as a "French natural" and bourgeois of the city.[6] But marriages usually conferred citizenship in the country as a whole only if the city or region in question had been recently incorporated into the kingdom, and if local practices were tolerated as part of that incorporation.

Jurists also did not consider that marriage permanently changed the citizenship status of either men or women in France.[7] In judicial treatises, court cases concerning the *droit d'aubaine,* and the applications of other laws affecting those deemed foreigners, immigrant men were referred to in terms of their origins, regardless of their marital status. More surprisingly, immigrant women were identified in terms of their foreign origins even if their husbands were French subjects. A woman was generally supposed to follow the juridical condition of her husband. Noble women, for example, became commoners if they married commoners, though they could petition to reclaim their former status if their husbands died.[8] However, jurists were explicit that marriage to Frenchman did not naturalize an immigrant woman and give her the same quality as her French husband.

This separation of marriage and citizenship status for both men and women did not completely prevent conflicts between family and citizenship status. But such conflicts were unusual, in part because French "citizenship" entailed limited rights, benefits, and duties in a world of privilege. Citizenship was often defined only to resolve specific practical conflicts. Most conflicts involving family and citizenship status focused on inheritance. But there were a host of exceptions to existing laws and the *droit d'aubaine,* which meant that where succession was an issue, individuals could often claim rights on the basis of those exceptions, rather than systematically addressing the benefits or limits of French citizenship status.

In most cases, conflicts also arose only after the death of a spouse or other family member, when the issue at stake was the status of the presumed heir or heirs. Choice between family and citizenship status seldom became an issue during the life of both partners. Indeed, if there were usually few reasons to force individuals to choose between nation and family, there were also few means of proving that a man or woman had done so while his or her partner was alive. Observers could speculate on the motives for marriage, as in Lescalle's case, but there was often no definitive evidence. Legal separations were limited, and divorce did not exist. Even the complete loss of civil rights in France through the legal fiction of civil death did not end marriage, since marriage was a religious bond that ended officially only with the literal death of a partner.[9]

There were also relatively few ways for individuals to choose between the bonds that connected parents and minor children and those that connected French subjects to their nation. A father often held real power over subordinates in the household, and children had few means of emancipating themselves from this authority. In areas of France governed by customary law before the Revolution, the age of majority had been fixed at twenty-five; in areas governed by written law, there was no age limit on a child's subservience to his or her father. It was also difficult to change family relations legally by adding new members to the household who were not products of a marriage; illegitimate children could not demand a share of their parents' estate, and despite the prevalence of the metaphor of adoption of foreigners, adoption was not part of French law.[10]

Paternal authority was, however, not necessarily a permanent obstacle to claiming citizenship rights in France. Just as women could return to France after their husbands' deaths and claim French citizenship status, so too could children of French parentage born outside the country, especially after their parents' deaths. As long as such children eventually returned to France, it did not matter if their parents had definitively abandoned the kingdom. As the legal scholar François Tronchet repeatedly insisted in the decades that preceded the Revolution, fathers could not deny their children the quality of a Frenchman.[11]

From 1789 on, revolutionaries fundamentally redefined many of the legal foundations of the family, particularly those that made it difficult to change familial bonds and those that curtailed the rights of women and children within the household more generally. They often rhetorically linked the "despotism" of the monarch to that of an abusive head of the household. In August 1790 the Constituent Assembly abolished *lettres de cachet,* an Old Regime institution that had allowed people, especially heads of households, to request that the king imprison their wayward relatives. It replaced such *lettres* with family tribunals, limiting a father's control over his family.[12] The National Assembly also abolished primogeniture in 1790, then decreed in April 1791 that intestate legacies had to be divided equally among children regardless of sex or birth order.[13] The new Constitution established in September 1791 made marriage a civil, rather than religious, contract. In January 1792 the National Assembly instituted adoption in principle, although legislators postponed defining the specific procedures and rights it would entail. In August 1792, just before overthrowing their father-king, legislators decreed the age of emancipation to be twenty-one for both men and women. They later limited a father's ability to bequeath his property at will or to disinherit wayward children.[14] Revolutionaries instituted divorce on September 20, 1792, after a vigorous campaign identifying indissoluble marriage with despotism and the dissolution of marriage with liberty.[15]

Revolutionaries expected such changes to bolster the new political order; they did not expect conflicts between familial and national bonds. One reason was that they continued not only to see the family as a political institution, but also to imagine the nation as a logical extension of the family. The rarity of such conflicts during the Old Regime also made it unlikely that legislators would think about the possibility of related tensions in a new order, much less make preventing them a priority on the crowded legislative agenda. Their lack of concern was also, however, deeply tied to the particular ways in which they defined national citizenship, and the related procedures for becoming or ceasing to be a French citizen.

Naturalization and Parental Permission

In late 1789 and early 1790, naturalization continued to follow the procedures and formulas of the Old Regime. Women, like men, petitioned for naturalization by asking "the very Christian King" to give them the same rights as "true *régnicoles* and French natives," like the Irish-born Susanne Creagh, who sought *lettres de naturalité* for herself and her daughters, both married and single, in order to allow them to inherit a small legacy in the French colonial empire.[16] But traditional procedures could not last indefinitely as France's political structures were fundamentally transformed. The National Assembly issued one of the first revolutionary decrees concerning national citizenship in April 1790, primarily to clarify which people living in frontier towns were entitled to vote in the new nation. A December 1790 law addressed a different group of people, and allowed the descendants of Protestants who had left the kingdom because of religious persecution to return to France and be treated as "naturels français." As de Longin observed, the 1791 Constitution established a systematic set of criteria for those seeking to become French citizens. It also established the possibility of automatic naturalization for individuals who met those criteria, as well as a separate possibility of special naturalization for exceptional individuals.

In institutionalizing these decrees, legislators occasionally considered possible conflicts between paternal authority and citizenship status. The December 1790 decree stipulated that "sons of families cannot use this right without the consent of their fathers, mothers, grandfathers, or grandmothers, unless they are adult or able to exercise their rights [*jouissant de leurs droits*]."[17] Although the authority of the nation, like that of the king, could trump the authority of individual heads of households, men petitioning for naturalization following the 1791 Constitution could also find it expedient to demonstrate paternal consent of their plans to change their national status. When William Priestley, son of the famous scientist and minister, Joseph Priestley, sought to be naturalized in the summer of 1792, he submitted a letter from his father establishing that he had paternal permission to become a French citizen. Similarly, the dossier for Fréderic de Hobe, a young Danish diplomat, contained a letter proclaiming that "no other motive led this young man to solicit this favor [of becoming French] from his father, than the love of our institutions and the most ardent desire to adopt France as his country and to make himself worthy of being a French citizen."[18]

Revolutionaries did not, however, imagine potential conflicts between national and marital bonds. They assumed that immigrants would want to become French. Legislators pictured immigrants like Priestley or de Hobe, eager to participate in the new revolutionary polity, rather than men like de Longin who feared the consequences of legal Frenchness. Although the April 1790 decree and 1791 Constitution included marriage as one of the qualifications for citizenship, most legislators did not, at last initially, conceive of marital contracts as transforming men into citizens against their will. Legislators also viewed some of these measures as distinct from naturalization. The December 1790 decree declared that all people (*toutes personnes*) who were descendants of an expatriated French man or French woman were French. But although certain men and women later claimed to have been "naturalized" by the decree, legislators did not usually think of it as a mechanism for naturalization, since such individuals were now considered to have remained French despite their ancestors' departure from the country.[19]

More importantly, lawmakers had difficulty conceptualizing the relevance of new forms of national citizenship for women. They were primarily preoccupied with the qualifications for political rights, rights that they usually assumed did not apply to women. Individuals like Condorcet, Etta Palm d'Aelders, and Olympe de Gouges demanded that women be able to exercise full political rights, while some organizations like the Cercle Social also championed women's rights. But most members of revolutionary government did not think of women as full political actors. Even if they debated such issues, they usually not think about such debates as they drafted legislation on national citizenship. Legislators were certainly aware that women had been naturalized during the Old Regime and that the articles of the new Constitution could be interpreted as naturalizing immigrants, but this was not their primary concern in the early 1790s.[20] The April 1790 decree addressed the necessary conditions for being considered French in order to exercise the political rights of a citizen; similarly, the 1791 Constitution focused on qualifications for active citizenship—namely the ability to vote or hold office—even as it established the means for foreigners to become French.[21]

Thus, when revolutionaries began to consider how much a woman could be affected by her husband's citizenship status in the new order, or vice versa, they did not immediately address Vanhoutem's concern: the status of those who were, or had been, literal foreigners. Instead, they considered the question of women's national citizenship more systematically in the context that de Longin discussed: the appropriate penalties for emigration, or leaving French territory.

Emigration

From 1791 through 1793, revolutionaries instituted increasingly harsh measures against émigrés. Legislators not only allowed the government to seize émigré property, but also permanently banned émigrés from returning to France, and in 1793 they condemned such expatriates to civil death, depriving them of any political or civil identity within France.[22] But it was more difficult to define who should actually be subject to these penalties. Lawmakers and administrators debated at length about who should be included in the category of émigrés and what exemptions could be considered acceptable. Scholars have tended to ignore these debates, usually seeing émigrés as counterrevolutionary nobles justly ostracized by a republic they had abandoned.[23] Certainly, many émigrés were from elite back-grounds and were outraged by the end of the old order; some were actively involved in campaigns to overthrow the revolutionary state.[24] But individuals from a wide variety of social backgrounds and political persuasions left the chaos of revolutionary France, including many who might not have been considered as enemies if they had remained in the country. Indeed the majority of émigrés, especially after 1793, can be identified as members of the Third Estate; and this was especially true for women.[25] Such diversity complicated the task of instituting measures against emigration; while revolutionaries themselves often imagined émigrés as corrupt aristocrats, socially, politically, and legally separate from citizens, applying laws often meant considering the complexities of emigration. Indeed, justifying and instituting laws on emigration forced revolutionary governments to assess what it meant to be a member of the nation, especially for those who officially lacked political rights. It also led authorities to confront conflicts between family and citizenship bonds for dependents within the family and to struggle with the legal consequences when the head of the household ceased to be a citizen.

The Opposite of Citizenship? Foreignness and Civil Death

The Constituent Assembly instituted the first laws against emigration in June 1791, arguing that such measures were justified because émigrés were citizens who had participated in the "social contract" creating the sovereign nation and then left. Such traitors refused to accept a pact that they had helped create and that required the submission of each individual to the laws of the polity. The law was briefly abrogated in September 1791, only to be restored by the Legislative Assembly, where the king's veto became a critical political issue. The law of April 8, 1792, instituted shortly before France went to war with Austria, systemized and extended measures against émigrés, and in October 1792 the new National Convention banned émigrés forever from returning to France. The law of March 28, 1793, one of the cornerstones of revolutionary legislation aimed at émigrés, proclaimed those who had left France to be civilly dead, not only permanently barred from their home country but also stripped of any property or legal identity within it.

In instituting these measures, legislators and administrators often echoed Old Regime rationales for punishing subjects of the monarch who had left the kingdom. They justified laws against émigrés by using the imagery of ungrateful children who should be chastised because they had turned against their nation-family. The anonymous author of the 1791 *Réflexions et autorités qui peuvent déterminer une loi contre les émigrans* contended that punitive measures were justified "when the nation [*patrie*] calls all of its children to its breast," and those children failed to respond.[26]

In a contemporaneous piece, the deputy of the Department of Aube argued that men who had abandoned France and assembled to make war against the nation could no longer be considered "children of the country [*patrie*]" and that to hesitate in attacking such renegades was itself a form of parricide.[27] Indeed, along with neologisms like "nationcide," accusations of "parricide" were often used to justify measures against French men and women who had left the nation. For example, the August 15, 1792, decree, which put émigrés' families in France under surveillance, began by lamenting the parricidal intentions of bad citizens who had abandoned their homeland.[28]

Immigrants in France, fearing reprisals if they left their adopted country, attempted to turn this rhetoric to their advantage, arguing that measures against émigrés were intended to affect only "ungrateful sons of the country."[29] But it was unclear whether resident foreigners like de Longin were sufficiently part of the revolutionary nation to be held accountable to it. There was a similar ambiguity in the relationship between the loss of citizenship rights in France because of emigration and the absence of rights because one was a foreigner. In instituting each stage of the measures against émigrés, lawmakers analyzed the loss of rights in France implied by banishment and by civil death in relation to literal foreignness.

Old Regime jurists like François Richer had also compared the loss of civil rights, especially civil death, to foreignness.[30] But the stakes of such comparisons had changed. Before the Revolution, civil death had not been a penalty for leaving French territory; now it was. Its role as a mechanism for depriving people of French citizenship status thus took on new importance. Men and women lumped together enemy foreigners and émigrés subject to civil death, linking them not only ideologically, as suspects and enemies of the Revolution, but also juridically, as outsiders who were subject to specific legal measures.

Early debates in 1791 over the justification of measures against émigrés often drew upon comparisons with foreigners. Thus one pamphleteer regretted that Old Regime laws forbidding subjects of the king to leave France had been motivated by religious bias against Huguenots. But he suggested that similar measures would be acceptable in the new nation if "we can limit ourselves, like the Romans, to declaring that those who abandon their country when it is in danger or put it in peril are deprived of citizenship rights [*droits de cité*]. We can declare them foreigners [*aubains*] and thus incapable of inheriting anything in France and, for even stronger reasons, of receiving any pension, salary, etc. from the public treasury."[31] Indeed, legislators initially considered treating émigrés identically with foreigners. In one of the key debates in October 1791, Condorcet argued:

> Every man has the right to change homeland; he can renounce the land of his birth in order to choose another. From that moment on, a citizen of his new

homeland, he is simply a foreigner in the first one, but if he should return there one day [and] if he has left his possessions there, he must fully enjoy his rights as a man; he has deserved to lose only those of the citizen.[32]

Others, however, contended that those who abandoned their homeland during Revolution lost both their civic and civil rights. It was this viewpoint, championed by Pierre Vergniaud, which persuaded the legislators to institute measures in 1792 against émigrés, and eventually to extend the Old Regime category of civil death to those who abandoned their country.

Legislators and petitioners also indirectly emphasized the "Frenchness" of those who remained in France by comparing émigrés to citizens and, after the declaration of the Republic in August 1792, to *républicoles*. The term *républicole* had implications for both political citizenship and juridical "nationality." It emphasized the political community that counterrevolutionary, or allegedly counterrevolutionary, émigrés had betrayed and abandoned. For example, an anonymous petitioner complained that the provisions of the March 1793 law affected patriotic family members in France more than émigrés, who had ceased to have rights on the territory of the Republic: the law "only strikes their relations who are républicoles; the weight of punishment falls on those who have not committed the crime."[33] But it also self-consciously echoed the Old Regime judicial term distinguishing French from foreigner: *régnicole*. For example, in 1792 a report on emigration by the Conseil Général of the Department of Seine Inférieure referred to the "civil effects, like those concerning property or the right to inherit, that can be granted to foreigners as well as *républicoles*"; it is perhaps particularly telling that the Conseil initially wrote *régnicole*, crossed out the word, and replaced it with *républicole*.[34] Individual petitioners also appropriated such language; as Marie Martin, a partially paralyzed woman who had been born in Brussels, later proclaimed when threatened by measures against those deemed to be enemy foreigners, "she has always fulfilled the duties of a citizenness: under the Old Regime, she was *régnicole*; under the new regime, she is *républicole*. Having married a French man, a Parisian who died before the Revolution, she must be considered French."[35]

In certain circumstances, foreign-born residents of French territory could be condemned for emigration.[36] However, they were not considered subject to the laws primarily because of their marriages or residence in France, or because they had implicitly satisfied other constitutional requirements for citizenship, but rather because they had participated in government. Certainly, exercising political rights in France had usually required becoming a citizen, but in the chaos of the early Revolution such requirements had not necessarily been enforced. The law of March 28, 1793, one of the centerpieces of revolutionary legislation aimed at émigrés, decreed that the category included "those who, though born in foreign countries, exercised the rights of citizens in France." Their absence from France was reprehensible because they had become part of the revolutionary political community—"citizens" in practice—and then betrayed that citizenship.[37]

Legislators explicitly exempted a few other groups over the course of the Revolution, including officials sent on diplomatic missions and the more nebulous category of businessmen whose commerce required them to travel regularly. Numerous other individuals affected by the laws on emigration also asked for personal or collective exemptions. Men and women often presented similar excuses. In 1792 accused émigrés usually maintained that they had been falsely included in lists of émigrés and had in fact never left French territory, that they had traveled for reasons of commerce or education, that they had been ill—an excuse invoked particularly by the seemingly endless number of French expatriates who claimed to have been dousing themselves in the healing baths of Aix-la-Chapelle—and had been physically unable to return to France within the specified period, or that they had not been informed of the relevant decrees. Such explanations mixed plausible reasons for leniency with the possibility of forging proof of residency or illness.

But apologists for women and children who left France also argued for specific exceptions on the basis of both gender and family position. Many claimed that women were French but not citizens: they could not "exercise the rights of citizens in France." They did not have public functions to fulfill or a political mission in France and were incapable of either making war against their country or defending it militarily. On the contrary, they were especially vulnerable to fear, and thus should be excused from the obligations of citizens, including the obligation to remain in French territory. Their champions also suggested that dependents within the family had not voluntarily left France but had been forced to do so: women and children followed "natural duty" by accompanying their spouses or fathers and were not able, or should not be obliged, to choose between family and nation.

Soliciting Exceptions Based on Gender

In a statistical study of emigration, Donald Greer has claimed that women made up approximately 15 percent of the total émigré population, with a larger percentage among the working classes and peasantry than among the elites, and a similarly large percentage from the areas that were most troubled.[38] All told, at least 14,000 women left France during the Revolution. The question of whether such women could or should be penalized as émigrés surfaced in 1791, but provoked more systematic consideration after the April 8, 1792, law. Instituted in a climate of impending war, the law was designed to allow the revolutionary government to sequester the goods of its enemies. It aimed at property rather than persons, and it effectively defined émigrés as all persons absent from the department in which they possessed property unless they proved that they had in fact remained in France. The law implicitly included women in terms like "the French" (*les Français*) or "people" (*les personnes*) but did not specify whether it applied directly to women and children as well as to men, and to resident foreigners as well as to those who were legally French.[39] In the maelstroms of revolution, it provoked both repeated queries from confused administrators and frantic petitions from women threatened by the measure.

Many women petitioners argued that they had left because their sex was unable to withstand revolutionary and wartime chaos. In the fall of 1792, Marie Louise Lambert claimed that she had fled because she was pregnant and overwhelmed by contemporary events: "she yielded to the impulse natural to her sex and her age, and a will that was not in her power to fight."[40] Lambert was, however, also careful to combine her pleas for clemency with the claim that she could teach her son republican principles and make him useful to his country if she were allowed to return to France. Similarly, in October 1792 the *citoyenne* Biron asked to be removed from the list of émigrés because she had succumbed to the fear natural to her sex; it was just that she be exempted "if nature refused my sex the necessary courage to rest firm in the middle of events that accompanied a bloody revolution."[41]

Like Lambert, Biron emphasized her own devotion to the revolutionary nation: she contended that she was a constant patriot who "never conspired against my country." However, she went one step further, asking not only for her own vindication as a revolutionary whose sex limited her obligations to the state, but also for a general exception aimed at women who had left "during the troubles of the last revolution and returned to France." Others made similarly comprehensive demands, like the author of an anonymous pamphlet, *Observations d'une femme sur la loi contre les émigrés*, who argued in late 1792 that women should not be condemned for emigration. Their nerves were too delicate for them to witness violence calmly, and they did not, and could not, exercise political rights.[42] Both men and women should be responsible members of the nation, but "if their rights are different, their duties are no less so." A woman would prove her patriotism and acquit her "duty to be useful to her country [*patrie*] . . . not only in paying taxes rigorously, but also in sharing voluntary contributions that circumstances make necessary; the country has nothing more to ask of her." Women could not exercise political rights, because of their weakness, but this inability also freed them from the duty of remaining on French territory: "the weakness that one attributes to women removes them from public affairs; this same weakness must excuse all the effects it produces when they are not contrary to moral laws." The author presented herself as unusually capable of overcoming fear, but she argued that such courage should not be demanded of other women, for "women whose nerves are more delicate, more susceptible to terror, would they be more guilty?" She made it explicit, moreover, that the law should treat women as a class in this respect; she desired not that "there be exceptions for some women, but on the contrary, that women in general be excluded from the decree."[43]

Certain administrators also considered the possibility that emigration was a crime committed by men who shirked their military and political duties in France and thus did not apply to women, who were not capable of, or subject to, the same duties of citizenship. For example, an unsigned memoir sent to the central government about the application of the law of April 8, 1792, began by asking whether the law applied to young women. The officials focused on widows and unmarried women:

> We ask first if this disposition applies to widows and to single adult women [*filles usant de leurs droits*] who left the kingdom, where, since they have no public function to fulfill, their presence is matter of indifference, and if they are assimilated to male children of émigrés whom the law does not punish if they are too young to carry arms.[44]

In certain cases, local administrations adopted different procedures for men and women labeled as émigrés. As part of an early and ultimately abortive move to allow émigrés back into the regenerated French nation, the Conseil Général of the Department of Bas Rhin explained in November 1792 that the department was treating women and men émigrés differently, in the belief that that only men should be treated as fully guilty of the crime of emigration:

> Without compromising the security [of a generous nation] we ordered that women were to be gathered in a common house in the seat of government [*chef-lieu*] of each district, and kept under the particular surveillance of the administration. This measure, dictated by a just compassion, could not be applied to men. They were truly the enemies of the country [*patrie*]. They are guilty.[45]

Marital Authority and Expatriation

Women accused of emigration attempted to present themselves not only as patriotic individuals who lacked political responsibilities but also as having been compelled to leave France because of their familial positions. Marie-Françoise Beudet went to Catalonia with her husband and children in 1791; there she had fallen ill and remained—or at least so she claimed—ignorant of the laws that required men and women to return to France within a set period. She argued that her decision to leave the revolutionary nation could not be counted as a crime, since it followed automatically from her position as a mother. Comparing her situation to that of a panther inextricably attached to her young, Beudet proclaimed: "I have no need to establish the motives that led me to leave France. I was a wife, I had to follow my husband. I was a mother; nature prescribed that I could not abandon my children. The guilty or innocent behavior of my husband is foreign to my existence, and is not for me to judge." After stressing that Spain was neutral rather than enemy territory, she went on to curse a law that branded as émigrés all who had left France "without regard for sex or age or circumstances; without distinguishing between those who abandoned their country [*patrie*] only because of a natural duty and those who had hostile intentions and took arms against their country."[46]

Other petitioners like Charles-Pierre Ducanel, the author of *Justice, humanité, les femmes absentes et les enfants appelans de la Convention Nationale à elle-même,* focused on married women's legal and natural submission in the family. Ducanel contended in 1792 that women were "political nonentities." But the bulk of his plea rested on the priority of familial ties over national ones: "Long before all the laws on emigration, there existed a more holy law, a law as imperishable as nature from which it emanates; I mean paternal and marital authority." He approved the severity of the laws for the few women who were conspirators but contended that in general, "women, like their children, ceded to marital authority in expatriating themselves"; they should thus be exempted from the laws.[47] In a similar but less benign view of the power of paternal authority, other petitioners asked the government to consider exceptions for women who had left because they were "threatened and tyrannized by their husbands."[48]

"All French, of Either Sex . . ."

The National Assembly itself briefly considered exempting women as a group from the laws on emigration. On November 17, 1792, the deputy Charles-Nicolas Osselin, the chief author of what would become the cornerstone of laws against emigration, proposed that the National Assembly make an exception for women who had left France for neutral territory:

> A man must, in critical circumstances, take arms to defend the law and not flee in a cowardly manner from the country [*patrie*], which requires the aid of his arms. But it might be just to make an exception for people of sex. (Laughter). But citizens, we each have a sex. (More laughter) . . . Ah well, I want to say that fear might be excusable for women, forced to flee their country [*pays*] momentarily because of bloody and disastrous events. In consequence, your committee asked me to propose an article stipulating that women who prove that they left France to go to neutral territory only after last September 2 will be exempted from banishment.[49]

Osselin's wording in this speech was perhaps unintentionally revealing: "people of sex" was a popular phrase referring to women; it suggested that they were defined by their biology, but men were not. His follow-up, "citizens, we each have a sex," was clearly designed to provoke salacious laughter from his audience, but also implicitly undermined his claim that women should be treated differently from men.

The proposed exception for women was dismissed without discussion, and the Committee on Legislation, led by Osselin, established a virtual code of law on émigrés, which was published definitively on March 28, 1793. The final version explicitly established that the definition of émigré applied to "all French of one or the other sex." The phrase was reiterated in each article defining émigrés in order to remove any remaining doubt or ambiguity. The only slight modification was for girls aged between fourteen and twenty-one who returned to France; they could be deported rather than executed. All others were subject to civil death and to literal death if they came back to France.

The new clarity in the law did not completely silence demands for exceptions based on gender or status within the family. Like the author of *Observations d'une femme*, the anonymous author of the 1793 *Observations sur les exceptions à faire à la qualification d'émigré* argued that that since women were not in a position to carry arms or to fulfill any public function, and since their only obligation to the state was financial, they should be excluded from laws against émigrés. The pamphleteer also contended that even if the government did not exempt women in general, it should still make exceptions for married women, since

> just until recently a married woman was so much under the authority of her husband that he controlled entirely her goods and revenues; she could not, without his consent, have another home than his; she was obliged to follow him everywhere. Could one consider it a crime for a woman to have followed her husband abroad, especially when this country was not at war with France? Could one punish as severely such a coerced act, one that was possibly strongly against her will? It seems that one must make a great distinction between those who were under their husbands' power and those who were not.[50]

Given the prevalence of such arguments, why were women held responsible for emigration? There is little direct evidence, since legislators dismissed proposed exceptions with minimal discussion. But part of the answer emerges in the discussion that ensued when Osselin proposed another exception, this one for servants, who, like women, could not vote or hold office.[51] He contended that servants had no political role in the revolutionary nation, and thus should not lose rights in France simply because they had left the country: "One will say that they were not attached to their country, but they did not have a *patrie*. The rights of citizens were refused to them; they were in some sense outside of society, and cannot be punished for not having fulfilled the duties that it imposed."[52] Such language closely paralleled the argument made by one anonymous petitioner on behalf of émigré women: "women did not abandon their *patrie,* because the rank that is assigned to them in the social order makes it impossible to draw this consequence from their absence from French territory. . . . women have not abandoned their *patrie,* since there is no abandonment when one is not use-ful, when there is no duty to fulfill."[53]

Osselin's proposed exception for servants was also dismissed quickly by other legislators. They feared that servants would be loyal to their masters and would follow their lead in stirring up conspiracies against the revolu-tionary nation. Such fears clearly played a role in the government's insis-tence that women could not be exempted from measures against émigrés. Married women's subservience in the family did not mean they should be excused for leaving France, but rather that they were likely to follow the *paterfamilias* in opposing the republic. There were also other strong practi-cal rationales for including women and servants: legislators feared that all those who left France, regardless of their political stake in the *patrie,* would take desperately needed property and resources.

But the decision to include women in the laws against emigration also rested on, and contributed to, the idea that women had personal responsi-bilities toward the sovereign nation. It implied that because they forfeited all citizenship rights for leaving France, women did in fact have a *patrie* in the revolutionary nation. Because married women had the same responsi-bilities as single women, responsibility to the nation also came before legal subordination in the household or loyalty to the family. As the Bureau des Lois would later conclude in a retrospective overview of the measures con-cerning émigrés: "The laws on emigration placed duty to the country above all other duties. A woman would try in vain to legitimate her absence by invoking the bonds that attached her to an émigré spouse; a child would have no more success invoking the sacred duties of filial piety."[54]

The radical nature of such a policy is especially striking if we compare it with similar measures during the American Revolution. In the United States, a married woman who went over to the enemy to be with her hus-band was not treated as a traitor, a foreigner and enemy of the republic. She simply needed permission from the sitting legislature or active committee of safety to join her husband, permission that was invariably granted.[55] In contrast, no man, woman, or child over the age of fourteen was allowed to leave revolutionary France.[56]

"Conjugal Love . . . Becomes in Them a Crime of High Treason"

While many men and women accompanied family members as they left France, others remained within the territory of the revolutionary nation. But the status of émigrés' wives and other relations was itself problematic. Determining the legal position of émigrés' relatives, like the task of estab-lishing the position of women émigrés, meant considering whether or how subordinates within the household could choose between family and national bonds. It also required assessing the implications of the loss of individual citizenship status in France on family members, particularly on the wife of an émigré man. How was the spouse of an émigré affected by her husband's status, once he became a traitor, "a permanent foreigner," or a man proclaimed to be civilly dead?

As with emigration generally, debate over émigrés' families was fueled by both practical and ideological concerns. Just as it appeared that some families had sent their children, particularly their sons, abroad to keep them from fighting for France or to encourage them to fight against their homeland, so too it seemed that wives of émigrés were likely to funnel money and information to their spouses abroad. As the citizens of the town of Nerac in the Department of Lot and Garonne proclaimed in August 1792, France had to be wary of a "woman whose body alone is in France but whose heart is in Coblentz . . . [and] prevent conjugal love from becoming a crime of high treason."[57]

But while the increasingly radical nature of the Revolution meant that potential traitors were often dealt with hastily, legislators in 1792 were also deeply concerned about clarifying the legal implications of this new category. They were torn between treating women who remained in France as "citizennesses suffering from their spouses' crime" or, in the later words of one revolutionary club, as "countesses, marquises, dames," whose pride and disdain for the revolution revealed their own crimes.[58] Administrators were often as confused about the appropriate effects of the laws on women who did not leave France with their husbands as they were about the implications of laws pertaining to French women who had abandoned their *patrie*.

In several cases, local officials suggested that the penalties for emigration should not apply to women whose spouses had left France, because they could not be held responsible for their husbands' crimes. The administration of the Department of Aisne wrote the central government about the law of April 8, 1792, congratulating the government on having acted promptly against émigrés. The laws were "effective measures to assure that a just and generous nation receives the indemnity owed to it by rebel Frenchmen who carry arms against their country [*patrie*] and force it to prepare for an immense and expensive war." However, the officials in the department believed that penalties for emigration should be applied only to men, who could be considered truly responsible for betraying their country, not to women: "You have not intended to extend the force of the law to a weak and timid sex that does not participate in the crimes committed by those who are united with them by conjugal bonds."[59]

Since the April 8, 1792, law focused on sequestering the goods of those who had fled France, administrators were particularly concerned about the property rights of émigrés' women and children. These became increasingly controversial if a woman sought a legal separation from her husband. Local officials in a variety of departments throughout France, including the Departments of Corrèze, Indre et Loire, and the Nord, sought to clarify if, as the *directoire* of the Department of the Nord put it on June 15, 1792, "separation is legally obtained, is the sequester placed on a woman's property lifted so that she can peacefully enjoy her income?"[60] The minister of public contributions submitted a query that extended and summarized many of these specific questions: "Is a husband's emigration a means for women to obtain a [legal] separation? . . . If a separation is granted, [and thus] a woman would be entitled to all her personal property, should she also enjoy henceforward all the advantages attributed to her by her marriage contract?"[61]

In these debates, the image of the nation as a family became striking. Legislators and administrators began not only to describe émigrés as children who had committed parricidal acts against the nation but also to imagine the nation as a literal substitute for individual male émigrés within the household. In defending the innocence of émigré women, administrators of the Department of Aisne claimed in June 1792 that such women had rights to their property because the powers of the nation were as limited as those of the *paterfamilias* it replaced: "Although the husband is the head of the household, he cannot dispose of the goods of his wife or his children without their consent; it's a maxim of the law that proves that the husband has no claim on these kinds of goods, and as a result, the nation has no more right than the émigré whom it represents."[62] The minister of the interior disagreed with such interpretations; on November 2, 1792, he proclaimed in a letter to the business manager of the Department of Cantal that "the nation is put in the place of the émigré from the very moment of his emigration to exercise all the rights that the émigré had previously enjoyed."[63] The minister went on to declare on December 26, 1792, that "before the law on divorce, emigration was not regarded as a sufficient motive for a women to request a separation from her husband, and as the husband has a tutelary jurisdiction over his wife and is the administrator of her property, so is the nation that represents him."[64]

The minister's proclamation, however, was in fact limited by the law of September 20, 1792, which legalized divorce and made the emigration of a spouse one of the legal grounds for ending a marriage. Although the law did not explicitly state that the wife should obtain full control of community property if she divorced her émigré husband, the courts usually reached this conclusion. Men and women who divorced émigré spouses were required to swear loyalty to the Republic; if they did so, their possessions could not be confiscated without other grounds for suspicion, even at the cost of losing property that would help the revolutionary state.[65]

Scarcely had the courts begun to wrestle with such issues than the new law of March 1793 went a step further and formally introduced the penalty of civil death for emigration. This penalty implied that the "widows" of émigrés might find their marriages automatically dissolved, since their husbands no longer had any legal status in France. In thinking through the possible consequences of a male émigré's status on his family, legislators struggled with comparisons between those who lacked rights in France because they were foreigners, and those who had lost rights because of emigration. The uncertainty over what family bonds meant for the loss of citizenship and the tenuous border between *étrangers* and émigrés is particularly clear in a set of questions that the Conseil Général of the Department of the Seine Inférieure posed to the National Assembly. It reviewed various laws relating to emigration and family, and contended that divorce initially provided the only valid means by which a woman could separate herself from her traitorous husband. If she did not take legal action to dissociate herself from him, it was fair to assume that "she preferred her loathsome spouse to her country [*pays*] and her country could thus envelop her in his punishment."[66]

The Conseil asserted that when divorce was first legalized on September 20, 1792, émigré husbands remained French citizens endowed with certain civil and political rights; "émigrés, although French traitors, were still French." Following the November 1792 law, which permanently banished émigrés from French territory, such exiled figures ceased to be French, but retained the same civil rights as foreigners:

> Civil effects, such as owning property and the right to inherit, can be accorded to foreigners as they are to members of the Republic [*républicoles*]; émigrés, banished forever from the Republic, were no longer French, but they were German, Prussian, or English, depending on the country that they adopted, and could inherit in France.[67]

But following the March 1793 decree that condemned émigrés to civil death, such traitors to the Republic ceased to be French or foreigners who retained limited rights in France. Instead, they were assimilated to people who were literally dead. This assimilation implied that women no longer had to dissociate themselves actively from their traitorous husbands. While the most prominent early champion of divorce, Albert Joseph Hennet, had argued that the existence of civil death was one of the strongest reasons for the legalization of divorce,[68] the Conseil contended that *mort civile* meant that such women had been effectively been widowed, their familial bonds automatically dissolved by their spouses' permanent exclusion from the "great family" of the nation. In short, "one cannot consider a woman to be married to a man who is civilly dead; she becomes a civil widow, and no longer needs to have recourse to divorce."[69]

However, despite the Conseil's lucid exposition of the laws concerning the loss of French citizenship and their impact on familial relations, the spouses of émigrés were not treated as widows, even after the March 1793 law. The formal effect of a husband's civil death on a woman's civil status did not absolve her of responsibility to demonstrate her patriotism. Throughout the

Revolution, wives of émigrés were required to divorce their husbands formally to have any hope of disassociating themselves from their husbands' crimes or alleged crimes. Indeed, divorce itself was scarcely adequate proof that French women had placed duty to their *patrie* over their loyalty to their families. Most legislators and administrators would become convinced that women were indeed using divorces as a means to protect their familial property and pass on goods and money to enemies of the Revolution abroad.[70] There were certainly grounds for such beliefs. Case studies of various cities suggest that divorces because a spouse had emigrated were almost universally initiated by women: 12 out of 12 in Limoges, 14 of 14 in Nancy and in Toulouse, 13 of 13 in Rouen, 17 of 17 in Metz, 5 of 6 in Lyon, 42 of 44 in Bordeaux, and 102 of 105 in Paris.[71] Various indicators, like the number of women who continued to plead for their husbands' removal from the lists of émigrés or who resumed life with their former spouses after the Revolution, suggest that such divorces were often, if not always, motivated by expediency rather than by marital differences or feminine patriotism.[72] But legislators' denunciations of émigré divorces were most frequent in the context of a new stage of the Revolution, the Terror, to which we will turn next.

Conclusion

If we return to Vanhoutem's question, "Is she not a citizen, and a citizen independent of the wretch [her husband] who abandoned her?," it is clear that in 1791 and 1792 revolutionaries were wary of the emotional and pragmatic bonds that bound suspect couples together, and often doubted that married women were, or should be, completely independent of their spouses. They did not address whether or how immigrant women like Vanhoutem could divorce their foreign spouses and become French citizens in their own right. Yet in the case of emigration, legislators were explicit that one of the key duties of revolutionary citizenship—that of remaining in French territory—applied to all women regardless of their marital status and that if women left their *patrie*, they lost all citizenship rights in France. At the same time, however, legislators also assumed that if *puissance maritale* did not excuse a woman who had left France, it also did not bind a woman who had remained in the country to a husband who had ceased to be a French citizen—as long as she actively demonstrated her own allegiance to the revolutionary nation by using the new institution of divorce to separate herself from her spouse.

Conflicts between family and citizenship rights thus surfaced unexpectedly in the wake of new revolutionary laws and practices. The Old Regime view that the authority of the sovereign transcended the authority of the head of household was carried over to a new world, in which both the meaning of the "sovereign" and the status of citizens were radically changed. In the choice between family and nation, the nation usually came first, outweighing gendered differences or legal subservience in the home.

As the Revolution became more radical in the summer of 1793, revolutionaries further extended the metaphor of the nation as a family and promoted new ideals of equality both within the family and among all French citizens. At the same time, the institutionalization of the Terror in the early fall of 1793 would add a new urgency and political importance to the attribution or denial of citizenship rights to men and women. Such developments would challenge anew the balance between family bonds and citizenship.

2 "Duty to the Patrie above All": The Terror

On 26 Germinal Year II (April 15, 1794), the Committee of Public Safety banished former nobles and enemy foreigners from Paris, maritime towns, and military strongholds. Hundreds of men and women rushed to petition the committee in the days following the decree, explaining both why they feared that they would be encompassed in the law and why they should be exempted from it. Supplicants sought to establish that they were in fact legal French citizens and commoners. They also contended that regardless of their origins or juridical status, they had acted as patriotic French citizens and should be treated as such.

In recounting their stories, petitioners identified themselves not only as former noble military officers or ex-*secrétaires de roi,* Dutch political refugees or foreign-born Jews, but also as widows, divorced couples, and children who had been born outside of wedlock. Some—especially women—feared that their family status meant that they would be encompassed in the law regardless of their personal actions. Such petitioners sought to separate themselves from the alien group their relatives threatened to incarnate, explaining why marital or filial ties should not label them. Others invoked family relations to prove the contrary: their familial bonds connected them to the nation as a whole and served as proof of their membership in the state. Such men and women claimed that they had established their citizenship when they married true citizens or that they were themselves progeny of the revolutionary state. As Foiselle, a self-proclaimed *homme de lettres,* put it, certain individuals were "adopted children of the republic," "necessarily born of the new regime."[1] The revolutionary government had to treat them as citizens regardless of their previous identities.

Equalizing Citizens and Expelling Foreigners:
The Dynamics of the Terror

To understand both the revolutionary government's rationales for exiling ex-nobles and enemy foreigners from key cities, and the arguments that petitioners used to claim their membership in the Republic, we need to look first at a series of changes instituted during the Terror. The ten months from September 1793 until Robespierre's fall from power in June 1794 were the most radical and violent of the Revolution. Revolutionaries began to extend the model of the "great family" of the nation in unprecedented ways. They instituted increasingly equalizing forms of family law and, at least in principle, dramatically extended citizenship rights. At the same time, the spread of both foreign and civil war and the institutionalization of state-sponsored violence fed a growing suspicion not just of émigrés and avowed counterrevolutionaries, but also of all who seemed to threaten the well-being of the Republic. Men and women deemed to be legally and socially "foreign" to the revolutionary nation appeared particularly dangerous. In this climate, conflicts between familial and national bonds took on a new intensity and importance.

National Adoption and the Family of Citizens

Although the revolutionary state continued elements of the Old Regime model of the nation as a family, the execution of the prerevolutionary "father" of the country, Louis XVI, in January 1793 appeared to have destroyed that model. Indeed, Lynn Hunt has argued that radical iconography in the period eschewed paternal imagery to celebrate a "band of brothers." She contends that whereas American republican imagery celebrated the father, French revolutionaries distrusted patriarchs of all kinds.[2] New revolutionary legislation increasingly limited the powers of the head of the household, often in tandem with reforms on the larger political scene. Revolutionaries thus abolished paternal authority over adult children on August 28, 1792, just before overthrowing the king and proclaiming a republic. But paternal imagery did not disappear; revolutionaries not only continued to describe the state itself as a great family, guided by the paternal benevolence of the legislators as a group; they also applied this metaphor in new and expanding ways after the king's execution.

Legislators established adoption in literal families in 1792, at least in principle, and maintained the term "adoption" to describe the process of incorporating foreign men and women into the nation. But the revolutionary government now also made native French girls and boys into "adopted children of the nation." In January 1793 the National Convention adopted the daughter of the martyr of liberty, Michel Lepeletier de Saint-Fargeau, after her father was assassinated for having voted for the death of Louis XVI.[3] It soon bestowed the same title on several other children of revolutionary martyrs. On February 2, 1793, the National Assembly adopted Basseville, the son of the assassinated secretary of the Legation of Rome. It formally embraced Auger and Azéma, two children of color, on June 15, 1793, and on 16 Vendémiaire Year II (October 9, 1793) adopted François Latour and the son of the adjutant-general Jouis, whose fathers had also died in the service of the nation.[4]

More general treatises on adoption suggested that there was a fundamental parallel between "national" or "public" adoption and adoption within families.[5] In June 1793 Michel Azéma, the author of a well-known project on adoption, proclaimed that "the country must, in all respects, act as a substitute father for those whose fathers died in its service." He invoked the wisdom of a legislator who was "truly a father in all of the significance of this expression." Azéma also contended that orphans should be declared "adopted children of the nation" (*enfants adoptifs de la patrie*), since "it is undeniable that such children are citizens, belonging to the city [*la cité*] at birth."[6] Following such logic, the revolutionary state adopted not only children of martyrs, but also certain other orphans and children whose parents were alive but unable to act in their offspring's interests. A decree of July 4, 1793, gave foundling children the title "natural children of the nation" (*enfants naturels de la patrie*). The following day the government proclaimed that such children should wear a national uniform to mark them as adopted children of the nation. On 15 Brumaire Year II (November 5, 1793), the National Convention officially adopted young children whose parents had had their property confiscated by the state.[7]

As Eric Goodheart has shown, the theme of the nation as adoptive parent was also prominent in the parliamentary debates on education, especially during the Terror.[8] Legislators insisted that even children whose biological parents remained living were first and foremost children of the nation. In a famous speech on national education on August 13, 1793, Danton proclaimed that "my son belongs not to me but to the republic."[9] Others were equally explicit. Calling for the formation of l'Ecole de Mars as a military school, Barère declared in June 1794 that "children belong to the general family of the republic before they belong to particular families."[10] Individuals also continued to solicit the parental benevolence of the government, like the widow Houbotte, who begged for the "paternal kindness" of the Committee of Public Safety, or Matthieu Risseau, who beseeched the fathers of the country (*pères de patrie*) to listen to his petition.[11] Petitioners even sometimes asked deputies to act as benevolent fathers who could, and should, intervene in their lives in place of their biological relations, like Josephine Letellier, who urged the deputies in February 1794 to help her become "a wife, mother, and *citoyenne*. . . . Can't I pass into your hands the power my father has over me?"[12]

Appealing to the paternal solicitude of authorities was certainly part of an old tradition, and one that would continue long after the Terror. But the language of the "great family" of the nation, while not unique to the period, was increasingly widespread in 1793 and 1794. It was accompanied by a growing emphasis both on literal family bonds as a means of establishing one's connection to the nation as a whole and on a suspicion of those who remained celibate. The National Convention received numerous letters from men and women who wanted to encourage their fellow citizens to marry. Petitioners often sought further to penalize those who remained single or to force them to contribute to the nation in other ways.[13] They often made direct connections between marriage and citizenship, especially as the Terror intensified in the spring and summer of 1794, contending that the government should limit the political rights of bachelors. In May 1794 the Popular Society of Condon called for the National Convention to declare by a solemn law that celibacy was a "political crime": "Celibacy has always been an outrage to nature; it has become a punishable crime in a republic."[14] They declared that a rich man or woman should be obliged to marry a poor *sans-culotte*. The term *sans-culotte* was a charged and multivalent one; often opposed explicitly to nobility or aristocracy, it implied both a social status as worker or small-scale business owner, and a fervent commitment to the republic. The Popular Society of Mayenne similarly linked republican devotion, hard work, and transformative familial bonds when it demanded "that single men and women [*célibataires*], priests, and all individuals whose laziness attests to their antirepublican sentiments be excluded from all public functions."[15]

Petitioners also tried to limit aspects of citizenship rights beyond political participation for single men and women. For example, Henry, *électeur du district de Montmédy,* proposed that those who did not marry or adopt children within a certain time frame should be legally stripped of the "quality of citizen." While he was concerned primarily with the rights to vote and to hold office, he also suggested that retrograde celibates should be deprived of civil rights often associated with French citizenship during and after the Revolution, such as the ability to gather firewood from the commons.[16]

The governments of the Revolution did not respond to all these suggestions, although they did tax bachelors over the age of thirty-five at a higher rate than married men and proclaim repeatedly that a good citizen was a good father.[17] But the logic that family bonds were associated with citizenship rights was applied directly to foreigners. As sovereignty was increasingly vested in the people of France rather than in the person of the king, strengthening family bonds among French citizens became an increasingly important means of becoming part of the national polity. In his speech on adoption in June 1793, Azéma proclaimed that "a bachelor is like a foreigner in society";[18] the Constitution of 1793 soon afterward established the converse: a juridical foreigner who married a French woman and established a family could easily become a citizen. Indeed, the 1793 Constitution went beyond the 1791 one, which had also mentioned marriage as one of the possible criteria for qualifying for French citizenship. Now not only marital bonds but also other family bonds could help integrate outsiders: an immigrant who adopted a child or nourished an elderly man or woman could also become a French citizen.

Instituting Equality in the Family

The extension of the metaphor of the nation as a family was accompanied by an increasing radicalization of family law. Revolutionaries further limited paternal rights over children and espoused equality among siblings. On March 7, 1793, the National Assembly mandated equal inheritance among children.[19] With this law, a father lost one of the most effective means of enforcing obedience, that of disinheriting a recalcitrant child. In June 1793 children born out of wedlock were allowed to inherit from both parents, while a controversial measure from 12 Brumaire Year II (November 2, 1793) allowed illegitimate children to inherit on an equal basis with their legitimate siblings.[20] In August 1793 the Committee on Legislation proclaimed that "the imperious voice of reason has made itself heard. It has said: *Puissance paternelle* no longer exists."[21] Such proclamations did not end paternal authority, but they limited it and helped change the basis of authority within the family, corresponding to a desire to introduce the same principles that governed political society into the family.

Projects for the Civil Code in 1793 and 1794 would have further limited marital authority. The main author of these projects, Jean-Jacques-Regis de Cambacérès, proclaimed on August 8, 1793, that common administration of goods belonging to a couple was the "mode that conformed best to the intimate union" of marriage, because "the principle of equality must regulate all acts of social organization."[22] Jean Etienne Bar, reporter for the Committee on Legislation, defended common administration of communal properties in the name of these same principles: "Ending the ridiculous principle of *puissance maritale* in marriage appeared just to the Committee and in conformity with the grand and eternal principle of equality. In the time of liberty, we cannot let any kind of despotism stand."[23] While these projects for the civil code were not instituted, unlike specific measures on paternal authority, ordinary men and women as well as legislators increasingly used the new language of civil contracts to discuss marital relations. As one anonymous petitioner described marriage in December 1793, men and women were "co-spouses," a term that echoed the equality implicit in the common term "co-citizens."[24]

Citoyennes, Members of the Sovereign Nation?

This conflation of family and nation and changes in family law combined with increasingly radical views about the nature of citizenship to help make women appear active members of the sovereign nation. The terms *citoyen* and *citoyenne* had become almost ubiquitous after the declaration of the Republic in 1792. *Citoyenne* was intended as a female counterpart to the universal designation of "citizen," rather than as a means to enfranchise women, and relatively few revolutionaries championed full political rights for women.[25] But the spread of the term unintentionally created a space that legitimated women's claims to be part of the national polity, claims that intensified during the summer of 1793.[26]

Well-known individuals like Olympe de Gouges and Condorcet had called for women's rights early in the Revolution, and women were involved in political insurrections from the famous October Days march of 1789 onward. But the general politicization of 1793 increasingly involved women. Certain administrators began to consider the suitability of women candidates for political office, especially on a local level; one example is the January 1793 query from administrators in a town in the Department of Seine and Oise asking if a prominent businesswoman could hold the position of mayor.[27] Claire Lacombe and Pauline Léon founded the Society of Revolutionary Republican Women in May 1793, an organization that would play an active role in Parisian politics in the following month.[28] Paralleling the March 1793 decree to explicitly include both sexes in measures against émigrés, the Jacobin Charles-Gibert Romme proposed a draft of a new constitution in April 1793 that repeatedly referred to "all men of either sex." He defined the nation as "all the members of a political body; it's the entire family, it's the *patrie*. The nation is composed . . . of fathers, mothers of families, or those who are of age to be."[29]

The version of the Constitution passed in June 1793 did not use Romme's language or explicitly include women. But by the summer of 1793 women were participated frequently in local electoral assemblies. Serge Aberdam has looked closely at this participation, and hypothesized that their involvement was due in part to particular circumstances. On June 10, 1793, the Convention issued a law on *avantages* or *biens communaux*, rights like the ability to pasture animals on town commons or to gather wood from the forest. It specified that an "equal right to undivided participation in *biens communaux*" applied "without distinction of fortune or sex" to "all inhabitants, married or not, in the same commune, with a real and fixed domicile for a year or more, legally French, registered on the list of those paying personal taxes, and heads of families or separate households." This law, which emphasized the social position as a head of household over sexual differences, coincided with public debates over the new constitution.[30]

The timing of the two events helped open the way for wider practices of suffrage for women and demands for their inclusion in the sovereign nation. Women often proclaimed their adhesion to the Constitution of 1793 alongside men, although the proceedings (*procès-verbaux*) sent to the Convention rarely mentioned their involvement.[31] Lists of potential electors also show that eligibility to vote was not determined strictly on the basis of gender. For example, a list of inhabitants of the commune of Baron from September 10, 1793, was divided into three columns, labeled "Men, Women, Children."[32] But under these three headings, "Men" referred to heads of households, including widows; "Women" to wives and daughters but also servants, including several who appear to have been men; and "Children" to all under twenty-four. Records from other departments suggest similarly elastic categories. The list of 196 "citizens fathers of families in the commune of Crouttes" (*citoyens pères de famille*) included 24 widows identified as such.[33] In this context, married women were excluded from voting and holding office because they were legally subordinate in the family, not simply because they were women. Such subordination was, moreover, subject to change with widowhood or divorce, and even with the measures instituting equality between spouses in the proposed Civil Code.

The openness of the summer of 1793 did not last; women were forbidden to form exclusively feminine political clubs after a dramatic political struggle in Brumaire Year II (October 1793).[34] Many scholars have seen this as the end of any viable claims to women's political citizenship in the revolutionary and early nineteenth-century nation.[35] But although the closing of women's political clubs limited the ability of women to participate in government, it did not eliminate the idea that women were part of the sovereign nation or end debate over the significance of women's citizenship. Women, even property-holding widows, did not vote after Brumaire Year II even in local elections—but neither did men under most circumstances; the Constitution was suspended during the Terror and most elections postponed. But *sans-culotte* women continued to act as citizens and to claim that they were part of the sovereign nation, participating in revolutionary uprisings and voicing a series of political demands; and numerous women played an active and directing role in the new mixed-gender sectional societies (the neighborhood political associations that existed primarily in Paris).[36]

Women also still retained full responsibility for certain acts as citizens, since they were recognized as guilty of political crimes. In a study of women before the Revolutionary Tribunal in 1793–94, Stephanie Brown has shown that the courts systematically considered women's political activities, not their gender, to be most salient in determining their fates.[37] Indeed, if we turn back to the Terror, and two categories of outsiders who were particularly suspect—foreigners, especially those from countries with which France was at war; and former nobles—the stakes of women's personal membership in the nation become clear.

Policing Foreigners during the Terror

If the legislators of the radical Revolution proclaimed new forms of civic and civil equality, they also turned against those who appeared to threaten the new nation. The laws of the Terror menaced all suspected of counter-revolutionary activity, whether professing royalism, hoarding grain, or communicating with émigrés. But literal foreigners and nobles—legally assimilated as a group to enemy foreigners—were subject to particular policing measures that intensified during the Terror.

The "caste of nobles" had been a touchstone of hatred from early in the Revolution. In June 1790 the Constituent Assembly abolished nobility and forbade the use of titles. But former nobles did not disappear from the list of enemies of the Revolution. Beginning in the winter of 1791–92, the revolutionary government took a series of measures against ex-nobles, designed to exclude them from the exercise of political citizenship, to keep them from "corrupting" the army, and in general to make them more vulnerable to laws aimed at potential counterrevolutionaries.[38] Individual ex-nobles were nonetheless welcomed into the government, and even the early laws of the Terror still made exceptions for patriotic individuals. The infamous Law of Suspects of September 1793 decreed the arrest of anyone simply suspected of having committed a counterrevolutionary act. Suspects included "those former nobles, together with husbands, wives, fathers, mothers, sons or daughters, brothers or sisters, and agents of the émigrés, who have not constantly demonstrated their devotion to the Revolution." The language of the law was dangerously vague and singled out ex-nobles. However, it also provided a means of escaping such identification for nobles who could demonstrate their personal patriotism, even if such patriotism was difficult to prove. Divorced spouses of émigrés were also exempted, as the government proclaimed on 28 Vendémiaire Year II (October 19, 1793): "considering that one cannot regard [a woman] as a wife of an émigré after she has legally ceased to be one, every divorced ex-wife of an émigré must, in the execution of the degree of September 17, be treated like other citizens, and arrested only if she has personally made herself suspect."[39]

Like certain former nobles, foreigners were also initially welcomed into the new nation as individuals. In the most famous example, both the American Thomas Paine and the Prussian Anarchisis Cloots became deputies to the French National Assembly in the autumn of 1792.[40] But starting in March 1793, the revolutionary government began to reverse its policy of accepting territorial outsiders into the community of French citizens. On 5 Nivôse Year II (December 25, 1793), Cloots and Paine were expelled from the Convention.[41] As the Jacobin government became increasingly embroiled in war with much of Europe, it began to keep track of all foreigners in Paris, ordering the arrest and confiscation of the property of

British and Spanish subjects. The government proclaimed in August 1793 that subjects of enemy powers who had not been domiciled in France before July 14, 1789, were to be arrested.[42] The decree quickly proved too sweeping to be applied easily, and it was replaced by somewhat more restricted measures in September and October 1793. Although these measures were applied rigorously to British subjects, they do not appear to have been systematically enforced against other foreigners.[43]

Substantial categories of foreigners were also explicitly exempted from the measures in the fall of 1793, particularly workers and artists and men and women from Liège and Brabant, who were to be regarded as legally French because they were part of the expanding French empire. Like former nobles who could demonstrate their personal commitment to the Revolution, *étrangers* who "since their stay in France have provided proof of their patriotism [*civisme*] and attachment to the French Revolution" were tolerated; they had demonstrated their personal adherence to the revolutionary community of citizens.[44]

Both men and women were encompassed by these measures, but the National Convention briefly debated the specific status of women married to men whose original nationality was different from theirs. It decreed in October 1793 that foreign-born women who had married French men were exempt from the law ordering the detention of British subjects unless they were personally suspect or married to French men who were under suspicion.[45] Proponents of the exemption offered two complementary rationales. Bertrand Barère justified the October exemption by drawing on the transformative principle of marriage for women and insisting that it applied to national citizenship. He declared that "when a French man marries a foreign woman, his wife immediately becomes French; it's a very well-known axiom, consecrated in the laws of all peoples, that a woman follows her husband's condition." Others emphasized that a woman's children anchored her to her new country. Antoine Louis Léon de Saint-Just, while contending that "independent and vagabond foreign women" were not to be trusted, proclaimed that women who had married good citizens and become mothers of French children had "no other country than that of their children."[46]

In responding to policing measures, individual women sometimes combined these arguments. The widow Dillon, who had been born in Britain, thus tried to demonstrate that both familial bonds and her own actions had made her French. She argued that both her husband and his father had been naturalized French, a fact that implicitly made her French. She had stayed in France after their deaths, thus demonstrating her own commitment to the revolutionary nation. To strengthen her argument, Dillon drew implicitly on the qualifications for citizenship in the 1793 Constitution, including both those of residence and those of the adoption of a citizen. She contended that she had brought her fortune to France and renounced England forever. She had also adopted a young daughter and tried to alleviate the situation of three young French citizens whose father, Général Théobald Dillon, had died in the service of France.[47]

Dillon's petition drew little attention. But when the revolutionary government attempted to apply broader policing measures against foreigners and former nobles, it was forced to consider similar claims by other women hoping to be counted as French citizens because of—or despite—their actions and familial connections.

The Germinal Law Revisited

The police measures of Germinal Year II (April 1794) against nobles and enemy foreigners reveal the growing challenges to early revolutionary visions of national citizenship as an individual and voluntary contract and the revolutionary state as the parent of new citizens and new "children." The decree, prompted by Saint-Just's reflections on the dangers facing the revolutionary republic, was only one of a plethora of measures taken by the government of the Terror to purge the revolutionary nation of its enemies.[48] But taken together with subsequent amendments and the exceptional number of individual petitions that survive in the archives—well over 1,000—it provides us with a rare opportunity to examine how the revolutionary state and ordinary men and women tried to make sense of the contracts of kinship and citizenship at a pivotal moment in the Revolution.[49]

With the decree, the Committee of Public Safety forbade former nobles and foreigners born subjects of enemy powers to hold public office unless they were explicitly "requisitioned" to do so. They were excluded from attending the meetings of revolutionary sections, *sociétés populaires,* and *comités de surveillance.* Moreover, they were ordered to leave key sites— particularly, but not exclusively, Paris—within a mere ten days of the decree. Leaving home was terrifying to men and women who had spent most or all of their lives in one locale and who often had no family, friends, or means of support elsewhere. Yet the penalty for disobeying the law was truly alarming: those who stayed, without having proved that they were both French and non-noble, were declared "outside the law" *(hors de la loi).* They would be defenseless in the face of revolutionary justice, risking prison or, as more than one petitioner discovered too late, the guillotine.

As in the October 1793 law, several categories of foreigners were explicitly exempted from the new police measure. But the Germinal law, though it allowed the government to requisition those deemed useful and created some exemptions for those who were too young or old and decrepit to cause real harm or those who were actively useful for the well-being of the revolutionary Republic, made no explicit provisions for those who could prove their attachment to the revolutionary nation. Indeed, Sophie Wahnich has argued that the decree marked an end to a model of integration through individual political adhesion. She claims that this shift involved ascribing communal identity before the Revolution to a "mythical origin" in which foreigners and nobles had not participated.[50] The shift was not as clear as Wahnich suggests, however, for the leaders of the Revolution in 1794 continued to espouse a contractual model of individual national citizenship even as they classed groups of men and women as inherently suspect. But the Germinal decree did intensify measures against enemy foreigners and appears to have been the first police measure that forced all ex-nobles to assess whether they were, or were perceived to be, permanently marked by their origin.

Indeed, questions and pleas from accused nobles are especially prominent in these collections. Unlike foreigners' familial bonds during the Old Regime, the family ties of nobles had been crucial to their status in the prerevolutionary state. Structures of nobility stressed family identity, often requiring several generations before full nobility was attained.[51] The members of the Committee of Public Safety did not initially consider whether children could be responsible for their parents' ambition in ennobling themselves, but they did proclaim that a woman's status should be enveloped in her husband's. Women who married commoners were to be rewarded for their virtuous decision, while women who aligned themselves with nobles were to be justly punished for their criminal ambition. Following earlier examples, the resulting exemption for foreign women who had married French men and noble women who had married commoners was passed with minimal discussion. As Barère explained, "this question did not concern the Committee, because it thought there was no room for doubt."[52] The revolutionary view that marriages were free contracts implied that marriage was a conscious decision by a woman to associate herself with the social and political community that her husband represented. The Germinal law further suggested that this was the only such act that she could perform in her life.[53] Families, once formed, were indissoluble units. Women remained permanently linked to their husbands, while children were forever marked by their familial heritage.

As Barère and the other members of the Committee must have known, the experience of eighteenth-century family life did not bode well for such a vision of domestic stability and harmony.[54] But more importantly, the emerging institutions and rhetoric created by the Revolution themselves militated against the assumption that families were unchanging units. Because the 1793 law had established exemptions for both men and women who could prove their patriotism, the converse of this exemption— the idea that a French woman who had married a foreigner was legally an *étrangère*—was not immediately problematic. But as the government of the Terror increasingly sought to label men and women in terms of an immutable origin, the question of how the marital bond affected women's citizenship status—especially for those who had been part of the "alien" community of nobles—suddenly became crucial.

Many threatened by the decree, particularly women, disputed the idea that marriage contracts should be read as emblematic of their personal ability or inability to participate in the community of good revolutionary citizens, especially if such marriages had been coerced or dissolved. They argued that they had legally dissociated themselves from their wayward spouses, breaking with the tyranny of Old Regime society and families to establish their personal involvement in the sovereign nation. Other petitioners emphasized the converse. Both ex-nobles and foreigners used the rhetoric of the "great family" of the nation to argue for their rights as adopted children of the new state. A law that permanently stigmatized them contradicted both natural laws and those of the newborn republic; it prevented outsiders from making new familial alliances that would allow them to find true homes in the revolutionary nation.

Widows, Divorcées, and the Contracts of Citizenship

Petitioners of both sexes portrayed themselves as patriotic. They invoked the testimony of their neighbors, referred to money that they had donated to the Revolution, pleaded that their status as workers or small-scale retail merchants should exempt them from the taint of nobility, or argued that the participation of their sons and brothers in the war effort demonstrated that they conformed to the social ideals of the Year II and deserved to be treated as members of the revolutionary community of citizens. They insisted that they should not be blamed for their parents' noble or foreign status; they should be judged according to their own actions, not the "stain" of their birth.

However, unlike men, women could be viewed as personally responsible for titles acquired through familial relationships, since they had chosen to ennoble themselves through marriage. Moreover, they could potentially end their membership in the alien caste of nobility with the dissolution of their marriages. Widows, divorcées, and women who had married "ex-nobles" after the formal abolition of nobility thus beseeched the government to consider their status as separate from that of their husbands. They argued that marriage could be understood as a contract symbolic of the desire to embrace or reject republican values only when it was made by freely consenting adults. Furthermore, such a contract, especially when it had associated petitioners with the despicable "caste of nobles," was not necessarily a permanent or irrevocable one.

Patrice Higonnet has rightly pointed out that nobles often tried to use the principle of individual responsibility to free themselves from accusations of familial or collective antirevolutionary behavior and that in the context of the Germinal decrees, the issue of non-noble relatives of "native" nobles was especially thorny.[55] But Higonnet does not discuss how revolutionary redefinitions of family might have contributed to making such associations particularly controversial, or whether men and women perceived familial and personal membership in the nation differently.

Certain supplicants, particularly women, tried to prove that marriages that branded them as nobles had been invalid social contracts from the beginning. They contended that they had not chosen to wed nobles but had been compelled to do so by laws that subjected them to their parents' wishes. They implicitly acknowledged that marriage, freely chosen, might demonstrate a woman's political choice and, by extension, determine her identity as a citizen or outsider. However, their exclusion from the community of citizens had been forced upon them. The *citoyenne* Ancerville, married to a Polish nobleman who had since abandoned her, argued that "if it were a crime for her to participate in this conceded nobility, it was involuntary on her behalf. Aged nineteen at the time of her marriage, submitted by her status as a minor to the wishes of her parents, she only followed the orders that she was given."[56]

It seems likely that many prospective brides had not, at least at the time, objected strenuously to their parents' choice of a rich, titled spouse. Most of these petitioners, like Ancerville, had celebrated their marriages at the age of eighteen or nineteen.[57] They were legally minors under both Old Regime and revolutionary law, but they were certainly old enough to have some idea of the possible consequences of their alliances. Stories of parental intervention, while clearly reflecting the family interests that often underpinned marital alliances, appear less as a simple reflection of their experiences than as a way to use revolutionary attacks on "despotism" to argue that their marriages were not legitimate social contracts.

As we have seen, women in the Old Regime had also portrayed their marriages as coerced when they wanted to separate themselves from their husbands' status; thus noble-born widows of commoner husbands sometimes sought to preserve their nobility by portraying themselves as victims who had been compelled as minors to marry commoner (*roturier*) husbands against their will.[58] But the Germinal petitioners took this strategy further as they sought to reject, rather than protect, noble status. They associated their forced marriages with a general time of tyrannical laws and practices, scattering their petitions with phrases like "an age in which the laws of despotism" had determined marriages. In several cases, petitioners even invoked the emblem of familial tyranny and state intervention in the Old Regime, *lettres de cachet*, to suggest that their marriages should not be read as free decisions to align themselves with a noble community.[59] For example, the divorcée Gotteville made a strong case that she had been coerced by parental pressure into marrying an officer in the marines. She stressed that she had been the victim of a *lettre de cachet*, issued a year after her marriage, which "gave her the choice to adore her husband and prove it to him, or to go to a convent." Her decision was simple: "Too honest to know how to dissimulate and wanting to spare herself the ordeal of a role she could not endure, she fled to a convent."[60]

However, unlike noble women concerned about *dérogation* through marriage in the Old Regime, petitioners in 1794 were often torn between showing that their marriages had been coerced and trying to prove that their husbands were not what they seemed to be.[61] The widow Daimous, after demanding to know if she could be held responsible for her parents' perverse ambition in marrying her to a noble, tried to argue that her husband had not really been a noble; rather, "a citizen without a fortune, a brave soldier, gifted with all the qualities that characterize a true patriot but descended from noble ancestors, her husband was as courageous in combat as he was a good father and citizen during peacetime." Marie Dubois was even more confused about what rhetoric to use or how to use it. She tried to present herself as a good republican and *roturière*, noting that she had been married at age sixteen to a forty-eight-year-old noble. But instead of a righteous denunciation of her spouse as a noble, whose status she rejected, she repeatedly testified to her devotion to her dead husband: "I made him the happiest of men, and I was the happiest of women for thirty-five years."[62]

Such confusion was often emblematic of more general uncertainty about how to use revolutionary concepts effectively. Dubois also undercut her efforts to portray her noble husband as a virtuous *sans-culotte*. She proclaimed that he had worked since the age of fourteen, teaching writing, mathematics, and music, and that "it is good to have children learn crafts and talents, because you never know what position you'll end up in life; that's a principle of Jean Jacques Rousseau, with whom my husband copied music for several people and for the opera." But rather than making the appropriate argument that her husband had "regenerated" himself with this work, she instead explained that his repeated attempts to obtain an honorific position in the government had been rejected because he did not have the money to bribe the appropriate officials.[63]

Even when petitioners used revolutionary rhetoric more effectively than Dubois, the government made no exceptions for women who contended that they had married nobles against their will, perhaps because it would have been almost impossible to prove whether or not a woman had freely consented to her marriage.[64] However, the Committee of Public Safety and the National Convention were forced to consider whether a marriage contract as social contract could be unmade, regardless of how legitimately or illegitimately it had been formed. More than 100 petitions in this collection were written by or for widows, while another 50 or so argued the cause of divorced women. The appeal made by one anonymous divorcée epitomizes a common fear that the Germinal law would prevent a woman from entering "a class in which she wants to live and force her against her will to remain the wife of a former [noble] when she no longer wanted to be one."[65]

Their pleas also raised a basic question of whether widowed and divorced women were in the same position. A spouse's death could not prove that a widow wanted to remain permanently attached to his name and reputation. At the same time, it did not, and could not (except in the dubious case of domestic murder), indicate that a bereaved wife had wanted to separate herself from her husband and the community that he supposedly incarnated. Several divorced women consciously highlighted this difference between their situation and that of widows. For example, the *citoyenne* Bouillard insisted that her divorce from a husband ennobled by his post as an accountant should free her from guilt by association in a way that widowhood would never have done:

> I ask you again if my divorce did not remove the stain of nobility, which my marriage to a noble gave me. It seems that it must have this virtue, since, in breaking the conjugal bond, it deprived me of all matrimonial advantages. How could it leave formerly honorific titles or qualities? One cannot compare divorce in any way to the natural death of a husband.[66]

Because divorce had been instituted for less than a year and a half, its legal implications were far from clear. On the day of the decree itself, 27 Germinal, C. F. Oudot, the deputy for the Department of Côte d'Or, proclaimed that further reform of divorce law was critical because "the Convention must hurry to destroy these sorts of chains; it owes this especially to those spouses who, beyond the work of the Revolution, have not ceased to fight an enemy of the Republic in their own homes and under the name of the most dear."[67] But other measures suggested that divorce was an inadequate means of disassociating oneself from a spouse, especially a husband, who was outside the revolutionary nation. The National Convention had proclaimed three weeks earlier, on 4 Germinal Year II (March 24, 1794), that no daughter or wife of an émigré, even divorced, could marry a foreigner and leave French territory, under penalty of being treated as an émigrée herself.[68] This decree was prompted by Barère's denunciation of an "infamous trade" in which women were being encouraged to marry foreigners and leave the country in order to cheat France of its rightful property. But it also heightened petitioners' uncertainty about whether they could separate themselves sufficiently from a noble or foreign spouse.

Responding to the "crowds of citizens" who besieged them, the Committee granted exceptions on 3 Floréal Year II (April 22, 1794, a week after the original decree) for "women born commoners who are childless widows of former nobles" and "women born commoners who divorced nobles before the law was passed."[69] At the same time the government exempted those who had purchased an ennobling office but who had not held it long enough to become noble in the standards of the Old Regime and nobles who had used the title *écuyer,* the lowest in the hierarchy of noble positions, and one that was often given to those straddling the boundary between noble and commoner.

In certain respects, similar logic underlay all these exemptions. Borderline nobles were exempted partly on the grounds that children who had had titles lavished upon them at birth by their parents could not be held responsible for such titles if they had since relinquished them; similarly, widows and divorced women could not be held responsible for the crime of their husbands' nobility if that bond had since been broken. However, these similarities also conceal a striking contrast. Children did not have to repudiate their relationships with their parents, whereas widows and divorcées often sought to dissociate themselves not only from their husbands' titles but often from their husbands themselves.

Furthermore, widows and divorcées were indeed treated differently. Widows were required to be childless in order to rejoin the community of *sans-culotte* citizens. As Higonnet has pointed out, the "legal status of the male line was the crucial variable."[70] With a husband's death, women who had not given birth to noble heirs returned to their maiden status and legally to the community incarnated by their parents. However, the obligation of childlessness was not imposed upon divorcées. At least in theory, they were able to erase their bonds with their former spouses and the "contemptible caste of the nobility" regardless of whether they had had children. In practice, this distinction was murky. The exception for divorced women inspired a second set of petitions from borderline cases: divorced women who had children over age fifteen and were not sure if they were truly exempted, women who had begun proceedings for divorce but had not yet signed the papers, and those who been abandoned or legally separated (*séparées de corps et biens*) during the Old Regime but not formally divorced during the Revolution.

Certain widows contested the requirement that they be childless in order to be considered part of the community of *sans-culotte* citizens. Others specified that their daughters—women who in Old Regime law would not have been able to pass on nobility to their husbands or children—should be considered incapable of retroactively staining their mothers with the sin of nobility. Thus the mother of a twelve-year-old girl demanded to know how her daughter's alleged nobility could affect her; since "this daughter could not, even following the prejudices of the outlawed regime, give nobility to her husband or children, how could she give this disastrous gift to her mother, especially in a time when all is personal, and when the ridiculous transmission of supposed 'rights of blood' is destroyed?"[71] Such widows argued that children should not count against a virtuous mother and citizen, often noting that their sons were in the armies of the revolutionary Republic. As one anonymous petitioner proclaimed, "to punish maternity would be too impolitic when celibacy is recognized more than ever to be one of the scourges of society."[72]

"As in Rome, One Sacrifices to the *Patrie* One's Father, Husband"

The Germinal petitioners were far from the only women to adopt such arguments; women accused of emigration during the Terror made very similar pleas. Supplicants highlighted their lack of civil and political power, past subordination to male family members, and their resolute identity as *citoyennes françaises*. One petition from 1794, by a young woman who wrote under the protective guise of anonymity, provides a particularly poignant example of these strategies.[73] Married at age sixteen, she and her infant son had been dragged to England three years later, in May 1791. She spent the next few years attempting to escape from paternal and spousal surveillance and to return to the revolutionary nation. French officials in London told her that she could not do so without her husband's permission; she dismissed the idea that she needed to submit to his authority, and continued to search for a means to return home. Prevented by the French plenipotentiary minister at the Hague from returning to France even after she left the marital household, the young mother made the agonizing decision to send her son back to his *patrie* without her. She finally managed to debark in France in March 1793 under an assumed name. She tried to return home, but her terrified mother refused to offer her shelter. By the time she pleaded her case with the government, she had spent over a year in France—during the height of the Terror—without a fixed residence, familial support, or news of her son.

In defending her case, the young woman repeatedly emphasized both her general weakness and subjection as a daughter and wife and her own unshakable identity as a "French citizen." Like the Germinal petitioners who tried to portray their marriages to noblemen and subsequent exclusion from the community of citizens as the result of parental despotism, she insisted that her exile from the national community was not of her own doing, but was a result of past subordination in the family. She presented herself as the victim of "the abuses of authority committed by fathers and husbands under the despotism of the Old Regime." Although her marriage had not directly made her a foreigner, the act that robbed her of her citizenship—her departure from French territory—had taken place against her will, and it had been possible only because of prerevolutionary laws establishing a husband's authority over his wife.

Like other apologists for women's emigration, the petitioner also focused on her powerlessness to harm her country. She had not left France with any intention to undermine the Republic, and as a woman she was unable to defend her country or to make war on it. Moreover, she claimed that the laws on émigrés actually acknowledged and excused the weakness of young women. She cited the March 1793 law, which specified that "émigré girls aged between fourteen and twenty-one who have returned or who will return to the territory of the republic will be deported." Although the article held young woman responsible for emigration, it treated them more mercifully than other émigrés, who, if caught after having returned to French territory, were condemned to death. She maintained that the exception encompassed her, since she had been only nineteen years old when she left France and twenty-two when she returned to her *patrie*. More important, the law seemed to suggest that "weak beings" should be exempted from political obligations, including the obligation to remain in France:

> The law wanted to exempt girls and women who are minors. These weak beings, subjected by their sex and education, without experience, considered to be incapacitated in their civil actions, were not subject to the penalties that belong only to a premeditated emigration with the intention to harm the rights of justice and the sovereignty of the people.

While emphasizing her gendered inability to harm the "sovereignty of the people," she also repeatedly insisted that she had in fact placed duty to her country over familial loyalties: "Disobeying paternal and marital power, I abandoned them to obey the laws of my country [*pays*]." The idea that she was sacrificing for her *patrie* allowed her to ignore criticism when she sent her son back to France without her: "I told myself that the prejudices, egoism, and abusive laws of our former government have changed; before, one owed nothing to one's country [*patrie*]; now, as in Rome, one sacrifices to it one's father, husband, and all others who must be dear to us only after it [*patrie*]." Her devotion to her *patrie* was linked to her firm belief that she was a *citoyenne française* and that her forced emigration under her husband's authority had not stripped her of her membership in the revolutionary nation. When the French plenipotentiary minister told her that she could not return to France, she had argued that she should be allowed to do so because "I am French and have never ceased to be." In concluding her case in her petition to the government, she contended that "I could not have lost the quality of a French citizen by a momentary sojourn." She demanded to know if "this quality so precious to my heart could have been taken away from me." It was a plea that would go unanswered.

Citizenship through Family Ties

Certain men and women threatened by the Germinal law went beyond the young émigrée's claim that she had placed *patrie* ahead of familial bonds to identify the nation itself as their family. Petitioners in 1794 talked of saving themselves in "the breast of their adopted country," proclaimed that they had "adopted the country as a mother," or argued that "born among the people, raised among them, am I not justified in considering them as my adopted family?"[74] Men and women also responded to the Germinal decrees by arguing that they were literally adopted "children" of the revolutionary nation-state. Illegitimate children, as well as certain monks and nuns who had been "civilly dead" during the Old Regime, begged the government to recognize them as its progeny. Other petitioners fretted that the decrees prevented them from forming new families and thereby contributing to the "great family" of citizens.

The new institution of adoption represented the most dramatic form of transforming family and civic bonds, substituting new, fictive relationships for those of birth. Adults were strongly encouraged to adopt. One writer on the topic, Oudot, who had also championed divorce reform, proclaimed in 1793 that adoption was a "sacred duty, indispensable for every childless citizen," and that various localities held festivals to honor those who had adopted children.[75] However, few cases of formal adoption are mentioned in these petitions, probably because children under fifteen were automatically exempted.[76] *Sans-culotte* parents who had adopted noble children were unlikely—for the most part—to worry about children who were still legally protected, while noble parents who had adopted *roturier* children had more pressing concerns than their children's status. Instead, the most vocal petitioners were those who, as adults, had become metaphorically "adopted children of the republic."

Such petitioners included men and women who had been born out of wedlock and given full rights as citizens by the revolutionary government.[77] Those with noble parents feared that their new ability to inherit from their parents would also make them inherit their parents' titles. The archives contain at least twenty petitions from such individuals, terrified that the rights granted to them by the revolutionary government had become a new title of exclusion, that they had been reborn not as citizens but as outsiders. Sophie Rousselet, whose father was the bastard child of a marquis, expresses their common fear and astonishment:

> My ability to inherit from a noble parent has been recognized; it's a blessing of the revolution, but could the laws of the Revolution have given me nobility? Neither my father nor I ever enjoyed [the status of nobles]: the former government did not find me noble. Judged as a commoner to share the humiliations and injustices poured with profusion on this class, will I be judged as a noble today for the first time in my life, to share the disgrace of the nobility?[78]

Men and women like Rousselet, however, could make a special case for their inclusion in the community of virtuous republicans. Several argued that they were the truest citizens of the new regime, "more closely tied than any others to the prosperity of the Republic."[79] The unprecedented recognition of their rights meant that they had actually been born—or in a sense "born again," this time legitimately—with the Revolution itself.

A few former nuns and monks caught in the confused tentacles of the Germinal decrees adopted a similar strategy to downplay their noble origins, portraying themselves as grateful citizens "reborn" with the Revolution from a state of social and political nullity. The position of natural children—unable to inherit from their parents and barred from public and military functions—was paralleled by the civil death of those who had taken religious vows. Thus August Malhau, who had joined a monastery at the age of sixteen or seventeen, asserted that his vows meant that he had lost all his civil and political rights during his religious confinement. But as a benefit of the same constitution that had destroyed nobility, he had been restored to "all his rights as a citizen." He contended: "Citizen Representatives, it's your constitution, it's you who gave me civil and political rights, and I am convinced that you did not intend to make me a noble." Similarly, the former nun Jacquet argued that as an innocent victim of her parents' vanity and ambitions, she had been thrown into a convent at the age of seven. There she had been forced to take her vows and renounce all civil rights. But the Revolution had restored her to liberty and all "the advantages of society."[80]

Jacquet made no reference to an impending marriage, simply asking that she be allowed to stay in Paris to make shirts for the army or otherwise do "what a woman can do with the work of her hands." Yet her story, that of a young girl forced by parental despotism and avarice into a convent, and deeply grateful for her release by a beneficent government, resonated with an important myth of the revolutionary government. When the members of the National Assembly suppressed contemplative religious orders in 1790, they had imagined nuns as beautiful young women kept from their natural roles as wives and mothers by the impenetrable walls of the convent. Marriage would reincorporate these lost women into society, allowing them to take up their true destinies as wives and mothers.[81]

Echoing the general celebration of marriage as an institution of citizenship, several petitioners explicitly referred to the threat that the Germinal decrees seemed to pose to this vision of domesticity and national fecundity. The widow Lauzanne argued on behalf of her daughters that the decree would have the effect of sending a large number of young people to isolated and little-populated corners of the country. Unable to meet potential partners, they would be forced to spend their lives in a lonely and unproductive celibacy, "which could not be the intention of the representatives of the nation."[82] Her argument paralleled those made on behalf of the former spouses of émigrés. The law of September 1792 forbade divorced couples to marry again within a year after the divorce. Individuals who wanted to remarry protested such restrictions: as one such woman proclaimed, she had got divorced because she no longer wanted to be "united to someone who had abandoned his country to arm himself against it" and should be allowed to remarry immediately, this time a patriot.[83] Others not only sought permission for the divorced spouses of émigrés to remarry, but insisted that they do so for the good of the nation; on 28 Nivôse Year II (December 22, 1793), another anonymous petitioner suggested that it would be "politic to add to this law a revolutionary article that would oblige all women who divorced because their husbands emigrated to remarry with three months."[84]

Petitioners who invoked the evils of celibacy often used language similar to that of the women who claimed that they had been forced to marry against their will. Like the young women married as minors, these petitioners cursed parental despotism. However, they pointed to a problem with the decree that was precisely the opposite: abuses of *puissance paternelle* did not, or did not only, coerce people into marriages and sociopolitical communities against their will. They also prevented citizens from forming new bonds and using those family ties to become part of the nation. The discursive continuities are particularly evident in a petition on behalf of a young noble-born woman who wanted to marry a *sans-culotte*. Because she was under twenty-one, she could not do so without her parents' permission. An anonymous supporter claimed that her situation was common: "Infinitely many ex-nobles are insistently and categorically opposed to their daughters' marriages with patriots . . . and tyrannically abuse the right accorded to them by the principle of the law."[85] Like the woman who described her marriage to a noble as that of "a girl under the power of her parents," the champion of would-be spouses of *sans-culottes* cursed the despotic power of their parents.[86] He even went a step further, suggesting that since the law had declared ex-nobles civilly dead, they were no longer French citizens and their paternal authority had ceased.

Integration or reintegration into the nation through marriage was particularly problematic for women who had married former nobles and for men. Some women noted that they had married ex-nobles—but emphasized they had married after the decrees of June 19–23, 1790, which had abolished nobility and forbidden the use of titles. Few of these petitioners specified the title to nobility that their spouses had previously enjoyed. It did not matter if a husband had been a military officer, a count whose family had held noble property for generations, or a newly ennobled *secrétaire de roi;* all forms of nobility had been suppressed. Petitioners contended first that nobles had ceased to exist as a separate and identifiable caste after the abolition of nobility in June 1790. They argued—like the ex-nobles who proclaimed that they had sat with the Third Estate in the Estates Générales and had thus thrown in their lot with the Revolution from its birth—that the Revolution had truly erased nobility. Second, such women contended that they had not intended to repudiate membership in the community of *sans-culotte* citizens by marrying former nobles. Such a marriage was not one of "criminal ambition"; instead, it represented the virtuous formation of a republican household, itself a proof of patriotic identity. The former widow Dumontier thus explained that she had refused the hand of a former noble officer until noble titles had been officially abolished and equality proclaimed, while Yolande Viel maintained that it was "not pride and vanity that determined my choice but public opinion that openly rendered justice to his wise life and conduct."[87]

The transformative power of marriage for men was also open to doubt, even as revolutionaries insisted that priests should prove their citizenship by abandoning their lives of celibacy. As one anonymous petitioner pointed out, the Germinal decrees did not seem to apply the same mechanisms of national integration to ex-nobles and priests:

> You regard as friends of the people priests who have taken a civic oath [*leur serment*], renounced their titles [*remis leurs lettres*], and married; we have also taken oaths, renounced our titles, and taken wives. Why establish a difference between men who have the same titles to the esteem of their fellow citizens?[88]

Another petitioner argued that the decrees were opposed to both the basic laws of nature and those of the republic, which made it a "duty for all citizens" to marry. No woman would voluntarily marry an ex-noble if it meant sharing his civil reprobation. In consequence, former nobles would remain forever isolated, deprived of the possibility of assimilating into a society of citizens. He proposed that the law be amended so that ex-nobles could marry *roturières* without fear of incriminating and endangering their prospective spouses.[89] His amendment would grant "all the rights of a French citizen" to noble men who were married to, or engaged to marry, *sans-culotte* women. This exception was subject to further qualifications. Such former nobles could not have émigré relatives and had to have public opinion in their neighborhood (*lieu habituel*) on their side. Their prospective wives had to be not only non-noble but also poor, with a dowry that did not exceed a limited sum; the petitioner left the exact amount up to the Committee to decide. But once "incorporated into the nation" by marriage, such people should no longer be considered as nobles.

Few other petitioners advocated such a general exception for noble men who had married *sans-culotte* women. Yet many were convinced, unlike the members of the Committee who had drafted the decree, that marriage should be understood as a social and political marker and moment of transformation for both women and men. Some petitioners simply mentioned their wives' status briefly in order to demonstrate that their lives were far from those of the great nobility. Marrying a laundress, an actress, or the daughter of an herbalist or journeyman clothmaker, although it might provide clean clothes or a few fragrant herbs, seldom prepared one for a career as a powdered aficionado of the court.[90] Others presented such marriages as incontrovertible evidence that they had turned their backs on their familial heritage: succinctly, "the proof that he [the petitioner] had no regard for the rank of a former noble is that he married a *sans-culotte* woman."[91] They implied that marriage was a form of national integration not only for the woman who had chosen to throw in her sort with a *sans-culotte* husband but also for noble men who had abandoned the cultural milieu of their birth to marry women of the working class.

Conclusion

The government of the radical Revolution wanted to establish clear-cut distinctions between citizens and outsiders. It thus attempted to treat families as immutable social units, in which a woman's status was fixed by her husband's. At the same time, however, it upheld and expanded earlier revolutionary laws that made it possible to transform the contracts of kinship through mechanisms like divorce and adoption. It also extended the idea of the nation itself as a "great family" that superseded individual familial bonds. Similarly, the partisans of the Terror sought to label people by their ascribed or juridical status—foreigner or French, noble or commoner—while still proclaiming the possibility of individual "rebirth" as citizens through personal patriotism, expressed in adhesion to the nation. The Germinal law and the responses it provoked provide one window onto the tensions created by these conflicting goals.

Given the chaos of the Terror, as well as the confusion of statutes inherited from the Old Regime and those created by the Revolution itself, it is not surprising that many requests to define individuals' citizenship statuses clearly received only limited clarification. But such ambiguity also reinforced the likelihood that national bonds would continue to trump familial ones. When faced with conflicts between individual citizenship obligations and hierarchical family relations, dependents often portrayed themselves as placing their duty to the state above legal subordination in the family. Although officials were often skeptical of such claims, they saw women as personally responsible for their actions as members of the state and not only recognized their ability to choose between family and citizenship ties, but often required them to do so.

Revolutionaries also began to consider the implications of marriage as a contract affecting both men and women. Lawmakers assumed that a woman's status would be subsumed under her husband's status, but were also forced to consider exceptions to that rule and ways in which marriage and citizenship status could be separated in a radical republic. They also began to consider more systematically the effect of marriage on men's place in a national community. Here they established an important difference between ex-nobles and literal foreigners. Male immigrants escaped the Germinal decrees if they had lived in France for twenty years, or ten if they had married a non-noble French woman. This exception implied that marriage to a French woman, unlike a nobleman's marriage to a *sans-culotte* woman, could affect an outsider's legal incorporation into the revolutionary community of citizens. This view was supported by the articles in the Constitutions of 1791 and 1793, which made marriage to a French woman one of the key factors that could expedite a foreigner's legal transformation into a French citizen; it would reappear in the 1795 Constitution in a new form. Indeed, as we shall see, debates over the implications of men's and women's membership in the nation-state and the effects of familial bonds in shaping that status, would persist long after the Terror.

Figure 2. Jacques-Louis David, *Portrait of Suzanne Le Peletier de Saint-Fargeau*, 1804, oil on canvas, 60.5 x 49.5 cm. The J. Paul Getty Museum, Los Angeles. Courtesy of the J. Paul Getty Museum.

Part II

Toward a Nation of Families:
Transitions of the Late 1790s

On 9 Thermidor Year II (July 27, 1794), Robespierre was arrested and then executed. His fall from power precipitated the end of the Terror. Revolutionaries began the slow and often painful process of trying to end the violence of the Terror and to assign responsibility for its excesses while still preserving the Republic.[1] They overturned some of the most abusive laws of the radical Revolution and repealed the 26–27 Germinal Year II laws on ex-nobles and foreigners on December 8, 1794.[2] They also began to reorganize the structure of government. Such changes were perhaps most evident in the Thermidorian period, the thirteen months that followed immediately on Robespierre's death. But while revolutionaries ultimately produced yet another constitution, in Fructidor Year III (August 1795), the resulting government did not bring stability.

Indeed, the next few years would be marked by political coups as the new Directorial government sought to create and protect a moderate republic. In 1796 and early 1797, France tilted toward a more conservative order. But the Directory reacted to the elections of royalists to the legislature with a left-wing coup on 18 Fructidor Year V (September 4, 1797). In its wake, the political leadership annulled elections and instituted the Directorial Terror of early 1798, a reprise of the earlier Terror, though it was far more limited in scale and primarily deported its opponents rather than executing them. The coup of 22 Floréal Year VI (May 22, 1798) struck in turn against movements that appeared to threaten the republic from the left. Throughout the period, France remained at war with much of Europe, annexing or establishing "sister republics," from the Low Countries through Switzerland and the Italian peninsula. In this climate of militarization and political turmoil, the general Napoleon Bonaparte seized power in Brumaire Year VIII (November 1799).

Historians have tended to see the Thermidorian period and the Directory either as reactions, codas after the drama and innovations of the radical Revolution, or as preludes to Napoleon's coup. Yet scholars have begun recently to demonstrate the originality and complexity of political ideas and experiments in the late 1790s.[3] Intellectuals and politicians sought to preserve the ideals and institutions from earlier in the Revolution, but also to redefine them. Revolutionaries struggled with pressing social problems, from inflation to persistent religious unrest, by changing or instituting specific measures. But they also began to rethink fundamental social and political assumptions that had undergirded earlier revolutionary practices and policies.

Many of these assumptions were linked to changes in the meaning of national citizenship. Revolutionaries sought to create new laws that would eliminate the ambiguities and contradictions embedded in earlier measures and clarify the distinctions among categories such as "French," "foreigner," and "citizen." At the same time, they increasingly questioned the usefulness and legitimacy of the idea of the nation as a whole as a family. In the wake of the Terror, the new political leadership rethought society explicitly in terms of hierarchical families rather than in terms of rights-bearing individuals. They began to argue that familial contracts were fundamentally different from other forms of contracts. For the idea of the nation as a family, they began to substitute one of the nation as conglomerate of families, separated from the society of citizens and represented exclusively by an adult male head of the household.

As they championed unified families, revolutionaries also increasingly limited women's political rights. After women led an invasion of the National Convention during the Germinal and Prairial uprisings of Year III (April and May 1795), the Thermidorian government went beyond banning women's political clubs, as their predecessors had done in 1793, to forbidding women to attend any political assembly. It is tempting to see these uprisings as the last gasp not only of the *sans-culotte* movement in Paris, but also of any effective movement for women's rights or substantial engagement with women's citizenship. Indeed, many historians have done so.[4] Yet contemporaries continued to perceive women as French citizens entitled to certain rights and obliged to perform certain duties to the French state. Authorities often faced serious challenges when trying to reconcile their desire for a paternalistic social order with the belief that women maintained an important status as French citizens. Such challenges, however, were often less evident in the political debates that historians have usually studied than in the courtrooms and administrative halls of the late 1790s.

Contemporaries also faced unexpected difficulties in defining men's citizenship in relation to their familial identity. The task seemed more straightforward than that of defining women's relationship to the state. Article 4 of the Declaration of Rights of the Constitution of Year III proclaimed: "No one is a good citizen if he is not a good son, good father, good brother, good friend, and good husband."[5] The article echoed Rousseau's rhetorical question in the 1762 *Emile:* "is it not the good son, the good husband, the good father who makes a good citizen?" The connection between citizenship rights and familial roles now, however, corresponded to particular policies; article 83 of the Constitution, for example, required that all representatives to the upper house of the legislature, the Council of Ancients, be married or divorced. It was also the subject of frequent orations; not surprisingly, it was a particular favorite at festivals devoted to marriage, which, beginning in 1796, the government promoted as part of its calendar of republican celebrations.[6] Yet in the wake of both political turmoil and territorial expansion, the categories of French, citizen, husband, and father did not always connect neatly or easily.

The following two chapters focus on the tensions and transformations of the late 1790s. Chapter 3 examines changing relationships between paternity and citizenship and different assessments of women's membership in the nation. It concentrates on two *affaires célèbres* from 1796 and 1797. The first reveals the sharply competing arguments for family and citizenship rights in the wake of the Terror. The second case, that of Suzanne Lepeletier, would also lead the legislature to debate whether the nation as a whole should be considered as a family capable of acting as a parent of an individual; lawmakers ultimately contended that there was a fundamental difference between literal families and the "great family" of the nation.

Chapter 4 returns to the problem of emigration, as residence in France was one of the most embedded patriotic duties required of both sexes. The exigencies of ongoing war and political crisis meant that women's obligation to remain in France persisted even as the civil courts and national legislature increasingly emphasized the integrity of the family in other domains. In the wake of the Terror, émigrés and their supporters reinforced earlier arguments. They pleaded anew with the government to grant a general amnesty for émigrés, or, failing that, at least one for women who had left France. They insisted that women were French but did not have the political rights or obligations of full citizens; hence married women should not be held responsible for the actions of the head of the household in leaving the country. They also suggested that marriage to a foreign man made a French woman into a full legal foreigner, freed of obligations to her homeland. When Napoleon came into power, he and his legislators would build indirectly on such arguments as they set out to establish a more definitive solution to contradictions between family and citizenship.

3 Fathers and Foreigners

In late 1796 a German businessman and a prominent French actress appeared before the Paris civil courts, at odds over the custody of their illegitimate daughter. The actress' admirers and critics gossiped avidly about the trial, which involved some of the most prominent lawyers of the period. Another case the following year drew even more attention. It concerned Suzanne Lepeletier, the daughter of a revolutionary martyr of liberty, who had been formally "adopted by the nation" by the French National Assembly in 1793. Now officially emancipated from her relatives' tutelage, she wished to marry a debt-ridden young Dutch man. Unable to prevent the marriage through more traditional means, her uncles demanded that the state fulfill its duties as father. They insisted that the National Assembly oversee the establishment of its adopted daughter and, with her, the fate of its revolutionary patrimony; Suzanne must be stopped from "denationalizing" herself through her planned marriage to a foreigner.

Both cases involved exceptional households: in one, the would-be *paterfamilias* was a foreigner and father of an illegitimate child; in the other, the extraordinary head of the family was potentially the nation itself. But precisely because of the unusual nature of such cases, they reveal otherwise implicit assumptions about the family and citizenship in the wake of the Terror. They highlight both key social and political changes in the late 1790s and the tensions that persisted as revolutionaries struggled to decide which elements of the radical Revolution could or should be perpetuated. They called attention to the rights and obligations women held as members of the French state, and the potentially problematic status of dependents in the family whose national identity and citizenship rights depended on the status of the head of the household. They also reveal the difficulties contemporaries faced when trying to equate fathers with citizens.

75

Both cases took place as authorities and prominent figures began to reconsider the general usefulness of the metaphor of the "great family" of the nation and attempted to clearly distinguish "Frenchness" from "citizenship." Women's national citizenship was increasingly circumscribed as officials proclaimed that women were not political members of the state and should not be allowed to act as such. But as the Hoppé-Lange and Suzanne Lepeletier cases showed, the idea of a woman's membership in the nation could still be taken seriously while contemporaries debated the basis of legitimate authority within both the family and the nation. The possibility that dependents could—and should—place national bonds before family ties was questioned but not abandoned.

The Great Family

In the aftermath of the Terror, revolutionaries continued to use both the concept of "national adoption" and the more general metaphor of the nation as family. On 26 Brumaire Year III (November 16, 1794), the National Assembly proclaimed that children from Saint-Domingue and other French colonies who were younger than fifteen years old and in France for their education would be received as "children of the *patrie*" if their parents had suffered from the troubles in the colonies.[1] In the same month the deputy Jacques Brival called for the daughter of the representative Charles-Nicolas Beauvais, dead at the hands of the English at Toulon, to be adopted by the nation as Suzanne Lepeletier had been in January 1793.[2] Men and women also continued to invoke the paternal solicitude of the state, like the citizen who beseeched the legislators on 28 Floréal Year III (May 19, 1795) to absolve him of guilt in his son's emigration. He addressed them repeatedly as benevolent "fathers of the people" who understood the responsibilities of a father—and also the potential limits of those responsibilities.[3]

But the persistence of such rhetoric in the immediate aftermath of the Terror masks structural changes taking place during the Thermidorian period and especially during the Directory. Revolutionaries increasingly rethought the appropriate relations between individuals, families, and the state. The emerging challenges to the concept of the nation as a "great family" are encapsulated in the title of a treatise published in Year V (1797), *De la famille considérée comme l'élément des sociétés* [Of the Family Considered as the Element of Societies]. The author, Charles Toussaint Guiraudet, was a former deputy to the Constituent Assembly and a close associate of Condorcet and Mirabeau; he was now the secretary-general in the Ministry of Foreign Relations. He insisted that families, not individuals, were the basic units of the French nation:

All other divisions [besides that of the family] can be neither elementary nor natural. Those who consider only the individual [the man] as an isolated being, and conceive of society as a collection of men, perform a division in which the last term is not complete. Man, so considered, is within the domain of the physics and morals, but only man in the family forms the element of society.[4]

Guiraudet contended that earlier revolutionaries had abused this principle and that destructive confusion about rights was the "necessary result of the principle that the nation is only a *collection of individuals.*" He reiterated that the nation was "neither a collection of isolated individuals nor a great family reunited under one or multiple leaders, but rather a collection of families."[5]

Guiraudet's contemporary, the ideologue Pierre Louis Roederer, reviewed the secretary-general's tract shortly after its publication. Roederer was also a well-known figure in the period: actor in the opening scenes of the Revolution, half-owner of the *Journal de Paris,* and founder of the *Journal d'économie publique.*[6] He claimed that the idea that the French nation consisted of individuals was a ludicrous proposition, one that Guiraudet had invoked only as a straw man:

It is doubtless only to animate his subject and to give himself an argument to combat that the author pretended to believe in the existence of a doctrine that the nation is only a collection of individuals, not of families. I have never known such a doctrine to exist. It seems to me universally recognized—especially in France—that the *chefs de famille* alone are citizens, if one uses this term, like the Roman *paterfamilias,* to refer not only to those who are currently fathers of families, but also to those who can be.[7]

Indeed, Roederer himself had equated the citizen with the *paterfamilias* as early as 1788 and continued to do so throughout the Revolution.[8] But Roederer's dismissal of the idea of the nation as an "aggregation of individuals" misses both the real innovations of the early Revolution and the transformations that were taking place as he wrote in 1797. The creators of a new social and political order had depicted the state as a population of individuals even as they often assumed that such individuals were adult men. In dismantling the corporate structure of Old Regime society in favor of rights-bearing citizens, they celebrated—and often mandated—personal relationships to the state. But by the Thermidorian Republic and especially the Directory, revolutionaries increasingly sought to reestablish families as hierarchical and unified social institutions, and endeavored to place family bonds before individual relations with the state. Prominent republicans hoped to avoid a return to the violence and chaos of the radical Revolution by establishing a more conservative social order. Wary of completely overturning revolutionary innovations in family law, they nonetheless slowly began to restore the authority of the *paterfamilias*. In Year IV (1795–96), legislators made primary schooling a matter of voluntary parental choice, suppressed family courts, and proposed a new version of a civil code that would limit the property rights of women; a year later they challenged divorce by mutual consent and began to consider restoring paternal control over inheritance, although they maintained the principle of equal inheritance among children.[9]

More important, they called into question the principles that had shaped earlier reforms and began to reformulate the relations between family and state. Rather than imagining the family and the society of citizens as qualitatively similar kinds of institutions, they began to treat familial relations as distinct from other kinds of social and political relations. Suzanne Desan has shown that hundreds of citizens petitioned the legislature about property and monetary disputes arising from the family reform laws passed during the radical Revolution. Litigants depicted the violence of the Terror in familial terms, emphasizing the ways in which the state had intruded into the home and attacked familial bonds. The leaders of the Directorial government often drew upon such petitions and rhetoric in their own efforts to make the family the foundation of society.[10] As Irène Théry similarly concludes from debates over marriage and divorce in the period, "concern over the rights of the individual yielded to concern over the government of families, the keystone of a system that sought to base public order on private order, social order on domestic order, the great country [*patrie*] on the little one."[11]

Legislators and intellectuals increasingly tried to replace the model of individual rights-bearing citizens, a model that they associated with the dictatorship of the Terror, with one of unified and hierarchically organized families. They emphasized that the citizen was a being within a network of social relations, especially familial ones. The Constitution of Year III's linkage of good citizenship to being a good family member came at a moment when lawmakers and administrators were becoming increasingly pessimistic about the individualism underlying doctrines of the social contract—a pessimism exemplified by Guiraudet's disdain for the idea that "the nation is only a *collection of individuals*"—and it reflected that pessimism.[12]

For dependents within the family, especially married women and children, these changes implied that their relationship to the state should be mediated by the head of the household. The emphasis on restoring hierarchical order within the home also implied that marriage should not transform male citizenship—or, more precisely, that while a man's status as a head of a household could affect his citizenship status, his partner's status should not change his. But establishing how family and state should interact meant deciding who should be defined as a citizen, and how the relationships between foreignness, Frenchness, and citizenship should be understood.

Separating Citizenship from Frenchness

In the aftermath of the Terror, legislators tried to clarify the place of different inhabitants of France in the body politic. Many of the laws of the radical Revolution had used "citizen" as an all-purpose word, one that not only erased social differences but also blurred the distinctions between legal membership in a national community, patriotic duty, and the exercise of political rights. While men and women of the Thermidorian reaction and especially the Directory revived distinctions like "monsieur" and "madame" to counteract the socially leveling "citizen," legislators also sought to limit the term "citizen" to those exercising political rights. As Michel Troper has observed, the Constitution of Year III, which founded the Directory, differed substantially from its predecessors. Unlike the 1791 and 1793 Constitutions, it avoided using "citizen" to refer to inhabitants of France who lacked political rights. Legislators, however, could not establish a consistent alternate term to identify such people.[13]

The articles on naturalization also continued to embed the definition of "French" and "citizen," outlining the conditions under which "a foreigner becomes a French citizen" and those under which "the exercise of the rights of citizen is lost."[14] The articles could be, and often were, read by jurists to indicate how foreigners would become French, rather than how they became full citizens.[15] They nonetheless maintained an important ambiguity, particularly in the eyes of the general populace. The conditions for naturalization were also more restrictive than in the 1791 and 1793 Constitutions. In the context of continual war, it was often easiest to blame domestic instability on foreign conspiracy and to equate foreigners with spies and disruption.[16] Legislators changed residence requirements from one year to seven years, and omitted any clause that would allow the legislature to award citizenship to a foreigner who had not been in France for a sufficient period.[17] Articles on national citizenship emphasized property and financial stability, as did the Constitution more generally. Social qualifications for becoming a citizen were changed from "lives from his work or has acquired a property in France" to "pays direct taxes and possesses immovable property or a commercial or agricultural business." Lawmakers did maintain marriage to a French woman as a possible qualification for French citizenship, but removed the clauses on the adoption of a child or caring for the elderly. Such changes, however, may have inadvertently emphasized the role of marriage; as Michael Rapport has observed, "the only concession to those who owned no property was the alternative of marriage to a French citizen."[18]

Authorities increasingly redefined and tried to limit the content of French citizenship in other contexts. In Year V (1796–97) legislators struggled to make the distinction between the categories "French" and "citizen" clear when they discussed the status of *religionnaires fugitifs*, Protestants born outside of France but descended from men or women who had fled France because of religious persecution. In 1790 such Protestants had been welcomed as fully French (*naturels français*) who would henceforward "enjoy all the rights attached to that title," implicitly including political rights. But in Year V, the government considered treating returned Protestants as legally French—possessing the title or quality of *français*—while barring them from political citizenship for at least seven years, the period now required for foreigners to become French citizens.[19]

Yet the distinction between Frenchness and political citizenship was difficult to establish. Many contemporary writings reveal a continued confusion about the distinctions between political citizenship and Frenchness and between the absence of French citizenship associated with being a foreigner and the further stage of civil death imposed upon émigrés. The authors of the 1797 *Mémoire pour les pères, mères, et ayeux des émigrés*, for example, seemed to miss the point that their children were being penalized for their emigration and not for their "foreignness" when they defended their sons by claiming that they "are born French. They are foreign only to the Revolution and to the faults that partisanship (*esprit de parti*) produced."[20]

Legislators not only argued about the place of foreigners, or alleged foreigners, in the nation; they also tried to clarify what citizenship meant for those who were legally French but unable to exercise political rights. In the immediate wake of Robespierre's fall from power and the effective end of the Terror on 9 Thermidor, on 29 Thermidor Year II (August 16, 1794), the legislature proclaimed that "the word 'citizen' is generic," including both men and women.[21] But they did so in response to a query about whether a specific law, which freed citizen workers and farmers who had been imprisoned during the Terror, applied to both sexes. The National Convention expressed a growing unease with the implications of using the term "citizen" to include women, especially in any political context. By November 1794, Pierre Claude François Mailhe protested such usages directly, proclaiming: "Misfortune to governments who introduce women into public administration!"[22]

After women led an invasion of the National Convention during the Germinal and Prairial uprisings of Year III (April and May 1795), the Thermidorian government went beyond banning women's political clubs, as they had done in 1793, to forbidding women to attend any political assembly.[23] Indeed, although women were massively involved in the 1795 uprisings, there was no notable feminine presence in the votes of September 1795 on the Constitution of Year III.[24] The Constitution itself reflected an effort to clarify and limit the meaning of terms like "citizen" and "sovereign," which had been ambiguous in many earlier laws. Pierre-Claude-François Daunou, one of key figures in the creation of the Constitution, proposed replacing the term "people," initially used to define the sovereign nation, with the "universality of citizens," arguing that women or children were not part of the French people and that sovereignty did not reside in the people as a whole.[25]

The Directorial government voiced growing doubts about the political rights and responsibilities of women. At the same time, individuals began to suggest that the very term "citizen," even in its modified form of "French citizen," should be eliminated for women. In his *Journal de Paris* in June 1796, Roederer protested the use "increasingly in fashion" of "monsieur" instead of "citizen"; his partner responded that "madame" was even more widely used. Roederer countered that that "is a different matter. Citizens, in the French Republic, are members of the State. To be a member of the State is to have political rights. The title of citizen is thus a political title. But a woman is only a member of the family. She has no political right in the State. She must not bear any political title." Roederer then explained to his opponent that "citizeness" could not be the feminine of "citizen" as "presidentess" (*présidente*) had been the feminine of "president" under the Old Regime: "When public offices were formerly obtained by patronage or money, Madame obtained them, and often exercised them at least half as much as Monsieur. But in the professions that depend on individual qualifications as in law or medicine, a husband's title did not pass to his wife. The duty of citizen is one that depends on individual qualifications."[26]

But while legislators attempted to clarify different forms of membership in the nation, they were unable to dismiss the morass of previous laws that had used the term "citizen" ambiguously or to nullify all the myriad and powerful associations of the word. Such confusion had substantive implications. Throughout the Thermidorian period and the Directory, the civil and political rights associated with membership in the French nation—and the associated distinction between citizenship and Frenchness—remained contentious. The cases of Hoppé-Lange and Suzanne Lepeletier, chosen from a number of contemporary trials and *causes célèbres* concerning relationships between French and foreign men and women,[27] allow us to probe the ways in which the revolutionary state of the late 1790s tried to reconfigure family and citizenship rights and the reasons why they remained controversial. The struggle between M. Hoppé and the *citoyenne* Lange starkly opposed the "natural" rights of fathers over their children with the rights a French child derived from her membership in the nation. As lawmakers and jurists debated whether young Palmyre Lange would, or could, be "denationalized" by her father, they confronted the question of what legitimated authority within the family. Their debates also reveal conflicting views about whether "French citizenship" for women was bound up, directly or indirectly, with membership in a political community of citizens, and the rights that such a title could or could not confer upon women.

Suzanne Lepeletier's case similarly highlights both the question of what legitimated *puissance paternelle* and the contested effects of a husband's or father's citizenship status on his legal dependents. But it also allows us to look more closely at the relationship between literal families and the "great family" of the French nation. Her case forced the French legislature to reconsider the metaphor of "national adoption" and the state's ability to create new "children" out of foreigners or orphaned French children. It reveals the collision of two very different views of what determined legitimate authority within the family and the degree of control the state should exercise over the private lives of French citizens.

Families and Frenchness in the Parisian Courts

In late 1796, M. Hoppé, a young businessman from Hamburg, and the *citoyenne* Anne-Françoise Lange, a well-known actress, appeared before the Parisian courts.[28] Both sought custody of their twenty-one-month-old daughter, Palmyre, who had been born out of wedlock. The case was one of a number of contemporary *causes célèbres* that littered the columns of contemporary newspapers, and the actress' admirers and critics relished the lurid tales of sexual and financial scandal that the trial revealed.[29] But the struggle between M. Hoppé and the *citoyenne* Lange also opposed familial and national bonds with particular clarity. Hoppé's status as a foreigner drew unusual attention to the case, but it also encouraged commentators to articulate otherwise implicit assumptions about the nature and significance of French women's and children's citizenship.

Prominent lawyers on both sides of the case were also directly involved in constructing a new social order and used the trial to dramatize their views. The *consultation* for Hoppé was signed by Portalis, Tronson du Coudray, Muraire, and Cambacérès, important actors in developing a new civil code.[30] All had participated in legislative discussions in the months previous to the case about the nature of the family and its relation to the state. Cambacérès had proposed a third project for a civil code on 16 Prairial Year IV (June 4, 1796), while Portalis had been appointed to the commission for revising inheritance laws on 25 Germinal Year IV (April 14, 1796), and had been president of the Council of Ancients during a heated discussion on changing inheritance laws, particularly the implications of equal succession for girls and boys. As the case opened in December 1796, legislators were in the midst of discussing whether divorce for mutual incompatibility should be limited, a position that Portalis would passionately support.

Honoré-Nicolas-Marc Duveyrier, the lawyer for the *citoyenne* Lange, was equally enmeshed in contemporary debates.[31] Indeed, he sent a copy of his brief to the national legislature, claiming that he was compelled to do so after reading an oration on divorce in the *Journal de Paris*.[32] Duveyrier contrasted the oration to the opening discourse of Cambacérès's contemporary project for a civil code, which decreed that if a father freely acknowledged a child born out of wedlock, the child would be placed in his care.[33] He sought to use the Hoppé-Lange case to demonstrate that granting rights to natural fathers undermined marriage and family as the basis of social order.[34] But to do so, Duveyrier defended the rights of an unwed mother, and a mother, moreover, whose profession as an actress made her morals suspect. In order to overcome this possible contradiction, he stressed the civil and political aspects of the mother's and child's rights in France.

The two opposing positions were laid out early in the case. Hoppé's champions concentrated on his inalienable, natural rights as a father, which they contended outweighed any formalities of citizenship.[35] Duveyrier's argument rested in part on a defense of the child's inherent Frenchness: "The girl whose education is being disputed is born French, of a French mother; our laws owe her protection. She cannot be abandoned to a foreigner without running the risk of being torn from her country and all the advantages that her country guarantees her."[36]

Such clear-cut conflict between a "natural father" and a French child could not have taken place in the Old Regime. Following the precedent of Roman law, French law had regulated the "nationality" of a child born out of wedlock according to the mother's status. An illegitimate child born of a French mother was thus unquestionably French, but the rights associated specifically with such Frenchness were limited.[37] The father—whether French or foreigner—had no official power over the child because of the legal fiction that a bastard child had no father. Since he could not bequeath familial patrimony to illegitimate children, he had no legal claim to control their upbringing.[38] Earlier revolutionary legislators had transformed laws on inheritance and paternal power, erasing distinctions between children born inside or outside of wedlock. By late summer 1796, as part of the more general rethinking of family relations, authorities—including lawmakers involved in the trial like Tronson du Coudray and Muraire—had overturned some of the most radical of these laws, especially a measure that had allowed illegitimate children to demand a share of their parents' estates retroactively.[39] But the status of bastard children remained murky. The courts had occasionally considered other cases concerning the custody of children born out of wedlock, but there was no law stipulating which parent was ultimately responsible for the education of such a child, and no law regulating the choice between a foreign father and a French mother in such circumstances.[40]

In Palymre's case, the contest between paternal and maternal citizenship status reflected both the increasing respect granted to the *paterfamilias* during the Directory and a persistent belief, which Duveyrier invoked strategically, that women and children could, and should, choose the polity to which they belonged. Hoppé's lawyers contended that a father's citizenship status necessarily determined that of the family as a whole. The *citoyenne* Lange had no right to complain if her daughter was taken away from her, because she should have known that a father's status always determined his children's fate and, with it, the nation with which they were associated. "The mother is afraid she will never see her child again. But she exposed herself to this risk by uniting herself with a foreigner. She has only herself to blame. She knew, or should have known, that the father is dominant in deciding the family's fate." The law, however, was not this clear-cut even for legitimate children, much less for those born out of wedlock. The lawyers' emphasis on the unity of the household and the preeminence of the father's status was instead informed by the belief that neither children nor married women could or should choose between familial and national bonds. Portalis and his colleagues granted that adults could not renounce citizenship rights in France against their will: "one can never become a foreigner except by a voluntary abandonment of one's domicile." But the ability to claim or forfeit citizenship status was restricted to independent adults and could not be opposed to paternal rights over a minor. A child "does not and cannot have another country than that of his father, or the country that it will please his father to choose."[41]

Lange's lawyer, Duveyrier, countered this argument by insisting that children had a right to choose their *patrie* over biological bonds and that Palmyre should not be entrusted to a father who could deprive her of rights as a French citizen because of her position of legal dependence within the family. Since there was no evidence that Hoppé intended to become French, he might well leave, taking the child with him. Such a forcible removal from French soil threatened to "denationalize" her in practice even if not in law. For "could it not happen that the child, taken to Hamburg, would there forever lose not the right, but the means to recover her country and the rights of her birth?" If her father eventually abandoned the child, died unexpectedly, or remarried, what would become of her in the cold wastelands of northern Germany? The future was grim: "Can the child, on this foreign soil, await anything besides abandonment and death?"[42]

Duveyrier's rhetoric tapped a strong vein of chauvinism in wartime France, but it also testified to a continuing belief that French children should retain the ability to choose and protect their identity as citizens. Contemporary newspapers such as *Messager du soir* and the *Journal de Paris,* which supported Lange's side of the case, singled out this section of Duveyrier's speech as particularly effective. As one columnist observed, Duveyrier "ended his brilliant discourse with a powerful and infallible argument. The father is a foreigner from Hamburg. The child is French, and as such must participate in the political and civil rights that the laws of her country accord to natural children; a French child cannot lose these advantages against her will."[43]

While this argument relied on the gender-neutral term "child," Hoppé's lawyers also contended that the value of French citizenship was inherently limited for the child because of her sex as well as because of her age. In short, French men enjoyed the "benefit of living under a government where each citizen is part of the sovereign nation. But this political advantage does not exist for the sex that does not participate in it."[44] The very fact that they could make such a claim hints at dramatic shifts in familial and political order. While it was widely accepted that women could not vote or hold office, the idea that women played no part, direct or indirect, in the polity would probably have startled many of the revolutionaries active during the Jacobin and early Thermidorian Convention.[45]

Even in 1796 and 1797, however, it was not as easy to establish that women were not part of the political nation as Hoppé's lawyers might have hoped. In this case, Duveyrier argued explicitly that French women did in fact "participate in the sovereign nation." He asserted, first of all, that women were represented politically through their male relatives: "Do not French women participate in it [the sovereign nation] through their husbands, their children, their sons, through all the benefits that the nature of the social contract has placed in common [*en communauté*]?" His claim echoed the theory of familial representation that his contemporary Guiraudet used to argue against rights for women as individuals: "All this confusion [over rights] results necessarily from the principle that the nation is only an aggregation of individuals. But when it is considered as a composite of families, represented in each case by the head of the household, there is not one member who does not have his place, not one who can complain about being deprived of his rights."[46] This form of logic was to become a commonplace in the nineteenth century, and it would be used far more often, as in Guiraudet's treatise, to deny women independent rights like the vote than to defend maternal custody. Indeed, the concept of women's citizenship through male representation was difficult to sustain in this case, since the women in question were an unmarried mother and her infant daughter.

Duveyrier thus rushed to make a second argument that fundamentally conflated aspects of political and legal citizenship. He contended that women had indirect political rights precisely because of the constitutional relationship between marriage and national citizenship. "Do not they [women] moreover participate in it [the sovereign nation] in the particular power of women to make foreigners into French citizens, without establishing a business or acquiring property?"[47] He alluded here to the clause in the Constitution of Year III, preserved from the 1791 Constitution and the Constitutional Act of 1793, that made marriage to a French woman one of the means by which a foreign man could expedite becoming a French citizen. He also played on the ambiguous language associated with citizenship and the specific ambiguity of the Constitution, which left open to question whether foreigners who fulfilled these requirements would become simply "French" or fully "citizens," capable of exercising all political rights. The combination of these factors implied that French women's membership in the nation was inherently political and that a woman's status could change her husband's. Such claims, however, threatened the emerging vision of social order based on patriarchal families.

The courts ultimately decided on a compromise solution. Wary of the intentions of the German businessman, they also suspected the morals of an actress who had given birth out of wedlock. Rather than deciding directly between the competing demands of family and national bonds, they ruled that the child should be placed in a state-run institution devoted to girls' education and directed by women whose morals and credentials were recognized by the government. Both parents were to have visiting rights at the school and were required to support their daughter financially.

But the very compromise nature of the judgment suggests the difficulty that men and women of the Directory faced when trying to reconcile an increasing emphasis on paternalistic family structures with an acknowledgment of the citizenship rights of dependents within the family. More important, the case shows that debate, both implicit and explicit, about whether women were part of the sovereign nation continued to have consequences not only for political rights, but also for the application of civil laws. Hoppé's lawyers combined the view that women were not part of the sovereign nation with an emphasis on the preeminence of the family. Duveyrier's arguments reflected similar assumptions about the importance of the family as the basis of social order, but he nonetheless portrayed women and children as a political part of the sovereign nation in order to contend that they should retain the right to be able to choose between family and *patrie*.

Suzanne Lepeletier, Daughter of the Nation

In 1797 two brothers brought an unusual case to the French legislature. Their niece, the daughter of the famous martyr of liberty Michel Lepeletier, had been "adopted by the nation" in 1793. She now wanted to marry an impoverished Dutch man. Her uncles opposed the marriage but could not do so directly because Suzanne had been officially emancipated from her relatives' tutelage. They thus turned to the state and demanded that the legislature fulfill its paternal duties by stopping its adopted daughter from marrying a foreigner.

Their demands and subsequent debates over the institution of national adoption reveal an extraordinary moment when the idea of a republican state as the father of a private individual was taken literally. Yet the case has received little attention. While scholars have made innovative use of court records to illuminate transformations of familial and public order in France, few have examined the *causes célèbres* of the late Revolution.[48] With the exception of one recent account, Suzanne's own story has been forgotten.[49]

But in debating the apparently trivial question of one young girl's engagement, men and women grappled with the nature of French citizenship and family-state relations during a moment of fundamental political and social reshuffling. When the Lepeletier brothers brought Suzanne's case to the legislature, they not only brought the daughter of a Jacobin martyr back into the public eye. Their public insistence on institutions created in the revolutionary fervor of 1793 also prompted legislators to address the assumptions that underpinned those institutions and to reassess their validity for a new republican order. Indeed, as men and women debated the institution of national adoption, they contested the very categories used to conceptualize family and state relations. Champions and opponents of the marriage articulated competing visions of the basis of familial relationships. Suzanne's engagement to a foreigner also led legislators to debate the significance of legal citizenship in the nation, especially for women, and the impact of marriage on a woman's citizenship status. The flurry over her adoption and proposed marriage further revealed deep conflicts over the appropriate relationships among the principles of publicity, liberty, and authority.

Perhaps most important, men and women used these different categories to uphold conflicting models of family-state relations. The Lepeletier brothers drew on the republican imagery of the radical Revolution to insist on unmediated relationships between individual citizens and the state. Champions of Suzanne's marriage contended instead that families formed natural and necessary intermediaries between the individual and the state. But in wrestling with the implications of national adoption for the social and political world of the late Revolution, both groups faced contradictions within their own assumptions. Proponents of a family-based model of political relations drew on a model of the family that subordinated the rights of married women and children to those of the *paterfamilias*. But they denied the need for paternal control in Suzanne's case and used the language of individual rights to champion the independence of a young woman. Conversely, the Lepeletier brothers and their supporters depicted Suzanne, the "first daughter of the Republic," as quintessentially French, but also as incapable of acting as an independent citizen.

Suzanne's Story

Suzanne's father, Michel Lepeletier de Saint-Fargeau, was assassinated on January 20, 1793, the day after he voted for the execution of Louis XVI. During the ceremonies honoring the murdered representative, his brother, Félix Lepeletier, held the orphaned child in front of the Assembly and proclaimed: "My niece, here is your father; people, here is your child!" Barère followed the gesture by demanding that Suzanne be adopted by the French nation, a motion unanimously approved by the Assembly. Although Michel Lepeletier became one of the famous "martyrs of liberty" consecrated by the Revolutionary Republic, his daughter disappeared from public view.[50] Since Suzanne's mother was also dead, her family appointed her uncle Félix as her tutor along with a governess, Madame Halm. Their family life proceeded quietly until Félix was accused of taking part in Gracchus Babeuf's 1796 Conspiracy of Equals and was brought to trial.[51] Since he did not appear before the court when summoned, he lost his civil rights, including the ability to act as a tutor for his minor niece. He was eventually acquitted, but in the meantime Suzanne was emancipated from familial authority at the age of fifteen.[52]

One of the conditions of Suzanne's emancipation was that her governess stay with her, and, at least according to the Lepeletier brothers, Madame Halm soon began to plot against her adolescent charge. She first brought Suzanne to a country house, allegedly for the pure air. Once ensconced, the governess filled the house with her relatives and those of a Dutch man, Jean-François De Witt, while preventing Suzanne's own family from reaching the girl. Soon afterward Suzanne announced to her grandfather that she planned to marry the young De Witt. Her grandfather and other relatives opposed the marriage. Suzanne then brought her case to a *conseil de famille*, an institution created by the Revolution to arbitrate conflicts within families. She invoked the law of September 7, 1793, which allowed minors whose parents were dead, exiled, or absent to marry. Four family members were summoned to the court and given a month to reach a collective decision. After the month's grace period, there were only two legal grounds for continued opposition to the marriage: "notorious disorder of *moeurs* or nonrehabilitation after a judgment carrying the penalty of infamy." If her relatives could not prove that De Witt was guilty of one of these two charges, Suzanne would be free to marry with or without familial approval.

Suzanne's relatives contended that since the legislature was about to reconsider the 1793 law, any judgment should be postponed until it was clear whether the law was still valid. In the short term, Pierre Bénézech, the minister of the interior, issued an *arrêt* forbidding the Parisian municipal government to register any act of marriage for her. While waiting for a conclusive decision, Suzanne's uncles sent a petition to the Directory arguing that the National Assembly, as Suzanne's adopted father, should intervene to stop her foolhardy marriage.

Unsure of what to make of this unusual charge, the Directory turned the case over to the Council of Five Hundred, the lower house of the legislature. A commission was appointed to study the affair and the more general ramifications of national adoption. A series of petitions and counterpetitions, memoirs, debates, and published discourses followed from December 1797 through February 1798. Several members of the legislature made particularly developed speeches about the case; Jean-Pierre Chazal presented the commission's reasoning in depth; Pierre-Antoine Laloy and Bernard Laujacq reacted to the specifics of Suzanne's situation and presented detailed proposals for new laws on national adoption; the deputies François Joseph Febvre and Julien Souhait and the Council's librarian, Rey, also published extended commentaries. The Lepeletier brothers issued direct ripostes to several of these speeches, while Suzanne herself also petitioned the government. Other deputies added their perspectives during several tumultuous legislative sessions, while numerous newspapers covered the affair.[53]

Participants' political leanings and experiences influenced their views on Suzanne's marriage and the institution of national adoption. The Lepeletier brothers, especially Félix, were deeply attached to the Jacobin movement, while several of their most outspoken opponents in this *affaire* were more politically moderate.[54] Personal considerations also played an important role. Suzanne stood to inherit 30,000 livres in revenues, a substantial sum in the late 1790s. Debates were thus colored not only by legislators' attitudes toward Jacobin arguments and institutions, but also by their assessments about whether those arguments masked other agendas, including Félix's alleged greed and romantic attachment to his niece. But differences over Suzanne's case cannot be ascribed only to political affiliations or accusations of personal interest. They also corresponded to models of family and state relations forged at different points in the Revolution, as legislators confronted institutions and ideas that had been shaped in a very different political climate but never officially abandoned. The issues raised by the *affaire* ultimately pushed men and women to struggle with potential contradictions within their own ideas about the basis of social and political order.

Competing Models of the Family and the Social Contract

Members of the Council of Five Hundred began by picking their way through the baggage of revolutionary laws and classical precedents. Deputies lacked any real model for deciding the case, and the models that did exist were increasingly at odds with the predominating political and social views of the late 1790s. When the Legislative Assembly reestablished the principle of adoption in January 1792, it did not stipulate how the law was to be instituted. Despite numerous proposals and petitions, the legal requirements and duties surrounding adoption were not to be fixed until the Napoleonic Code came into being.[55] "Public" or "national" adoption was even less clearly defined. Suzanne's acclaimed adoption had been the first such case. In honoring her with the title "daughter of the nation," the National Convention had charged the Committee on Legislation to prepare a report on the laws of adoption and their relevance for Suzanne's case. However, the report never materialized. Although the National Assembly subsequently bestowed the title of "adopted" child of the *patrie* on several other children, it never articulated the consequences of such adoption.

In the social and political climate of the Directory, an institution that appeared to conflate familial and state authority was problematic in any form. But several aspects of Suzanne's case made it particularly controversial. Not only was she the first "adopted daughter of the nation," but her father's name was one to conjure with. Michel Lepeletier was perhaps the only martyr of the radical Revolution who remained a politically viable hero in the late 1790s. The fortune that Suzanne stood to inherit—and possibly transport permanently outside France—also whetted public imagination. Legislators tried repeatedly to distinguish the specific circumstances of Suzanne's case from the question of general laws on national adoption, and often failed to do so. But both the peculiarities of the case and its wider resonance combined to make it a forum for debating the nature of citizenship and authority in the post-Thermidorian Republic.

To decide whether the metaphor of the state as a father could be taken literally, legislators attempted first to define what legitimated paternal authority within households. Politicians and legislators advanced two opposing models of the basis and extent of *puissance paternelle,* models that corresponded partially to different moments of the Revolution but also reworked existing ideas and vocabulary. The Lepeletier brothers emphasized the model of a benevolent tutor to replace that of a despotic patriarch. In contrast, those who ridiculed the idea that the republican nation could act in the same way as Suzanne's "natural father" drew on many of the same arguments used in the late 1790s to justify the need for literal fathers to exercise authority within the household. They emphasized the importance of patrimony, the ability to pass on one's name and possessions. This definition of the family had its roots in the Old Regime. But it was also key to the late Revolution as men and women sought to make property the basis of familial and social order.[56]

Reporting in the name of the commission, the deputy Chazal noted on 22 Frimaire Year VI (December 12, 1797) that certain collectivities, such as Lyonnais orphanages, and individual sovereigns, like princes, had been able to exercise parental rights over their "adopted children."[57] But unlike orphanages and princes, the French Republic was a large "immortal" collectivity, which exercised its rights not through individual actions but through collective scrutiny. Since the Republic could not die and bequeath its patrimony to its children, it was unimaginable that an individual citizen could be the son or daughter of the country in anything beyond a honorific sense.

Subsequent commentators made this theme more explicit. On 30 Frimaire (December 20, 1797), the archivist Rey demanded to know: "Does the Nation have a first name, a name and a last name, that its adopted children can take? Never dying, can it transmit an inheritance to its children? These are nevertheless essential conditions, without which adoption cannot exist."[58] On 3 Pluviôse (January 22, 1798), the deputy Laujacq mocked the idea that the French people could be imagined as a father on the same grounds:

No act of her family records their wish that Susanne Lepeletier pass under the *puissance paternelle* of the French people. A gigantic and ridiculous idea that it is nonetheless necessary to consider. But *puissance paternelle* no longer exists. Can the French people be Susanne Lepeletier's father? Can she take the name of the French people? Can she inherit from the French people? Can she will her possessions to the French people?[59]

The legislators who advanced this definition of the family took the next step for granted: if Suzanne Lepeletier could not inherit from the French people, the nation and the assembly that represented it did not have the power to interfere in her marriage. Their logic rested on the unarticulated but traditional notion that a father's right to approve or disapprove of his children's marriages was based on protecting the familial patrimony.[60] If there was no national "familial" patrimony that could be passed on to Suzanne Lepeletier, then there was no justification for the state to intervene in her affairs.

This definition of the family did not preclude concern for paternal affection. Indeed, Chazal also dismissed the Lepeletier brothers' claims on the grounds that a legislature could not adequately provide paternal love for a child, suggesting both that such love had to be demonstrated and that it could be exercised by only one father at a time. Chazal and Laujacq argued that during none of the formative moments of Suzanne's life—and especially not in the appointment of her tutor or in her emancipation—had Suzanne's family looked to the state for advice on raising its "adopted" child; they could thus not invoke the state's authority at this juncture. This strategy allowed the deputies to belittle the Lepeletier brothers' intentions in bringing the case, since Suzanne's uncles had not done so before money had become an issue, but it also implied that a child could never have more than one father.

As Eric Goodheart has observed, this argument suggested a fundamental difference between "individual" and "national" adoption.[61] Children who were adopted privately were completely removed from their birth families, but children who were adopted "publicly" by the "nation" remained with their blood relatives and lived under their immediate authority. Several members of the legislature endorsed this perspective. On 6 Nivôse (December 27, 1797), Laloy proposed a new law stating: "National adoption grants the nation no special rights over its adopted child. The child does not cease to belong to his family."[62] On 3 Pluviôse (January 22, 1798), Laujacq presented essentially the same article: adoption "changes nothing in the relations that exist between an adopted child and his birth family."[63] If it were possible for a child to belong to the nation in a special way, he or she could not also continue to belong to a "natural" or biological family.

In contrast to the traditionalist claim that *puissance paternelle* was justified by the task of preserving the family name and possessions, the Lepeletier brothers and their supporters used a conception of the family that had been institutionalized during the early years of the Revolution. They argued that being a father primarily involved acting like one, providing for children's basic needs, education, and, above all, moral guidance. Both individual fathers and the state could thus act as benevolent parents. They echoed Chazal's invocation of paternal love, but recast it in the terms of the radical Revolution: consent or rejection of marriage should be based only on a father's concern for a child's well-being, not on the preservation of familial property. Like their opponents' claims, such arguments had a strategic value; in this case, they allowed the Lepeletiers to claim that they were not motivated by greed. However, they also drew centrally on Jacobin conceptions of the tutelary authority of parents and the state.

Their model further implied that familial bonds were malleable and not necessarily exclusive. Souhait, a neo-Jacobin deputy who supported the Lepeletier brothers, acknowledged that public or national adoption differed from private adoption in that "it preserves a child's name, family, and fortune." However, he saw this factor as unimportant in determining the Assembly's responsibilities toward Suzanne: "both [forms of adoption] otherwise resemble each other . . . notably in that the country [*patrie*] and the adopted father have the same duties as natural fathers." Souhait used the language of the radical Revolution to voice suspicions of the political trustworthiness of biological families in contrast to the wise surveillance of the nation itself: "are you sure that you can find in these families the wisdom and patriotism that must guide the education and establishment of the children of the nation?"[64]

However, the Lepeletier brothers and their supporters did not simply recycle earlier views about the essence of the family. They also added a new twist to the interpretation of what legitimated familial bonds. While they downplayed the idea that familial authority was defined by the transmission of property, the Lepeletier brothers focused on a more intangible form of familial patrimony, but one that had also been part of the Old Regime definition of what justified *puissance paternelle:* familial honor. Not only was this a form of heritage that the French people, collectively, could give to the "adopted daughter of the nation"; it was obligatory that the representatives of the nation—her substitute parents—fulfill the responsibilities created by such a patrimony. Suzanne Lepeletier must be made to be worthy of both her natural father, the brave martyr Michel Lepeletier who had sacrificed his life for her country, and her adopted father, the great French people. The young girl must not be seduced into forgetting her position or be allowed to marry someone who would diminish this heritage, least of all a foreigner. The brothers argued repeatedly that "if it is true that every good father does his best to make his children worthy of him, and if he can do so only by surveillance, would it not be infinitely ridiculous if the French people did nothing to ensure that the name of its adoptive daughter not be worn by one unworthy of it?"[65]

"Denationalized" Daughters

These competing interpretations of the role of patrimony in legitimating *puissance paternelle* were particularly important because Suzanne planned to marry a foreigner. Although the Batavian Republic had been created in 1795 as a sister republic of France, Dutch men and women were not legally considered to be French citizens.[66] By marrying the Dutchman De Witt, Suzanne threatened to expatriate and "denationalize" herself, as well as the material and ideological inheritance that she had received from her father and the nation.[67]

The Lepeletier brothers advanced multiple reasons for opposing the marriage, ranging from the youth of both parties to the fact that Suzanne Lepeletier was a Catholic and Jean-François De Witt a Lutheran. However, the brothers returned most often to the possibility of Suzanne's expatriation, a possibility that newspaper commentators also seized upon as a central element of the affair.[68] In the brothers' eyes, Suzanne's governess aimed to trick the girl into marrying a foreigner and abandoning both her homeland and heritage. Succinctly, "this woman hurls her [Suzanne] into the arms of a foreigner, alienates her from her country, makes her fall short of the memory of her father and scorn the glorious national adoption."[69]

Both champions and opponents of Suzanne's marriage used the term "foreigner" in ways that conflated political and territorial identity. For the Lepeletier brothers, *étranger* implied an enemy of the Revolutionary Republic. They used a Jacobin vocabulary linking De Witt's foreign origins with other reprehensible qualities, such as stealth, cowardliness, greed, and treachery.[70] They and their allies suggested that if the daughter of the man who had "died for all" was seduced into the "bed of a foreigner" she would not merely become a Dutch, rather than a French, woman. Instead, her marriage would intimately link, and thus betray, the heart of Revolution and its opposition.

Like her uncles, Suzanne and her supporters used a politically charged definition of citizenship. Suzanne herself denied her fiancé's "foreignness," presenting him as a member of an international community of republican citizens that took priority over formal distinctions of nationality. By marrying him, she was remaining true to her father's wishes and her heritage. Jean-François De Witt was, at least in her version of his lineage, a descendant of Jean De Witt, the *grand pensionnaire* of Holland who had been killed in the seventeenth century for his patriotic opposition to the house of Orange.[71] According to Suzanne and her supporters, their marriage would be "the union of heirs of celebrated names in the annals of two new-born and allied Republics."[72] Her supporters in the legislature similarly emphasized De Witt's identity as a Batavian—rather than as a generic *étranger*—and as a member of a shared political community.[73]

Legislators, however, also addressed the legal effects of a French woman's marriage to a foreigner to argue that Suzanne's marriage would actually add to, rather than subtract from, the community of French citizens. Chazal insisted that a fortune should not become a chain binding French women to their homeland. He contended that because the Constitution of Year III stipulated that foreigners who married French women could expedite the process of becoming French citizens themselves, it actually encouraged such unions: "The Constitution does not forbid it [such a marriage]; indeed, it forbids it so little that it has made these sorts of marriages a means of acquiring the rights of citizenship among us; it [the Constitution] thus authorizes a foreigner to marry a French woman."[74] Some others made similar arguments; the librarian Rey, for example, dismissed the Lepeletier brothers' fears with the declaration that "far from expatriating herself, she [Suzanne] will undoubtedly give France a new citizen in the person of her husband."[75]

Chazal's and Rey's uses of the constitutional clause were less controversial than Duveyrier's invocation of the same article, as they used it to champion the incorporation of foreigners into France rather than to argue that French women's membership in the nation was inherently political. However, the idea that a woman's national status could change her husband's still threatened the growing consensus among officials that the family should be an organic unit, defined and represented exclusively by the adult male head of the household. Most other legislators favorable to Suzanne's marriage passed quickly over the legal ramifications of her marriage.

Liberty, Publicity, and Legitimate Authority

Suzanne's case was finally decided on the intersecting grounds of liberty, publicity, and familial honor. The young woman and her supporters repeatedly emphasized that she was the daughter of a martyr of liberty. They concurred with the Lepeletier brothers that she shared in a glorious heritage, but argued that betraying her heritage meant preventing her from acting freely, exercising a tyrannical authority over the very woman whose father had died for freedom.[76] Suzanne thus presented herself as a French woman with rights common to all members of the Republic while lamenting the cruelty of singling out the "daughter of the martyr of liberty" for special constraints. She proclaimed that "daughter of Michel Lepeletier, a French woman, I have the right to the Constitution of the French people, to the liberty and equality that sprang from the blood of the creator of my days [i.e., her father]." Moreover, she contended that "my father is dead for the nation; the nation promised to replace him for me, and the nation now destroys my choice."[77]

In contrast, the Lepeletier brothers and their supporters argued that it was possible to preserve liberty only if those in authority acted openly. In calling for the legislature to exercise its true duty as a father, they emphasized the importance of surveillance. Such surveillance meant watching the adopted daughter of the French people closely to prevent her from being embroiled in dangerous plots. Her uncles criticized the fact that the couple had been brought together secretly, away from the eyes of her family. In their original petition to the Directory, they described repeated familial efforts to reach the young woman, and the literal as well as metaphorical blockading of the country house where Suzanne and her governess resided. They sought to brand the governess, Madame Halm, as a "despot" who had "seduced" her student through treasonous plots and "clandestine intrigues."[78] By stressing the governess's deception, the Lepeletier brothers, as in their condemnation of the *étranger* De Witt, echoed Jacobin rhetoric. In the revolutionary celebration of transparency, dissimulation had become synonymous with the misuse of power.[79] It was furthermore a characteristically feminine trait and suggested the dangers of feminine authority. The brothers contrasted this secretive tyranny of a mischief-making governess and a scheming foreigner with the legitimate and open authority of the paternal revolutionary state over its children.

During the first substantial legislative session on the topic, the deputy Chazal attacked the letter from the minister of the interior that forbade the Parisian municipal government to register any act of marriage for Suzanne Lepeletier. Like Suzanne herself, he called the order a "true *lettre de cachet.*" The term was loaded. Such letters had been used in the Old Regime as a mechanism for state intervention in family affairs, a mechanism that provided a discreet means of removing individuals who had disgraced familial honor.[80] The revolutionary legislature had abolished the use of *lettres de cachet* as symbols of arbitrary and intolerable authority by the state. In applying the term to the minister's order, Chazal was deliberately stretching its definition, equating the indeterminately long postponement of marriage with prison.[81]

Chazal then advanced his own version of the appropriate relations between family and the state. For him, the potential tragedy was not the mismarriage of a young woman, but the exposure of her dreams to the prying eyes of the legislature. Her destruction began with the despotic "imprisonment" implied by the *lettre de cachet* and ultimately ended with her death at the hands of an inept assembly after her dreams of love were crushed.[82] His depiction of Suzanne's ruin suggests a reversal in the way family relations were conceived—a reversal not only of the principles of the radical Revolution but also of those of the Old Regime. It was still crucial to preserve familial honor and secrecy. However, this preservation no longer entailed a pact between monarch and families like that instituted in the practice of the *lettres de cachet*. Instead, it required the protection of a domestic sphere from the intrusion of the state.

Other legislators followed up on Suzanne's and Chazal's arguments. They inverted earlier revolutionary denunciations of the shackles of marriages in order to portray the prevention of Suzanne's marriage as itself a "chain" and a breach of liberty. Laujacq denounced the "arbitrary" nature of the ministerial act preventing Suzanne's marriage and insisted on the responsibility of the state not to fetter its citizens by preventing marriages.[83] During the closing discussions of the case, the deputy Febvre similarly insisted that "it is time to resolve the case, since one cannot, without harm to the fundamental principles of civil liberty, leave individual rights in suspense any longer."[84]

Their portrayal of the fifteen-year-old Suzanne as a shy and blushing virgin, but also as a woman entitled to her rights and capable of deciding her own fate, conflicted with legislators' rhetoric about the need to control willful minors and irrational women in other circumstances. The Lepeletier brothers systematically depicted Suzanne as a child, usually referring to her as "the minor Lepeletier." Their opponents rarely used the term, and alternated between depicting Suzanne as a child not yet capable of consenting to her adoption and as an adult capable of contracting marriage. This terminology was in part legal formalism.[85] According to a model of adoption that required adoptees to ratify their adoption when they reached adulthood, Suzanne had not consented to the binding contract and could not do so. Rey summarized this view: "Suzanne Lepeletier was adopted when she was a child; still a minor, she is incapable of all legal consent except that which the law permits."[86] What the law permitted was consent to her marriage. As the Lepeletier brothers noted, this logic was potentially inconsistent: it refused the fifteen-year-old the power to consent to one life-determining relationship, adoption, while insisting that she had the right to consent to another such bond, marriage.[87] Although legislators never addressed the topic directly, the specter of divorce may have played a role in such logic; the marriage contract could be dissolved later; once both parties had formally approved adoption, it was final.

But members of the Council of Five Hundred also contradicted themselves on a more fundamental level. In championing Suzanne's marriage, they drew on and contributed to the contemporary trend of protecting family life from the perceived intrusions of the state. But such families were usually defined by male heads of household. In order to deny that the National Assembly had any particular paternal duty to the *citoyenne* Lepeletier, they ultimately downplayed the authority of fathers in general. They suggested that a fifteen-year-old girl was fully capable of acting independently, making what was the possibly the most important decision of her life without the advice or intervention of an adult guardian.

It was an exceptional characterization, made possible only by the absence of Suzanne's real father and the difficulties of directly addressing the idea of national adoption. Indeed, the singularity of the case is striking in light of the Council of Five Hundred's debates over the law of September 7, 1793, which allowed minors whose parents were dead, exiled, or absent to marry in certain circumstances, the law that underpinned Suzanne claims to marry against her relatives' wishes.[88] Although legislators differed about the composition of the *conseil de famille* that should judge such cases, they were consistent about the need to prevent minors from marrying unwisely. In this context, Laujacq, one of the firmest opponents of taking the metaphor of the paternal state literally in Suzanne's case, proclaimed that "we must truly take the place of fathers of family and invest the marriages of minors with all the formalities that can guarantee their duration." In one of the final, though ultimately inconclusive, discussions on the 1793 law before the creation of a new civil code, the deputy Guillaume Robert declared that the authority of familial tribunals had to be increased: "surrounding this fictitious paternity with confidence is the only way to make it worthy. This is why the commission thinks that the deliberation of the *conseil* must not be subject to any revision." He went on to deny the possibility that young men and women could invoke the demands of liberty against familial control, contending that "if you cannot specify all the cases that could motivate the *conseil de famille* to refuse their consent, which we believe to be impossible, the minor, blinded by his passion, will always accuse his relatives of tyranny."[89] While legislators listened to Suzanne's pleas that she was being "despotically" prevented from marrying by the state, they had little patience for such accusations against more immediate substitutes for paternal authority.

Suzanne's Fate

The Council of Five Hundred ultimately decided that Suzanne's enemies were not those who sought to steal her away from the metaphorical family of the French nation, but rather a state that would arbitrarily destroy her chances of marital bliss by intruding into the realm of the natural family. Suzanne's marriage took place on 9 Germinal Year VI (March 30, 1798). The presidents of both the Council of Five Hundred, where her case had been debated, and the Council of Ancients attended her wedding—implicitly giving a stamp of public approval to her choice even as they disavowed the ability of the state to intervene in her family life. By all accounts, the wedding was a spectacular affair.[90]

Although the legislature planned to review the laws on national adoption after dismissing Suzanne's case, it never did so. The case, however, reveals the contradictions implicit in the institution in the last days of the Revolutionary Republic. The Lepeletier brothers claimed that Suzanne embodied a special political position in the nation—but also depicted her as incapable of acting as an independent citizen. Proponents of her marriage scorned the Lepeletier brothers' rhetoric of "denationalization" and dismissed the idea that Suzanne had a special relationship with the state—but nonetheless insisted on her identity and rights as a French woman. Legislators who elsewhere insisted that the authority of fathers and husbands must be reinforced argued here that marriage to a French woman would integrate a foreigner into France, not subordinate a woman's national status to that of her husband's. Champions of paternal authority in the home, they rejected the paternal authority of the state.

Except for Suzanne and her immediate circle, the case had few direct repercussions. Suzanne's own life after the trial ironically paralleled the long-term turn to a more conservative social and political order in the wake of the Revolution. On March 22, 1802, a justice of the peace pronounced a divorce between Suzanne and Jean De Witt. Meanwhile Suzanne, following the rupture with her uncles, began to associate closely with her royalist cousins, and in 1809 married the aristocrat M. le Mortefontaine. She ceased to be the embodiment of a national patrimony of revolutionary radicalism and became instead one of the leading ladies of the royalist party.

Conclusion

In the longer term, Suzanne's case both reflected and reinforced the emergence of a new model of family-state relations. The view articulated by the Lepeletier brothers' opponents was triumphing: families served as both natural and necessary intermediaries between individuals and the state. The nation was not itself a great family, but rather a nation of families, a state in which only a *paterfamilias,* or potential *paterfamilias,* could be considered a full citizen.

Nonetheless, contemporaries still believed that women could and should retain the right to choose between family and *patrie.* This right, however, could be supported both by invoking a connection between women's juridical nationality and political membership in the sovereign nation and by insisting on a disjuncture between the two aspects of national citizenship. Duveyrier argued for the right on the basis of a French girl's implicit, if indirect, connection to the political body of citizens. Conversely, champions of Suzanne's marriage justified her ability to choose marriage over her *patrie* by arguing that her rights as a French woman were separate from, and more important than, her honorific political position as the "adopted daughter of the nation." Though Suzanne's case was unique, this disjuncture between political and civil aspects of national identity would become increasingly common in contemporaneous arguments over an amnesty for women émigrés, arguments that, as we will see, usually emphasized not the right, but the obligation to choose between family and nation.

4 *Gender and Emigration Reconsidered*

The governments of the Thermidorian period and the Directory maintained and sometimes even expanded laws forbidding emigration. The National Convention instituted a new and comprehensive law against émigrés on 25 Brumaire Year III (November 15, 1794). In contrast to the explicitly inclusive term "any French [person] of either sex" [*tout français de l'un et l'autre sexe*], which had appeared in the March 1793 decree, most articles now used the more ambiguous expression *tout français*, which could be read as meaning "any French person" or "any French man."[1] The Constitution of Year III (August 1795) expressly forbade the return of the émigrés, but also used the ambiguous expression *les français*, "the French," without making it explicit that it applied to both sexes.[2] Officials nonetheless continued to treat women as émigrés if they left the country and to hold those who had left earlier responsible for their expatriation.

Indeed, in the context of ongoing war with most of Europe and recurrent political crisis, laws against emigration appeared to be an essential policing measure throughout the 1790s. While legislators heralded the unity of the family elsewhere, in the domain of emigration law they still held individuals responsible for their absence from France, regardless of their sex or position within the family. Nevertheless, pushed in part by contemporary petitioners and pamphleteers, officials also revived debates about the validity of these laws and the principles that justified them, especially during the later years of the Directory. As in the Hoppé-Lange trial and the *cause célèbre* of Suzanne Lepeletier, revolutionaries considered whether women as a sex or as dependents in the family could lose citizenship rights in France.

Legislators debated the status of the family members of émigrés with particular passion in the immediate aftermath of the Terror, focusing especially on the question of parental responsibility for children's emigration. In championing measures against émigrés, politicians and leaders combined the remains of the older model of the nation as a preeminent family with the resurgent emphasis on the authority of individual heads of households. Petitioners rejecting these measures emphasized the limits of parental control over their children. But in doing so, they continued to assert the priority of family over nation and to maintain that there was an important difference between political membership in a community of full citizens and the civil membership of women and children in the nation. These arguments were even more pronounced in 1797, when apologists for émigrés called for a general amnesty, and, failing that, one for women and children. They argued both that a child's or woman's departure from revolutionary France under the authority of the *paterfamilias* did not constitute a voluntary and irreversible forfeiture of French citizenship rights, and that women should be allowed to return to France precisely because they had only partial citizenship rights.

In late 1797 and early 1798 the Directory reactivated certain measures from the Terror, aimed especially at émigrés, priests who had refused to accept the Civil Constitution of the Clergy and to take a loyalty oath to the French state, former nobles, enemy foreigners, and other apparent foes of the Republic. In this context, apologetics on behalf of émigrés met little sympathy. But in applying these measures, jurists and administrators, like their predecessors in the Revolution, struggled to establish how people became or ceased to be French citizens, and the relevance of different aspects of citizenship for men and women. They were particularly concerned about whether women who had married foreigners and left France were still responsible for emigration. While the government initially proclaimed that duty to the nation superseded all other duties, officials increasingly incorporated arguments made earlier during the Directory to emphasize the importance and strength of marital bonds and the different positions of men and women in the nation.

Emigré Families

Some of the most passionate debate about emigration in the immediate wake of the Terror focused on the status of the family members of émigrés rather than the émigrés themselves.[3] Officials were particularly concerned with the parents of émigrés. As we have seen, divorce provided a partial means for spouses of émigrés to separate themselves legally from their wayward partners. The revolutionary government regarded such divorces with suspicion, but nonetheless accepted them as legitimate, if insufficient, proof of individual loyalty to the state. It was trickier for the parents of émigrés to prove that they had disassociated themselves from their offspring, and their responsibility for children's emigration became controversial. Certainly, as parents of émigrés and their supporters repeatedly pointed out, the Revolution itself had created legal forms of emancipation that removed a child from his parents, particularly the age of majority. But the government did not necessarily view these forms of emancipation as relevant. Other factors, such as their children's marriages or establishment of separate households, suggested independence, but did not necessarily prove parents' lack of complicity in their offspring's plans.

Debate in the late 1790s explicitly reassessed earlier measures concerning the family members of émigrés. These had begun with the first laws against emigration. In 1791 and 1792, parents whose sons had emigrated were required to pay for food and clothing for a French soldier. This indemnity was soon increased to the obligation to provide two soldiers with basic necessities for every son who had emigrated. Parents were assumed to be complicit in sending their children abroad. In theory, they could be cleared of guilt by association if they could prove that they had actively tried to prevent the emigration of their adult children. However, such proof was difficult to establish. The law of March 1793, which codified and extended measures against émigrés, gave the nation the right to collect for the next fifty years inheritances that would have gone to émigrés. As it explicitly applied laws against emigration to both men and women, it also now held parents responsible for the emigration of both sons and daughters. It nonetheless made two exceptions: those whose children had married or were domiciled separately before July 1, 1789, and those who earned less than 1,000 livres per household and had earned a certificate of *civisme*. On 17 Frimaire Year II (December 7, 1793), Danton introduced a new law. It allowed the government to seize the property of all relations of émigrés and declared them to be charges of the Republic (*pensionnaires de la République*) who would be provided with a basic living wage by the government. It exempted parents of adult children who had emigrated if they could prove they had actively tried to prevent their children's departure.

Danton's law was repealed in late 1794, as part of the general overhaul of the legislation of the Terror. But the end of the Terror did not end measures against the relatives of émigrés: the Frimaire law was followed by the infamous law of 9 Floréal Year III (April 28, 1795). Championed by Chazal, it required that parents of émigrés declare the value of all their possessions. The state then claimed the portion of property that in the normal course of events would have constituted the legacy bequeathed to children who had emigrated. The National Convention overturned the Floréal law only a few months later but continued to institute other legislation against family members of émigrés.[4] The infamous law of 3 Brumaire Year IV (October 25, 1795) excluded relatives of émigrés from holding political office; it potentially encompassed parents, sons, grandsons, brothers, brothers-in-law, relations by marriage, uncles, and nephews. In the winter and spring of 1796, the Council of Five Hundred and the Council of Ancients vigorously debated relaxing measures against émigrés. Instead, in May 1796 they revived much of the earlier Floréal law and continued to allow the state to liquidate the assets of émigrés' parents and to seize what it claimed was the Republic's portion.[5] After the elections of Year V, which temporarily brought more conservative deputies into power, the legislature abrogated the law of 3 Brumaire. Laws concerning the seizure of émigré property nonetheless remained in effect until 8 Messidor Year VII (June 26, 1799).[6]

The complexity of these measures often overwhelmed contemporaries and has rebuffed historians. But the arguments over the laws reveal some of the changing assumptions about the appropriate relationship between family and state and the citizenship capacities and duties of individuals, particularly women. Debates over the responsibility of parents for their children echoed certain earlier apologetics for women's emigration and fed indirectly into arguments that would be used in the late 1790s to call for an amnesty for women and children émigrés.

Justifying Measures against the Parents of Emigrés

Legislators continued to justify measures against émigrés' families by depicting the nation as a whole as a family and émigrés as parricides who had tried to destroy it. Just as the Lepeletier brothers, especially Félix, had tried to portray the nation as a great family that took precedence over individual families, former Jacobins and their supporters often depicted the nation as a family threatened by its renegade émigré children. On 19 Nivôse Year IV (January 18, 1796), the regicide and deputy to the Council of Five Hundred Pierre-Jean Audouin berated those who proposed "to imitate these parricides who destroy everything in France for the honor of nobility and the high clergy." In an influential speech, he proclaimed on 28 Ventôse Year IV (March 18, 1796) that "the Republic justly possesses the portion of the goods that parricidal French would have inherited." The speech helped turn the tide in favor of renewed measures against the parents of émigrés.[7] Deputies echoed similar sentiments as part of the "Directorial Terror" two years later. On 18 Nivôse Year VI (January 7, 1798), Jacques-Antoine Creuze-Latouche, in charge of a commission to examine a fresh resolution on the fathers and mothers of émigrés, proclaimed anew that "émigrés are no longer anything for us except defeated criminals, rebuffed parricides, traitors rejected from the breast of our country never to return."[8]

Even those who were less inclined to perpetuate a Jacobin model and vocabulary for defining the state were concerned about prematurely undoing some of the changes made during the Terror. Their concerns were especially acute as war continued and the Directory faced ongoing political uncertainty. Because the Constitution of Year III (August 1795) forbade the return of the émigrés, it indirectly confirmed that they would never be able to reclaim inheritances in France, and thus justified state seizure of such inheritances. Legislators also had strong practical motivations for maintaining laws that allowed the state to claim the property of émigrés' relations. They desperately needed the revenues such property provided. Moreover, men and women who remained in France but had contacts with family members outside the country posed a constant threat to the Republic. Seizing their property might dissuade others from encouraging their relatives to emigrate.

"I Am an Unfortunate Father, but I Was Never Guilty"

Like the men and women who petitioned to be exempted from the Germinal Year II laws on ex-nobles and foreigners, those affected by the laws against the family members of émigrés insisted that the Revolution had made responsibility for crimes personal and not collective.[9] Petitioners often argued that their own continued residence in France should be sufficient proof that they had placed personal duty to their country above all other duties or legal statuses. The widow Chastillon in April 1795 claimed that her daughters were married and in their thirties; she had "done all she could to retain her daughters in their country, she preached by example by staying in France herself, but she could not win over daughters under the power of their husbands." Similarly, a woman who had stayed in her home near Angoulême when her husband emigrated with their sons protested indignantly in June 1795 that "she preferred her country to her family, she stayed in its breast, she abandoned herself to the support of her fellow citizens, and now she would be punished for this confidence!"[10]

But while such proclamations echoed the claims to patriotic devotion made by former nobles, alleged foreigners, and accused émigré women, other petitioners attempting to dissociate themselves from their children's emigration seem to have adopted an opposite argument. These women often justified their absence from France by referring to their subjection to their husbands or fathers, like the anonymous petitioner who portrayed herself as fighting against "the double power of a father and a husband acting together to overpower all her wishes."[11] In contrast, parents and grandparents of émigrés stressed the limits of *puissance paternelle*. Considered responsible for their children's emigration—often regardless of the age and marital status of their sons and daughters—they adopted a discourse of parental powerlessness. But they also argued that holding parents responsible for their children's actions after the age of majority actually undermined *puissance paternelle* as a principle of social order. For example, a group of "fathers of families" from Arras contended in October 1796 that legislation penalizing the parents of adult émigrés would be "immoral and imprudent; it would strike the final blow to paternal authority, the sacred base of any society, since it would make fathers and mothers dependent on their children."[12] Such arguments resonated with contemporary proclamations about the importance of unified and hierarchal families, from Guiraudet's claim that families were the basis of society to the debates about how to bolster the authority of the *paterfamilias* in the proposed civil code.

Both parents of émigrés and apologists for women émigrés made many of the same arguments in the late 1790s. They claimed that women should not be penalized for the emigration of their male relatives, whether spouses or sons; insisted that émigrées had left France only out of obedience to their husbands; and reiterated that French women had the right to leave or return to France precisely because they lacked any significant political or military identity. Women, especially widows, wrote a large portion of such petitions, maintaining that they had been unable to control whether their adult sons and daughters remained in France.[13] The petition for the widow Longchamp from April 1795 was typical of their mixture of specific evidence of their children's willfulness and strategic invocations of revolutionary laws. She demanded to know whether she could be held responsible for her thirty-seven-year-old married son, a son whom she had not seen for eleven years and who had run away from his paternal home seven times. She asked further how she could be expected to restrain a son "enjoying all the rights of Man, which make him master of his will and his actions? It would be a great contradiction with the law that removes all power from the parents of adult children over the age of twenty-five."[14]

Polemicists similarly tried to inspire pity for the relatives of émigrés and a relaxation of the laws aimed at them by invoking the image of a powerless mother unfairly penalized for her son's defection. André Morellet, one of most prolific and articulate champions of the rights of the family members of émigrés, described a woman unable to stop her children from leaving and punished for her husband's crime of encouraging their emigration:

> One must be astounded to see even a mother held to such a responsibility. A woman under her husband's authority has neither the legal right nor, most often, the reality of any power over her children. Even in cases in which the father has consented to children's emigration, the crime of this consent is not hers but that of her spouse, for how could she oppose a resolution of this nature if the father approved it? Will she fight her son and her husband?[15]

Those whose daughters had emigrated also revived the theme of the military and political insignificance of women and their gendered inability to witness the violence of the Revolution. In this vision, emigration was not the crime of leaving French territory; rather, it was a transgression that entailed the loss of French citizenship because émigrés had failed to conform to the declaration in the Constitution of Year III that every French citizen was a soldier. Emigrés forfeited their citizenship by refusing to defend the Republic with arms or by threatening to fight against it. Thus the fathers and mothers of émigrés in the Department of Meurthe argued that a law against them "could derive from Article 24 of April 8, 1792, which gave to the profit of the nation successive rights to come due for émigrés; but this law affected only children who were old enough to carry arms, and several among them are being pursued for the emigration of their daughters, even those who left under the authority of their husbands."[16] Similarly, the authors of the later *Mémoire à la convention nationale pour les pères, les mères, et ayeux des émigrés* bewailed the fact that laws punished mothers whose daughters had left France:

> And you punish this unfortunate mother whose daughters weren't brave! They feared executioners and war—war of which women are often innocent victims, but which they never provoke and always abhor! If I were to talk again of this crowd of fathers and mothers whose daughters, under the power of their husbands, left because [their husbands'] authority on the one hand and fear on the other led them to do so, against the wishes of their parents, who were powerless to retain them since they lacked the right to do so.[17]

As the émigrés' champion, Morellet, put it in 1796, the government might penalize sons who could fight for France, but not "émigré daughters, who do not fight and have no contracts to fulfill."[18]

Such arguments were most prevalent in the immediate wake of the Floréal law and its successors, but continued afterward. For example, in 1797 Pierre-André Despommerais of Caen, held responsible for the emigration of his adult daughters, maintained that he had done his best to prevent them from leaving France and that they could not act against the Republic because they were women. It was "commonly known in the area where he lives that one of them emigrated alone and the other to follow her husband, and that neither one nor the other can carry arms against her country." Despommerais reiterated later that their gender disqualified his daughters from acting against France: "What could they do, given their sex, to oppose the will of the Republic?"[19]

Women who remained in France were obliged to demonstrate that they had placed their loyalty to the revolutionary nation above legal or emotional bonds with their families and the enemy communities that their spouses now potentially represented. Even after the Terror there were, however, no clear means for other relatives of émigrés to prove that they had dissociated themselves from their outcast relations. Such men and women, like émigrés themselves, thus often focused on the gendered significance of emigration and the role of *puissance maritale* in coercing young women's flight from France. These arguments would reappear more explicitly when revolutionaries began to consider an amnesty for women émigrés in 1797.

An Amnesty for Emigré Women? Debates in Year V (1796–97)

Although émigrés were still formally ostracized in Year V, more and more returned to France, where they lobbied for a relaxation of the laws against them—and especially for women and children. Not only did individuals petition for exceptions or changes to the laws, but the lower house of the legislature, the Council of Five Hundred, itself battered the Directory with proposed legislation, while the upper house, the Council of Ancients, debated those proposals at length. Reassessing laws on emigration forced the government to consider what it meant to be a citizen and to confront potential conflicts between family and citizenship bonds for dependents in the family.

The government had already stipulated a number of exceptions to the category of émigrés when the Constitution of Year III forbade their return to France. Many of these echoed exceptions to the Germinal laws, especially those for laborers who worked with their hands and their wives and children under eighteen. Such exemptions required that émigrés had not left France until after May 1793 (the date now seen as the beginning of the Terror) and had returned shortly after the decree.[20] In the wake of the new Constitution, in September 1795, the government declared an amnesty for many of those who had left the city of Toulon, which had been captured by the English in the summer of 1793. The amnesty affected sailors, bakers, artisans working with their hands, workers in military hospitals and the arsenal, women, children, and old men.[21] In 1796 and 1797 revolutionaries debated additional exceptions for those from Toulon and from the Alsatian departments of Haut and Bas Rhin.[22] Speechmakers often used the term *fugitif* (or the feminine *fugitive*). The term was a favorite among apologists for émigrés trying to portray those who had left France as forced to flee from violence and an illegitimate government, rather than as voluntarily "emigrating" from their country. It echoed the term *religionnaire fugitif,* used to describe Protestants who had left France for religious reasons during the Old Regime and who had been encouraged to return by the 1790 law, which restored them to citizenship rights in the revolutionary nation. The government's use of the term, albeit with periodic skepticism ("supposed fugitives" in some speeches), suggested the possibility of further legitimate exemptions.

Apologists for émigrés during the Directory resurrected or echoed older arguments about the political insignificance of women and the inability of dependents to choose between family and national bonds or the undesirability of their having to do so. But such claims began to appear with particular frequency after Thermidor, as legislators, philosophers, and writers increasingly sought to portray unified families as the basis of a new social order. By 1797 they had become a common trope among writers trying to locate a domestic haven of innocence, praising women as beings who could neither perform nor witness the violence that had marked France during the Terror.

Champions of émigrés also sought to use the case of women émigrés to challenge the laws on emigration. Earlier apologists had tended to argue that the laws were essentially valid, but that exceptions should be made for women and others who lacked political citizenship or who had left under another's authority. Pamphleteers and political writers in 1797 criticized the principles behind the measures against all émigrés. However, they still made a special case for women. Trophime-Gérard de Lally-Tolendal, a former member of one of the Old Regime sovereign courts or *parlements,* an important member of the National Assembly in 1789, and later a prominent figure in the Restoration, spearheaded the appeal to allow émigrés to return to France and reclaim their rights as French citizens. His *Défense des émigrés français* appeared in at least four editions in 1797 and was reprinted several times during the Restoration.[23] Many of Lally-Tolendal's arguments were common themes among the apologists of the émigrés. He reviewed the various laws on emigration, contending that émigrés had not ceased to be loyal Frenchmen, since the government of the Terror had been fundamentally illegitimate, and that those who had left France had been forced to flee rather than voluntarily abandoning their country. While calling for a general amnesty, however, he also insisted that "the case of women and children must be treated separately from all others." He justified such special treatment by focusing on women as a distinctive group whose relationship to the French nation was inherently different from that of men because they could neither defend nor make war on their native country. Their absence from French territory could not be defined as a crime: "Can any one deny that all *women* émigrées are obviously innocent of *treason* and *cowardliness?* Can women be accused of having carried arms or not having done so?"[24]

Other pamphleteers echoed Lally-Tolendal's insistence that émigrées had not committed a political act by fleeing France. Exploring the connections between citizenship and gender more systematically, the anonymous author of *Défense des femmes, des enfans et des vieillards émigrés, pour faire suite à l'ouvrage de M. de Lally-Tolendal* made one of the strongest pleas for pardoning women for emigration. Her fundamental claim was that "political impotency is proven for women, and must militate in favor of their return."[25] Lally-Tolendal had simply lamented the "lists of exiles filled with the names of women." She, however, took this a step further, contending that such prescriptions really did presume in a novel way that women were citizens endowed with political rights. "No people, ancient or modern, enveloped women in the most vast of political banishments, as if women were, or should be, something in the political order."[26]

The pamphleteer contended that the laws had already begun implicitly to differentiate between men and women. For Lally-Tolendal, an amnesty for women had been necessary precisely because the laws continued to treat émigrées and émigrés as equally guilty. He ranted that "old laws explicitly included women, and the new law leaves them there irrevocably."[27] In contrast, the author of *Défense des femmes* suggested that the proscription of women was the work of the radical Revolution and that the laws on emigration themselves had now begun to treat French men and French women differently. She argued that because the Constitution of Year III did not specify that the ban on returning to France applied to both sexes, it represented a change in policy:

> Although it is true that the Constitution is stained, in spirit and letter, by an absolute condemnation against innocents and guilty alike, it cannot be accused of having included women, since it said that the nation would not suffer the return of French men [*français*] who abandoned it, etc.: If it had meant to include women, it would have added "nor French women [*françaises*]." Either women are nothing politically, in which case they are neither named nor included in a particular political sentence, or they are something important, in which case a constitution refers to them at least by a generic name that can encompass them, when it is a question of an article or a law that does not include the totality of the citizens of the empire.[28]

She suggested that women should be considered as political nonentities; to treat women as émigrés was to falsely disguise (*travestir*) "their persons as political members of the republic."[29] Her language echoed Roederer's claim that a woman had "no political right in the State" because she was "only a member of the family." It also echoed the claim made by Hoppé's lawyers a few months before the publication of this treatise that women did not participate in the sovereign nation. However, rather than arguing that women's distance from the political sphere meant that the head of the household could and should choose the nation in which the family lived, the pamphleteer called for a dissociation between political and civil rights that would allow women to return home regardless of the actions of the *paterfamilias*. She contended that precisely because French women lacked political rights and were now often recognized as lacking those rights, they should not be banished from their homeland and lose their civil rights in France.

Other participants in this debate reemphasized the priority of family over citizenship bonds for dependents in the household and implicitly supported a model of the nation as a conglomerate of families. Lally-Tolendal himself argued that the government could not place duty to the country above loyalty to the family since "the country [*patrie*] is born from the family, [and] nature precedes the city [*cité*]." Emigré husbands and fathers were exonerated because they had fled an illegal regime; their daughters and wives were exonerated because they had followed the tender call of familial bonds.

Lally-Tolendal contended that in other circumstances, judges and juries had already "solemnly proclaimed that the daughter who nourishes her father, the mother who nourishes her son, the wife who nourishes her husband in exile, fulfill a duty rather than committing a crime."[30] While he did not elaborate on the context of such proclamations, he implied that they should translate easily to the realm of emigration.

Even those opposed to an amnesty for women used many of the same arguments. In another tract directly inspired by Lally-Tolendal's work, Jean-Jacques Leuliète, professor and *homme des lettres,* sought to justify selected measures against those who had left France. He agreed that most émigré women were not guilty of abandoning their country under their own volition but had left because of their subordination to their spouses. He acknowledged that "it is cruel, doubtless, to close the gates of the country [*patrie*] irrevocably to so many women, whose only crime was an overly faithful attachment to the opinions of those mortals dearest to them, to whom they were tied by sacred bonds." While such logic could have been applied to other family relations—such as sons over the age of majority who followed their fathers out of France—Leuliète explicitly referred to those who were legally dependent within the family and who were, in his view, incapable of acting independently and politically. Women could not be regarded as traitors to France, since they were not, and had never been, opposed to the Republic: "You plead for an amnesty for women, but I misspeak; one should not say amnesty, since they were never our enemies."[31] The author of *Défense des femmes* had depicted women's return to France as a return to their families:

> There, mothers who have remained alone, missing the presence of their daughters with young children. Here, sisters who sigh for the return of their sisters; here again, five children who have lacked their mother since she fled with the oldest daughter whose age made her fear danger; there, husbands deprived of their wives; they are waiting for you to reunite what heaven and society never intended to separate.[32]

In contrast, Leuliète portrayed a partial amnesty as destroying rather than restoring familial unity, for "what charm could there be for a sensitive woman in a land from which her husband would be eternally banished?" Precisely because their loyalty to the family preceded loyalty to the state, women would not want to return to France without their spouses, and they should not be allowed to do so. It would be an "illusory mercy, to misjudge the noblest sentiments of nature, to recall a wife and close the door to her husband."[33] He praised the courage of French women, defining women like Charlotte Corday and Madame Roland as revolutionary heroines. However, he contended, it was precisely such courage, which when combined with their fundamental familial loyalty, that militated against the return of émigré women.

Leuliète's tract was not the final word in this debate. An author who signed himself only as "F. T-D." took up Leuliète's arguments directly and rearticulated Lally-Tolendal's rationales for an amnesty for *émigrées*. F. T.-D. joined Leuliète in praise of Charlotte Corday, associating the unmarried assassin of Marat with Andromache, the epitome of a loyal wife in Greek legend. However, he argued that women's loyalty to their families would make them forgive their country for its excesses. He adapted the common term *fugitif* to claim that women were "naturally" inclined to flee from the violence of revolution and war. F. T.-D. expressed astonishment that such innocent beings could be permanently cursed with "political anathema" "only because of the pretext that sacred bonds have united them to their [husbands'] fate!" He argued that in championing their return, he offered "a homage more worthy of them and the sacrifice they made of everything that attached them to France, to follow their husbands, the patience and resignation that they showed in the rigors, dangers, and misery of expatriation."[34]

The Directorial Terror and Its Limits

The 1797 debate did not immediately lead to an amnesty. Indeed, the Directorial Terror, which was instituted soon after this controversy in Fructidor Year VI (September 1797), reactivated and intensified prosecution of émigrés. In January 1798 the Directory reinvigorated laws against émigrés that had been increasingly ignored, attacked nonjuror priests, and formally assimilated nobles to foreigners (*étrangers*), depriving them of political citizenship. In the year that followed, 160 returning émigrés were executed, and 1,800 priests were either shot or deported. But the Fructidorians themselves drew implicitly on the preceding reconsiderations of the place of women in the nation as they put together their position on émigrés. In April 1798 the minister of justice suspended the automatic death penalty for émigré women, suggesting that women and men should be treated differently.[35] Although military commissions had exiled sixteen women, this directive seemed to put an end to the prosecution of most émigrées.

In the wake of the Fructidorian coup, the Bureau des Lois, an advisory committee for the minister of police, attempted to suggest the correct interpretation of measures pertaining to emigration, foreigners, and the incorporation of conquered territories into France.[36] Members of the Bureau repeatedly confronted questions about the relevance of French citizenship for women and especially about the implications of marriage to a foreigner for French-born women who had left, or sought to leave, their native country. They sought to clarify not only the general role of familial bonds in determining responsibility for emigration, but also the specific implications of Frenchness and foreignness for both men and women.

In applying some of the measures of the Directorial Terror, lawmakers and administrators sought to distinguish clearly the *qualité de français* and that of *citoyen*, as legislators and jurists had done implicitly in court cases like the Hoppé-Lange trial and explicitly in various arguments about the exercise of political rights in France during the Directory. When they debated whether the Knights of Malta should be subject to all the penalties for emigration, they tried to distinguish between the title of "French" and that of "citizen" and declared that the *chevaliers* had forfeited their political rights but not their "Frenchness" when they joined the religious order.[37] However, other measures of the Directorial Terror blurred the definitions of foreigner and citizen further. In Vendémaire Year VI (September 27, 1797), the legislature formally equated ex-nobles and foreigners. Former nobles were obliged to undergo the same constitutional requirements as immigrants before they were allowed to exercise political rights in France, including a period of seven years in which their commitment to the Republic would be established.[38] The decree echoed debates in the winter of 1796–97 about whether returned *religionnaires fugitifs* should be required to undergo a similar seven-year hiatus before being allowed to vote and hold office. But rather than distinguishing between Frenchness and citizenship, as the earlier debate had done, the law on ex-nobles used the term *étranger* loosely to encompass former nobles born in France and residing in French territory. Indeed, various administrators were sufficiently confused by this designation to ask if the status of former nobles as foreigners meant that they required special passports.[39]

In explicitly and legally defining former nobles as foreigners, the decree was harsher than the Germinal Year II (April 1794) measure exiling ex-nobles and enemy foreigners from France. It also did not have the same provisions for requisitioning useful ex-nobles. On the other hand, it pertained only to political rights, and not to residence in Paris and other key localities in France, and there were few means of enforcing the law. Patrice Higonnet has defined this measure as a part of a resurgent antinoble ideology, linked to the return of the common equation of émigré and noble from 1791 and 1792. In contrast, Howard Brown has shown that the Directory applied the decree very selectively, making distinctions based on the threat that a specific subgroup posed to the immediate domestic stability of the Republic rather than antinobility as such.[40] The limited application of the measure suggests not only the political challenges of the moment, but also that administrators soon became reluctant to use the term "foreigner" as loosely and inclusively as the law implied.

"Duties That Bound the French to Their *Patrie* above Those . . ."

The question of whether French women married to foreigners could leave the country remained controversial in the late 1790s. A law from 25 Prairial

Year III (May 7, 1795) had annulled the decree of 4 Germinal Year II, which forbade daughters or wives of émigrés, even those who had divorced their spouses, to marry a foreigner and leave France. But there was no decree clarifying whether French women in general could accompany foreign husbands outside France without penalties.

The Bureau's initial decisions suggest that it continued to place duty to the country above hierarchical familial relations. The Bureau proclaimed that paternal authority did not override children's "duties toward the country [*patrie*]." On 13 Frimaire Year VII (December 3, 1798), it considered the case of François Le Roux, also known as La Serre, a French émigré who had become a professor in a school in Saxony and wanted his illegitimate thirteen-year-old daughter to join him. The Bureau ruled that Le Roux's rights as a father did not justify sending young Aglée out of France:

> Following normal laws, and consulting only the principles of paternal power, there is not the slightest difficulty in granting Serre's wish, since according to these principles, one cannot justify separating a child of only thirteen years of age from her father; such a child is far from being freed from paternal authority. But the laws on emigration placed the duties that bound the French to their country [*patrie*] above those that attached them to their families. That is necessarily the base of paragraphs 1 and 2 of article 2, title 1 of the law of 25 Brumaire Year III, which counts children who have not returned to France as émigrés at an age where they still lack political rights and legal will and when paternal power has all its force. Consequently, however natural the desire of a young French girl to join her father may be, it is not a legitimate motive for leaving France.[41]

The Bureau voiced further suspicion of Le Roux's motives and ability to raise his daughter as a French patriot, echoing, in a very different context, the argument that Julien Souhait had made for legislative control over Suzanne Lepeletier in February 1798: "are you sure that you can find in these families the wisdom and patriotism that must guide the education and establishment of the children of the nation?"[42] The Bureau's emphasis on the untrustworthiness of such families also resembled the views expressed by the regicide Philippe Laurent Pons de Verdun a year earlier, on 15 Frimaire Year VI (December 6, 1797). Pons de Verdun had argued more generally that children of émigrés should not be educated by their parents. Following the logic used by people like Danton and Barère in 1793 and 1794, he proclaimed: "These children belong to their country before belonging to their fathers, and if the latter do not raise them for it [their country], you have the right to restrain them or to have the children raised by others."[43]

Le Roux's petition to have his illegitimate daughter join him outside France also paralleled certain aspects of the Hoppé-Lange trial in December 1796, although it drew far less attention than that case. Hoppé's champions had contended that a foreign father's authority over a French daughter was justified because the value of French citizenship was inherently limited for girls; it mattered less if Palymre left the country with her father than it would if she were a boy. In Le Roux's case, duty to the nation applied regardless of sex. The Bureau ultimately refused to allow the thirteen-year-old to leave France and join her émigré father, proclaiming that "young French, whatever their sex, should not be sent to foreign countries to be raised by their parents [who are] presumed enemies of the French."[44]

The Bureau similarly emphasized duty to the country over familial bonds when it considered the case of Marie Montbéliard, the French-born widow of a Swiss merchant. Marie's property in the Department of Lot had been seized as that of an émigrée because she and her husband had moved to Switzerland during the Revolution. She vehemently protested this seizure, contending that her marriage had made her an *étrangère* and thus liberated her from the civic duties imposed on French men and women. She insisted that her property should be restored to her, rather than taken for a crime that an *étrangère* could not have committed. The Bureau des Lois responded on 27 Prairial Year VI (June 15, 1798) that simply marrying a foreigner had not released Marie from her obligations as a member of the French nation. A woman's subordination to a French husband in no way pardoned her from the crime of emigration. By the same logic, her subordination to a foreign husband had not excused a French woman from abandoning her *patrie*:

> A French woman would attempt in vain to excuse her disobedience to the law by insisting that she needed to follow her French husband; such devotion, which compromised the interests of the country [*patrie*], was a crime against it in the eyes of the law, [so] it could well be in the spirit of the law to consider as an émigrée a woman who left France to follow a foreigner who had become her husband since the Revolution.[45]

Foreigners before the Revolution

Yet the Bureau went on to state that such obligations applied only during the Revolution. It had in fact been possible for a French woman to have become a foreigner through marriage before the Revolution. In such circumstances, her "foreignness" freed her from the responsibility of staying in, or returning to, a country that was no longer the one in which she belonged. The Bureau thus ruled that Marie Montbéliard should be provisionally allowed to retain her property in southern France because her wedding had taken place before 1789. It specified that the obligation to remain in France applied only when the foreigner had "become her husband since the Revolution." Generalizing from Montbéliard's situation, the Bureau proclaimed that a "French woman married to a foreigner before the Revolution thus has the right to invoke the principles of common law; she follows the condition of her husband, she is thus only a foreigner, and is at least in the same position as individuals naturalized or established in foreign countries before July 15, 1789."[46]

In subsequent cases, the Bureau reiterated that a French woman married to a foreigner before the Revolution did not have the responsibilities of a woman who had married since then. On 29 Pluviôse Year VII (February 17, 1799), it considered the situation of Catherine Nicole Desland, who had married an Italian optician before the Revolution and had moved with him to a small town near Milan in 1783. When she attempted to claim an inheritance bequeathed to her by her father in France, her case came to the attention of the Bureau. In contradiction to Old Regime law, Desland's position was actually strongest if she was viewed as foreign and not French. If she was legally an *étrangère*, she was legitimately entitled to her father's property, since the restrictions on the ability of foreigners to inherit in France had been abolished in 1790. However, if she was a French émigrée who had left the Republic and not returned when the revolutionary government decreed that all loyal citizens belonged in France, then she had no rights in her home country. The Bureau stated categorically that marriage to a foreign husband provided no reason for pardoning a woman's emigration:

> The laws on emigration placed duty to the country above all other duties. A woman would try in vain to legitimate her absence by invoking the bonds that attached her to an émigré spouse; a child would have no more success invoking the sacred duties of filial piety. . . . absence from France to follow a foreign husband is nowhere recognized in the law [of 25 Brumaire Year III] as legitimate, and we are persuaded that it is an exception in neither the spirit nor the letter of the law.[47]

But as in the case of Marie Montbéliard, the Bureau went on to clarify that it was only since the Revolution that "abandoning France has become a political crime." It argued that women like Desland were attached to their new countries not by a business or property that could be sold or by potentially fickle service to a prince—the evidence of changed national allegiances for men—but by more fundamental and permanent ties: "Surely one will not believe that a woman established in a foreign country by bonds quite otherwise respectable than naturalization or the establishment of a business should be forced to break those lines in order to return to her former country."[48] The members of the council suggested that, for women, marital bonds were stronger than national ones and less dissoluble. They implied that this was a universal truth—but nonetheless one that did not apply to women who sought to wed during the Revolution.

"Purely Personal Interest"? Marriage and Naturalization

Indeed, the Bureau applied such principles when it directly considered the case of French women who wanted to marry foreigners. It scorned the desire of an Alsatian woman who wanted to wed a subject of a German prince newly allied with the Republic. It decided on 5 Fructidor Year VI (August 23, 1798) that the woman's relationship with her would-be husband provided no excuse for leaving France:

> There is no reason to treat a woman who, purely out of personal interest, wants to abandon her country to live in a foreign land, more favorably than any other individual. . . . Until the law forbidding French to leave the territory of the republic is lifted, a French woman cannot leave France on the pretext of marrying a foreigner and go live with him in a neutral or allied country, without running the risks of being considered an émigrée.[49]

The wording of the judgment is revealing. In forbidding the Alsatian woman to follow her fiancé, the Bureau stressed that "a French woman cannot leave France on the pretext of marrying a foreigner." The members of the Bureau seem to have presumed the point in question: that a woman who married a foreigner during the Revolution remained French—or that any "foreignness" that she acquired did not override the duties she owed to the revolutionary nation. In contrast to Montbéliard's and Desland's situation, marriage did not bind the Alsatian woman more closely to her new home than naturalization would have done; during the Revolution, her connection to her native *patrie* came first.

The Bureau, however, seemed to reverse its policy completely when, on June 25, 1799, it considered the case of Antoinette Goets, a woman who had been living in Mont Terrible—an annexed department on the east bank of the Rhine—and who wanted to marry and move to her intended's home in Switzerland. Members of the Bureau debated whether she could leave France with her fiancé without being considered an émigrée. In this case, the Bureau did not deride the "purely personal interest" that might lead a woman to abandon her country to join her future husband, as it had done a year earlier when it refused to let an engaged Alsatian woman leave French territory without suffering the penalties of emigration. Instead, it proclaimed that Antoinette Goets's engagement was not simply "a preference that she gives to another country [*pays*] over France," but rather "an affair of the greatest importance for her that leads her to leave her country [*patrie*]." The Bureau concluded that "since the establishment of the constitutional regime, the marriage of a French woman in an allied or neutral country no longer has the character of a reprehensible abandonment of France" and that such marriages were now legitimate reasons for French women to leave their country.[50]

It is difficult to give a definitive explanation of why the Bureau reversed its policies and, especially, why it shifted ground when it did. Part of the answer must lie in the complexities of contemporary politics, as the Directory lurched between more conservative and radical policies while attempting to ward off challenges from both the left and right. By the time the Bureau considered Antoinette Goets's case, the government was leaning back toward the right and may thus have been more lenient toward those accused of emigration.

But this does not provide a full answer to our questions. The Bureau's change in policy also seems to correspond to the increasing tendency to distinguish between "foreigners" and "émigrés," and between the titles of "French" and "citizen." Like those calling for an amnesty for émigrés, the Bureau drew upon the Constitution of Year III to justify its stance. The Constitution forbade the return of émigrés to France but restored the right of French citizens to travel in and out of their country's borders as they saw fit. Just before considering Catherine Desland's case, the Bureau debated whether Frenchmen who had accepted employment from a foreign government after the proclamation of the new Constitution should be categorized as émigrés.[51] They concluded that, according to the Constitution, such men had lost their political rights or *droits de citoyen* in France, but now simply became foreigners, rather than men who were completely "dead" to their country.[52] By the same logic, French women who married and left their native country should simply be treated as foreigners—especially as they had no political rights to lose.

The Bureau further justified its shift by stressing the issue of permission, arguing that "it is only French women who left their country without permission who are émigrées." In the case of the Alsatian woman, the Bureau had ruled that "until the law forbidding French to leave the territory of the Republic is lifted, a French woman cannot leave France on the pretext of marrying a foreigner and go to live with him in a neutral or allied country, without running the risk of being considered an émigrée." It now suggested that the previous judgment was valid but insufficient; it was simply necessary to add the qualifier "unless she has obtained permission from competent authorities."[53]

Members of the Bureau now lauded the formation of new marital alliances "so fitting to strengthen the bonds of natural affection between nations." They suggested that French women's departure from—or implicitly their return to—France should not be seen posing the same problems as the movements of male citizens. The Bureau did not, however, consider whether women might naturalize as individuals. Nor did its members consider whether emigration was a crime defined less by its territorial nature than by its political and military character. Raising such issues would have made it difficult to enforce more general legislation against émigrés. But the Bureau did imply that naturalization and marriage were functionally equivalent means for men and women to renounce their *droits de citoyen* in France, as long as they had official permission to do so. Invoking the problem of "permission" was clearly a face-saving maneuver, and one that must have come naturally to an advisory committee for the minister of police. However, the Bureau also continued to suggest that women participated in some kind of contract of citizenship with the sovereign and could not leave without obtaining permission to break that contract—even if they were legally covered by a husband's citizenship status. Marital bonds may have been more respectable forms of establishing national allegiances than naturalization or establishment of a business and increasingly took priority over other loyalties, but they were not indissoluble or transcendent bonds.

The Amnesty of Year IX: "If a Woman Prefers Her *Patrie*"

The twin ideas that family should take priority over duty to the state for women and that women should not have the duties of citizenship incumbent on men were vindicated when Napoleon declared a partial amnesty for émigrés on 28 Vendémiaire Year IX (October 20, 1800). It allowed for the legal repatriation of some 52,000 émigrés.[54] The first categories of people granted amnesty were primarily those who had, in some sense, already been cleared. These included men and women who had already been provisionally or definitively removed from the list of émigrés, foreigners who had been previously allowed to remain in France, manual laborers—the subject of various earlier laws pardoning workers and peasants who had fled during the Terror—and those who had been listed collectively, rather than individually, as émigrés.[55] The "wives and children" of such émigrés were allowed to return to France with them, as an extension of the amnesty granted to the head of the household.

Article 5, however, aimed specifically at women. It granted amnesty both to women who had left France under their husbands' authority and to those who had left on their own, regardless of whether their spouses had been cleared of charges of emigration. Joseph Fouché, the minister of police, explained that in addition, "other articles concerned women under the authority of their husbands or children still under paternal authority or who left only to complete their education. . . . That could not be considered as a crime of emigration. A married woman obeyed her husband's orders, she left her country with him without calculating the consequences of the path along which he took her, and without knowing the laws that menaced her."[56]

The registers of those who took advantage of this article in the following year record close to 13,000 names, or roughly a quarter of all those who took advantage of the amnesty, far more than any other group singled out for a special reprieve.[57] The government did retain the right to deport women whose spouses or children were still considered as émigrés if they proved themselves to be dangerous: "Women whose names were eliminated from the list because of article 5 of the first title, even if their husbands or children remained on the list of émigrés, can be expelled from French territory by an order of the government if they trouble public tranquility."[58] The qualification, however, was rarely applied.

The amnesty built on the consular decree of March 3, 1800, which closed the lists of émigrés; no one else would be added to revolutionary lists of men and women condemned to civil death for leaving French territory. But many remained in a state of limbo, provisionally, but not definitively, cleared of the charge of emigration. As the lawyer for Bernard-Henri-Joseph Montagnac, an ex-soldier accused of being an émigré, complained in a tract pleading his case, such men became "an enigma to themselves, unsure whether they are French or foreigners." His political and civil "paralysis" was particularly troubling to him since the twenty-five-year-old soldier wanted to marry and was unsure whether he could do so legally, despite having being provisionally removed from the list of émigrés and having fulfilled all the "formalities prescribed by the law in order to preserve his *qualité de français* and all his rights of citizenship."[59] It was a common dilemma; indeed, the tract that defended Montagnac's case, *Sur l'importante question du mariage des prévenus d'émigration*, struck a chord throughout France, going through at least three editions in Year IX (1800–01).[60]

Louis Eugène Poirier, the young veteran's lawyer, presented a series of arguments in defense of the lovelorn man. He claimed that Montagnac should be given the benefit of the doubt since he had been provisionally cleared of the charge of emigration, that marriage was too "natural" and important a phenomenon to be restricted by legalistic quibbles, and that the French population as a whole would suffer from laws restricting marriage and in consequence the birth of new citizens. But Poirier also insisted that such marriages would not harm native French women and children. He restated many of the arguments about women's ability to choose between their family and their country that had been articulated during the Revolution. If women were transformed into foreigners through marriage to an émigré or supposed émigré, they forfeited their membership in the French nation by their free choice; it would be "by a voluntary abjuration and their personal actions that they would be henceforward foreigners in France." More important, women could always place national bonds over familial ones even after marriage: if "a woman prefers her country [*patrie*] to her spouse and children prefer their country to their father, a woman can ask for a divorce and find a new spouse; the children, aided by their mother and her family, can form useful establishments and become excellent citizens."[61] In short, dependents in the family could choose between allegiance to the head of the household and to the nation.

In a decision that was published in later editions of the tract, the minister of the interior proclaimed that Montagnac and other supposed émigrés in his position could be allowed to marry. The minister's decision, however, was based on technical grounds: municipal officials had no authority to judge personal status (*l'état des personnes*) and should thus proceed with the appropriate ceremonies. He left it to others to decide the validity of Poirier's argument about the relationship between family and citizenship bonds.

Conclusion

Throughout the 1790s, laws on emigration continued to mandate that men as well as women remain on French territory, to forbid the return of both sexes to France, and to penalize the family members of émigrés. During the Directory, revolutionary governments instituted amendments and exceptions to laws against émigrés. Their attitudes were shaped in part by the political fluctuations of the period. Governments were more willing to relax measures when elections had brought relative conservatives into office, and upheld measures more stringently when the Republic lurched to the left, especially after the Fructidorian coup.

But officials also began to consider special policies for women and children, policies that would be put into place with the partial amnesty of Year IX. Not only apologists for émigrés, but also legislators and administrators began to depict women's membership in the nation as sufficiently different from men's to excuse them from the crime of emigration. Paralleling the emphasis on the limits of the nation as family articulated in the contemporaneous Suzanne Lepeletier case, they increasingly emphasized the hierarchy and unity of literal familial bonds.

Yet, while the Bureau des Lois's equation of marriage and naturalization suggested that naturalization had a different relevance for men than for women, its formulations also continued to imply that women, even married women, had some kind of independent contractual relationship with the French nation. Similarly, Poirier's pamphlet for Montagnac suggested that by 1801 women no longer had the obligation to put *patrie* before family, but retained the ability to do so, even after marriage. The Napoleonic Civil Code would institute more dramatic change that would fundamentally challenge these assumptions, as legislators would soon attempt to move beyond limited solutions like those offered to Montagnac to a more systematic and wide-ranging assessment of familial and citizenship relations.

CODE

NAPOLÉON.

ÉDITION ORIGINALE ET SEULE OFFICIELLE.

A PARIS,

DE L'IMPRIMERIE IMPÉRIALE.

1811.

Figure 3. Code Napoléon. Courtesy of Archives & Special Collections, Mount Holyoke College, South Hadley, Mass.

Part III

The Napoleonic Solution
and Its Limits

In 1799 Napoleon overthrew the Directory and, with it, the Republic. He declared himself first consul; soon afterward he became consul for life. In 1804 he proclaimed himself emperor, a reign that would last until 1814, with a brief revival in 1815. As Napoleon waged war with most of Europe, the French territorial empire expanded; at its height in 1812, it included France, Belgium, the Netherlands, Spain, the Italian peninsula, and many central and eastern European lands.

Historians have struggled to make sense of the relationships between the revolutionary and Napoleonic epochs. One of the key points in their debates is the Civil Code, one of the most lasting and influential productions of the Napoleonic era, and one that has served as a model for law codes in more than twenty nations around the world. For historians of gender and family relations, it often appears as the conclusive denial of women's rights.[1] The Code reinforced the power of husbands and fathers over their wives and children. It did not completely abolish revolutionary innovations in family law, but it limited them substantially. In probably the most infamous example, it preserved divorce, allowing men to divorce their wives for adultery, but permitting women to divorce their husbands on the same grounds only if infidelity had taken place in the conjugal home. For historians of nationality and citizenship, the Code has served as a landmark of a very different sort, the consolidation of revolutionary laws on civil equality and the foundation for future measures on the acquisition and loss of French citizenship.[2]

Few scholars, however, have examined the Code both as a means of defining and systematizing modern forms of "Frenchness" and as a turning point in institutionalizing hierarchical familial relations. Yet legislators were often deeply concerned with both domains. They sought to create a solution to revolutionary conflicts between national citizenship and family bonds by emphasizing the unity of the family after a couple's marriage and the qualitatively different nature of familial bonds from other contracts.

But the new legislation was almost immediately challenged in practice, and its interpretation and application were often as important as its initial formulation in shaping the long-term impact of the Code. While scholars have also usually focused on making of the Code, administrators' and jurists' struggles to decide on its relevance both for the past and the future were often critical in shaping its impact.[3] Many revolutionary measures had been superseded, but they still had real consequences for determining citizenship status in the early nineteenth century, and did not always fit easily with the principles of the new Code. At the same time, applying new laws on the loss or acquisition of French citizenship to both men and women required addressing aspects of national citizenship that legislators had rarely considered.

Chapter 5 examines more closely the Napoleonic "solution" to conflicts between family and citizenship rights; it looks at debates over whether laws concerning national citizenship should be aimed at individual men or women or at families, and how individualized measures could be reconciled with the authority of the head of the household. The subsequent chapters explore the important changes that were institutionalized in the law courts and administrative halls of the Napoleonic empire. Chapter 6 examines the problems that lawyers and judges faced when confronting the heritage of the Revolution and its implications for citizenship rights in the Napoleonic era. Returning émigré men claimed that they had been "reborn" from civil death and restored to all their rights as citizens, including those of fathers and husbands; their reintegration into the "great family" of the nation entailed their return to a position of power in the home. They hoped to challenge acts that dependents in the family had undertaken in their absence, including divorces initiated by their spouses and the emancipation or marriages of their children. In judging their cases, the courts sought to preserve the legal ramifications of civil death, as well as to redefine the relationships among marriage, literal foreignness, and *mort civile*. But their desire to establish paternal authority within the household and to protect literal families from perceived intrusions of the state could also lead them to decide that civil death had temporarily suspended, rather than ended, an émigré's position and rights as the head of a household.

Chapter 7 turns from Napoleonic judgments on the past to explore what it meant for new immigrants to become French citizens and for women to lose their citizenship rights in France. Citizenship law in the Napoleonic era included not only the Code, but also exceptional forms of naturalization and loss of citizenship rights. Indeed, during the height of the empire, these mechanisms were used more often than the Code itself in the acquisition or loss of citizenship. Applying both the Code and related legislation contributed to the disappearance of women's exercise of political rights and participation in the formal mechanisms of national citizenship. While women had petitioned for and received *lettres de naturalité* during the Old Regime, naturalization in the Napoleonic period was linked to military service and political citizenship. Women who asked for French citizenship were told that naturalization conferred political rights for which they were ineligible. An 1811 law punishing French citizens for leaving the empire without permission explicitly excluded women, in contrast to both prerevolutionary measures and revolutionary laws on emigration that had been applied to both men and women. At the same time, foreign women who wished to marry French men—a class of women who had been initially subject to the same procedures for access to civil rights in France as men, at least in certain regions—were now automatically subsumed under their fiancés' or husbands' status.

But the very disappearance of *étrangères* increased the visibility and perceived importance of liaisons between immigrant men and French women. Chapter 8 turns to the end of Napoleon's rule and the return of the Bourbon monarchy. It shows the embedded contradictions between law and practice; relationships on France's frontiers were often viewed not as a means of turning French women into foreigners, as the Napoleonic Code dictated, but rather of turning foreign men into French men.

5 Tethering Cain's Wife: The Napoleonic Civil Code

Napoleonic legislators created a comprehensive Civil Code to regulate personal and property relationships, and accompanied it with extensive penal and commercial codes. Unlike earlier proposals for a civil code during the Revolution, the Napoleonic version would not only be adopted, but would shape both French and international law for much of the following two centuries. Lawmakers sought to end the ambiguity and diversity of earlier measures. They redefined the legal basis of citizenship, officially separating the *qualité de français* from political rights. They attempted to establish the unity and internal hierarchy of the family over the citizenship status of dependents in the home, subordinating a woman's legal identity to her husband's and reinvesting fathers with extensive powers over their children. Legislators also went beyond their predecessors during the Directory in divesting women of political rights and defining family bonds as qualitatively different from other contracts.

But the process of establishing a uniform legal order was not as simple as it might appear. Legislators struggled to decide how best to combine individual titles to national citizenship with their desire for a clear familial order. One problem particularly vexed them: what to do when a head of household did not have citizenship rights in France, but his wife and children did.

The Architects of the Code

The creators of the Napoleonic Civil Code addressed the relationships among the *qualité de français*, gender, and familial status most explicitly in the opening sections of the Code on the exercise and loss of civil rights. The Conseil d'Etat debated these parts of the Code for several sessions during the summer of 1801; debate then moved to the legislature and the Tribunate, which met in December 1801 and January 1802. Discussion resumed in the late fall of 1802 and winter of 1803. The final version of the first section of the Code was promulgated in the *Bulletin des lois* on 17 Ventôse Year XI (March 7, 1803).[1] All the relevant legislative debates have been preserved, and they allow us to trace both the logic behind the final version of the Code and the most heated points of contention in producing it.[2]

The makers of the Code represented a variety of political views and agendas.[3] Napoleon himself intervened frequently when the outline of the Civil Code was under examination by the Conseil d'Etat, especially when the legal rights of women were being discussed. The second consul, Jean-Jacques Régis de Cambacérès, had been the principal artisan of three proposed versions of the Civil Code in 1793, 1794, and 1796, but had changed his views from some of the more radical propositions of his earlier projects. Four jurists, Portalis—whom we have encountered in the Hoppé-Lange trial—Jacques de Maleville, François-Denis Tronchet, and Alexandre-Etienne Bigot de Préameneu, were charged with the final production of the Code. All were sympathetic to the principles of 1789 but were critical of the civil legislation of the Revolution. The political views of other members of the Conseil d'Etat and the Tribunate were more mixed; in general, while often leery of the legislation of the radical Revolution, they were anxious to preserve certain changes wrought by the early Revolution, particularly those affecting property. In making the Civil Code, however, they also introduced substantial innovations affecting both the significance of membership in the French nation and the legal basis of the family.

Redefining Membership in the Nation

In the opening section of the Civil Code on *la jouissance et la perte des droits civils*, legislators began by weighing the competing principles of *jus soli* or *jus sanguinis*, that is, whether to privilege birthplace or descent in determining national citizenship. Napoleon argued that the interests of the state mandated that all children born in France be considered French. They would add to a population that could be subjected to conscription and other public obligations. Opponents of unlimited *jus soli* insisted that birthplace could be accidental; would-be French citizens needed to demonstrate their desire to be part of the French nation.[4] Influenced in part by Tronchet's defense of *jus sanguinis*, legislators reached a compromise on this point. All born of a French father, inside or outside French territory, were declared to be French; children born in France of a foreign father could claim French citizenship status when they reached the age of majority.[5]

Building on the efforts of certain intellectuals and officials from the Directory onward to define citizenship more clearly, Napoleonic legislators also instituted another vitally important change, a rupture with both the Old Regime and the Revolution. They distinguished the civil rights associated with the *qualité de français* from the exercise of political rights. For the first time, "Frenchness" was officially regulated separately from political "citizenship." The *qualité de français* was to be defined and regulated by civil law, not by the founding laws of the national polity.[6] Article 7 of the Civil Code spelled out that "the exercise of civil rights is separate from the rights of [political] citizenship, which are acquired and preserved only according to constitutional law."

The distinction changed the significance of the Constitution of 22 Frimaire Year VIII (December 13, 1799). The Constitution, inaugurated after Napoleon's coup d'état of Brumaire Year VIII (November 1799), had itself made some significant alterations from the Constitution of Year III. It changed residence requirements for becoming a French citizen from seven years in French territory to ten years and suppressed all other qualifications for citizenship, including property ownership, civic oaths, and marriage. Article 2 of the Constitution of Year VIII proclaimed that "any man born and residing in France, who is at least twenty-one years of age, who has enrolled on the civic register of his communal arrondissement and lived for at least a year on the territory of the Republic is a French citizen." Article 3 decreed that "a foreigner becomes a French citizen after having reached the age of twenty-one, having declared his intention to settle in France, and having resided in the country for ten consecutive years."[7] Before the institutionalization of the Civil Code in 1804, these articles, like those in earlier constitutions, established who was legally French as well as who was legally a citizen. After the promulgation of the Code, the 1799 Constitution remained in effect but served officially only to define the citizen entitled to political rights.[8]

Article 13 of the Napoleonic Code also proclaimed that foreigners formally authorized by the government to establish their domicile in France would enjoy all civil rights as long as they remained in the country, even if they never became fully French. The Conseil d'Etat further decided that a foreigner who wanted to become French was obliged to obtain permission from the government to establish himself in France. As a result of these transformations, the procedure of *admission à domicile* became a step toward acquiring the *qualité de français* and potentially, but not necessarily, the full rights of citizenship.[9]

Redefining the Family

The Napoleonic age has often been seen as one of bourgeois individualism, but it inscribed the individual in the family. As Anne Verjus has shown, the electoral laws of Year X (1802) made familial, rather than individual, property the qualification for voting and holding office.[10] Only the 600 wealthiest citizens in each department could participate in the highest levels of elections, the departmental electoral colleges. But these citizens were not defined as individual property owners. Instead, their eligibility was determined by the property owned by the entire family. This rule applied even when a couple was separated; electoral laws now explicitly stated that the "all taxes paid by a wife, even if legally separated [*non commune en biens*], would count toward a husband's eligibility" (art. 66). "All taxes paid on the property of minor children" were similarly included when determining a father's eligibility (art. 67). Property-owning relatives could also designate their property to count toward a man's eligibility to vote. A citizen "whose father pays a total sum of taxes sufficient to be among the 600 wealthiest people in the department can, if his father consents by an authentic declaration, be registered in his place on the list of those eligible" (art. 38). Finally, "if a widowed woman who has not remarried pays sufficient taxes to be among the 600 wealthiest individuals, she can designate one of her adult sons to be included on the list of those eligible" (art. 69).[11] Politically, an elector was treated as if he was the universal heir of both his parents and children, and of his wife and her family.

While family property implicitly determined eligibility for political citizenship, the Napoleonic Codes, especially the Penal Code of 1801, also considered the family as an institution separate from and protected by the state.[12] This institution was deeply patriarchal. Sections of the Civil Code, often strongly influenced by Napoleon's direct intervention, institutionalized a rigid hierarchy inside the family. They limited the ways in which individuals, especially dependents, could challenge familial order or dissolve familial bonds. Women could not enter into legal agreements without the participation or written consent of their husbands, even if they were legally separated; they also could not plead in court under their own name, act as civil witnesses, or own property without the consent of the man of the family.[13] Divorce was allowed in only a limited number of cases: adultery, sentencing by a court, or cruelty and grievous insult. Even these cases were often limited further. Women, for example, could prosecute for adultery only if the husband's infidelity had taken place in the conjugal home.[14] Similarly, the Civil Code consecrated both the ideology and practice of *puissance paternelle*. Although legislators retained a universal age of majority, fathers were reinvested with the power to punish minor children for various misdeeds, to accord or withhold their consent to marry to sons younger than twenty-five and to daughters under twenty-one, and to bequeath property as they chose.

Napoleonic family relations were also qualitatively different from other kinds of social and political relations. Marriage was still defined as a civil contract between two free and equal individuals, but it was now constituted differently from other contracts.[15] In the case of common contracts, a civil officer observed the will to form a binding contract; in this case, he declared the spouses united by marriage. A minor could marry with parental permission (art. 148), while he or she could not otherwise enter into a contract, even with permission (art. 1398). Moreover, marriage was public, whereas other contracts were often private. The dissolution of marriage also took place on different grounds than that of other contracts. Fraud, a primary factor in the annulment of contracts in private law, was excluded as grounds for the dissolution of the marriage contract. If the application of contract law had led to divorce in 1792, divorce could no longer be considered as the mark of the contractualization of marriage. Even if both spouses wanted to separate, they could do so only by meeting particular conditions (art. 1132). Legislators preserved "divorce by mutual consent," but it now served only to protect familial honor by hiding the causes of divorce from the public eye.[16] Finally, although article 686 explicitly prohibited the establishment of rights over the person, marriage granted each spouse rights over the person of the other.[17] Once individuals were married, they were constrained to act according to the roles determined by their position within the household. They became spouses with different rights and duties, a rule that they could not change even if they wanted to do so.

Balancing Familial and National Rights

Following the general emphasis on a woman's subservience to her husband, legislators agreed that a married woman had to share her husband's citizenship status. This decision eventually resulted in article 19 of the final version of the Civil Code, which proclaimed that a French woman who married a foreign man would follow her husband's condition. Like Barère in 1794, the architects of the Code believed that this policy was natural, and thus did not require debate. It followed logically from the idea of marriage as a special and binding but unequal contract. Lawmakers made exceptions only for widows, who could apply to "recover" their original status as French women, if they chose.

Legislators also removed the possibility that marriage would legally transform male foreigners into French citizens, a possibility that had existed in all the revolutionary constitutions except that of Year VIII. They did not discuss the rationales for this change, and it may have been motivated in part simply by the elimination of other social qualifications for citizenship within the Code itself. However, it was also clear that lawmakers envisioned the hierarchical contract of marriage as changing a woman's citizenship status, and not her husband's.

The Code's emphasis on modified *jus sanguinis* was also compatible with the lawmakers' beliefs that all members of a family should have the same national *qualité* and that citizenship status should be determined by the head of the household. Except in unusual circumstances, children had the same citizenship status as their father, at least until they reached adulthood.[18] Legislators generally assumed that, with the exception of widows, the people granted or stripped of French citizenship would, and should, be male.

But the architects of the Civil Code found it more difficult to establish the consequences when the head of a household in France lacked, or had lost, his title as a French citizen—precisely because such circumstances implied a need for married women to chose between family and nation after marriage and to do so while the *paterfamilias* was alive. The Conseil d'Etat considered this problem briefly in Vendémiaire Year X (September 1801) when it proclaimed that married women had to live wherever their spouses chose. Legislators debated whether this obligation applied only to continental France or to the colonies as well, and it discussed whether a husband had a right to make his French wife into an *étrangère* by forcing her to live abroad.[19] Following revolutionary policies on emigration, the first version of the article made an exception for those who left the country:

> The wife is obliged to live with her husband and to follow him wherever he judges fit to reside; the husband is obliged to receive her and to furnish everything that is necessary for basic needs, according to his abilities and position. If the husband wants to leave the territory of the Republic, he cannot force his wife to follow him, unless he is charged by the government with a diplomatic mission requiring residence outside France.[20]

The Conseil briefly considered other possible motives for absence for French territory that would not necessarily affect a wife's status. Regnaud proclaimed that a man did not have the right to make his wife into a foreigner, but nonetheless he should not be forced to live without her if his business affairs led him outside French territory.[21] Napoleon ended the discussion abruptly by proclaiming that a wife's obligation to live with her husband was absolute. If a woman did not want to follow her husband out of France, he could simply deprive her of food. At this point, discussion was adjourned, with the unrealized intention of returning to the topic when legislators addressed the issue of divorce. Article 214 of the final version of the Code would mandate that a married woman had to live wherever her husband chose; it did not explicitly state that this obligation applied outside France, but it also presented no exceptions to the law.[22] Although the wording of the law retained an important ambiguity, as we will see later, the very possibility that women could be legally forced to follow their husbands out of the country represented a dramatic break with revolutionary policies on emigration. It was also a rupture with Old Regime practice, which usually had not constrained a married woman to live with her husband outside France.[23]

The architects of the Civil Code struggled with the implications of the citizenship status of the head of household at more length when debating two other issues: *mort civile,* or civil death; and the *droit d'aubaine,* the sovereign's traditional right to limit a non-naturalized foreigner's ability to inherit or bequeath his property and goods in France. When the *paterfamilias* was sentenced to civil death, he abruptly ceased to have any civil or political rights in France. The rights of his wife and children were also suddenly threatened by his changed status. Legislators struggled to decide what should happen to them, debating whether women and children retained a meaningful relationship to the state on their own, and whether they should or could be asked to choose between marital and national bonds. Conflicts between citizenship and family rights were less obvious in debates over the *droit d'aubaine,* as many lawmakers concentrated on issues of high politics, such as the French state's relationships with its neighbors or the long-term consequences of immigration for the French economy. But they also wrestled with the implications for family and citizenship law if the head of a household was unable to bequeath his property to his dependents in France.

Cain's Wife?

The potential impact of civil death on familial bonds was in the public eye as legislators opened debate on a definitive Civil Code in 1801. Napoleon had closed the list of émigrés with the consular list of March 3, 1800, and declared a partial amnesty for émigrés on 28 Vendémiaire Year IX (October 20, 1800). But, as we have seen, many alleged émigrés remained in a state of limbo, provisionally, but not definitively, cleared of the charge of emigration. Decisions like those that allowed the ex-émigré Montagnac to marry resolved the immediate concerns of émigrés, but did not clearly define familial boundaries between "Frenchness," foreignness, and civil death. These issues preoccupied the architects of the Napoleonic Civil Code, when—less than two months after the minister of the interior's decision on Montagnac's proposed marriage—the Conseil d'Etat opened debates on 6 Thermidor Year IX (July 25, 1801) about who was entitled to civil rights in France. When discussion moved to the Tribunate in December 1801, lawmakers struggled at even greater length to establish the relationships between civil death and familial bonds.

The legislators' discussions, however, were formulated in slightly different terms than in the Montagnac case. Rather than considering whether an émigré or supposed émigré condemned to civil death could marry, lawmakers fretted over the plight of the wife and children of a married man condemned to *mort civile* for criminal acts rather than for emigration. The stumbling block was not whether such women and children should themselves be considered civilly dead, as émigré women and children over the age of fourteen had been. The architects of the Civil Code presumed that the penalties involved with losing one's membership in the French nation would henceforward apply to women only in terms of their relations to their male family members. They thus struggled to resolve whether the bonds of marriage and paternity should be dissolved by the penalty of civil death.

The possibility that civil death could automatically end marriage was unprecedented. In principle, Roman law, the basis for much of French law, stipulated that civil death dissolved marriage, but Roman jurists had repeatedly concluded that those condemned to deportation continued to enjoy all civil effects of marriage.[24] The penalty of civil death had existed during the Old Regime, but it had not ended marriage, since marriage was legally a religious as well as a civil bond and could be completely dissolved only by death.[25]

The 1791 Constitution redefined marriage as a strictly civil contract, while the 1792 law on divorce established that marital bonds could be definitively broken. But because women were required to actively demonstrate their loyalty to the revolutionary community of citizens, even the most radical revolutionary laws did not equate *mort civile* with the automatic or complete dissolution of marriage. As we have seen, local administrators occasionally raised the possibility that it might. Their views were exemplified by the opinion issued by the Conseil général of the Department of Seine Inférieure that émigrés had originally been made into foreigners, but that the 1793 law declared them dead and thus definitively ended their familial ties, for "one cannot consider a woman to be married to a man who is civilly dead; she becomes a widow and does not need to ask for a divorce."[26] The law of 24 Vendémiaire Year III, which spelled out the procedures for divorce in the case of emigration, made it clear that a spouse's emigration and subsequent civil death did not, in and of itself, legally end marriage in France. Women could not only choose between familial and national bonds; they could be required to do so.

The men who created the Civil Code depicted two dismal plights for the wife of a man condemned to civil death. In one scenario, marriage was automatically dissolved; humiliated and scorned for her continuing loyalty to her outcast husband, a woman would become a concubine and her future children bastards. In an alternative scenario, the marriage bond was maintained despite a man's civil death. In this vision, the condemned man's wife and children would be permanently subjected to a monster, forced to remain with a man cast out of French society and deprived of legitimate authority inside the home or out of it.

Lawmakers who argued against the dissolution of such marriages praised Cain's faithful wife and alluded to the general obligation of a woman to remain with her husband. They contended that the dissolution of a marriage was a poor reward for a woman's steadfast loyalty to her companion: "From a legally married woman she abruptly becomes a concubine. What fate is she reduced to, if she continues to feel affection for her husband, sentiments that could be reinforced because she believes him innocent!"[27] Making such a woman a "concubine" because of her husband's changed status implied both creating general social and political disorder and punishing her for a crime that she had not committed. Proponents of continued marriages accused their opponents of a "desire to multiply the number of concubines, immolate the sacred right of innocence, and sacrifice the honor of a woman to the punishment of another's crime."[28]

While the makers of the Civil Code lauded the unity of families and the general subordination of women to their spouses, they were uneasy about leaving French women under the authority of men who no longer deserved to have power inside or outside the family. The status of the women and children of such exiled figures was especially vexing, as their prescribed subordination to the man of the family clashed with their personal entitlement to rights within France. As the tribune Théodore Huguet proclaimed, "a husband's sentence will indirectly affect his wife, because, continuing to live under the authority of a man incapable of exercising civil rights, she herself will be deprived, which would be unjust to her and prejudicial to her rights."[29] The consequences would be equally disastrous for children, as Louis Roujoux exclaimed: "You don't want the civil contract to be dissolved! You thus want to allow a father branded with infamy to retain his paternal authority, the administration of his family, and the protection of his children, their morals, and their education. For those are the consequences of your system."[30]

Such a stark choice between cruel subjection and public shame would appear to be easily surmountable. As we have seen, revolutionary laws had made the emigration and the subsequent civil death of a spouse a legitimate reason for divorce, and indeed required such "widows" to formally renounce their connections with their "dead" spouses in order to preserve their property and rights in France. The Directory had increasingly emphasized familial unity over national duty, but it did not legally restrict the possibility for women to choose between their spouses and their country, even after marriage. Indeed, even in 1801 Poirier had argued for the ability of ex-émigrés to marry on the grounds that if a woman ultimately chose her country over a spouse deprived of rights within France, she could always divorce him.

Several Napoleonic legislators argued that the state could not end a marriage against the wishes of the couple; the appropriate solution was to allow the couple to choose to remain together or to separate. Jean-Pierre Chazal, the same lawyer who several years previously had championed Suzanne Lepeletier's right to marry, argued again that the state should not prevent or destroy marriage against a couple's wishes: "The law must limit itself to according divorce or separation if they are requested, but it must not impose them on a couple who want to remain united."[31] Similarly, the tribune Louis Faure contended a few days later that "a contract formed by the will of two people under the protection of the law must not be broken against the will of these two people."[32]

Most of the makers of the Civil Code, however, disapproved of divorce, especially divorce initiated by women. In discussing the loss of civil rights in France through civil death, they portrayed divorce as an act deeply repugnant to a woman. A law that automatically dissolved a marriage would thus save women from the agonizing choice of remaining under the authority of a man who had no rights or rebelling against her natural superior. Jean-François Curée, for example, ranted that "a woman will either have to live with a man who exudes criminality and the infamy of crime, or raise herself in judgment against him, asking for divorce. Raise herself against whom? Against her condemned husband, against the father of her children. You force her to be unhappy or unnatural."[33] In their view, a woman's choice between her family and her country had to be made for her.

The Tribunate initially rejected the proposed version of the section of the Code on the *jouissance et la perte des droits civils* on 11 Nivôse Year X (January 1, 1802). But Napoleon reacted strongly to this challenge and soon afterward purged the Tribunate of legislators judged to be overly republican or otherwise troublesome, including François Andrieux, Nicholas-François Thiesse, Jean-Pierre Chazal, Joseph-Marie-Blaise de Chénier, and Benjamin Constant.[34] In the process, he removed some of the tribunes who had been most opposed to the idea that civil death would automatically dissolve marriage against a couple's wishes.

When the Tribunate resumed discussion of the Civil Code in 1803, legislators ultimately decided that the civil death of a spouse dissolved marriage, at least legally, if not socially or emotionally. In its final form, the Code established that during civil death, a condemned man was unable to contract a marriage with any civil effects, and that any marriage he had contracted previously was dissolved "as to all its civil effects."[35]

The legislators reached this decision in part because they viewed women as dependents. But they also equated French citizenship and paternal rights. Or more precisely, being a potential or actual father and being French were necessary if insufficient conditions for being a citizen. The complete loss of citizenship rights entailed the converse: the loss of paternal rights. As the tribune Thomas Mouricault put it in December 1801, "this criminal, justly banned from the great family, is necessarily cut off from the private society that forms one of its elements; he no longer exists (civilly at least) for his wife, his children, his parents, his fellow citizens; in short, for no one."[36] When the tribune Alexandre Gary presented the final speech of the legislators before the relevant section of the Code was promulgated in the *Bulletin des lois* in March 1803, he justified the dissolution of marriage on precisely these grounds; a man who had been deservedly expelled from society "was no longer a citizen, a father, or a husband."[37]

The *Droit d'Aubaine* and the *Paterfamilias*

Even as they debated the implications of civil death, the architects of the Napoleonic Code argued whether to restore the *droit d'aubaine*. The *droit d'aubaine*, the key legal distinction between foreigners and French subjects in the Old Regime, had traditionally limited a non-naturalized foreigner's ability to inherit or to bequeath his property and goods in France.[38] The Constituent Assembly had abolished the *droit* on August 6, 1790, but by 1801 the French state was ready to consider reinstating it, at least on the limited basis of reciprocity with other countries. Much of the legislators' debate focused on the diplomatic and economic consequences of restoring the *droit*. But as in their deliberations over civil death, legislators also wrestled with the question of how much fatherhood and French citizenship were intertwined, and how to reconcile laws that made the *qualité de français* a personal title with their vision of a society based on families.

As we have seen, the ideological rationale for the inability of foreigners to inherit or bequeath property during the Old Regime had depended partially on the idea that they had no legal family ties in France. The absence of legal family bonds went hand in hand with the "legitimation" of a foreigner through his naturalization and "adoption" by the sovereign. The fiction of new birth in France through the king's favor was accompanied by a certain respect for literal birth in France; children born in the kingdom were often allowed to escape the *droit d'aubaine*.[39] The gradual dissociation of family and the nation had made such assumptions difficult in the late Revolution, and the fiction that a foreigner had no legal family in France without the sovereign's approval perturbed some of the drafters of the Civil Code. The tribune Chazal suggested in December 1801 that the justification of the *droit d'aubaine* hinged on a distinctive concept of the *père de famille*, or "father of the family," which had existed in classical times but not in regenerated France.[40] He explained that the *droit d'aubaine* had existed in Rome because the right to bequeath one's property as one chose was a right that belonged only to full citizens entitled to act as *pères de famille*: "The right to bequeath one's possessions was in Rome one of the attributes of political paternal authority."[41] Thus, it had made sense for Romans to exclude foreigners from a right that was intrinsically political. But the right to control the transmission of property was not, in France, a power limited only to those who exercised full political rights, but rather to all members of the nation, even if they did not vote or hold office.

J. P. Mathieu, one of the members of the Tribunate, was especially concerned. Like Guiraudet in *De la famille considérée comme l'élément des sociétés*, Mathieu proclaimed that the family, rather than the individual, should be considered the fundamental unit of the nation. But Mathieu took this a step further and tried to apply such a family-oriented vision directly to the legal definition of French citizenship. He contended that the *droit d'aubaine* focused purely on individual status and thus fundamentally violated the familial basis of order that legislators sought to establish. The law imposed a

> toll that tax collectors claim unjustly . . . to the detriment of the widow and the orphan; interposing themselves between the individual who has just died and his family. . . . It is always a family that is hit and plundered, to the great scandal and distress of native [French] families. . . . [The *droit d'aubaine*] introduces a bad example into the law; it accustoms one to see only individuals, which is a kind of cruel abstraction; the law must always see in the individual—or rather in the man—a husband, a father, a brother; in a word, a complex being, modified by his familial relations.[42]

Mathieu's arguments against the *droit d'aubaine* also echoed many of the claims made on behalf of the relatives on émigrés. As we have seen, a series of revolutionary laws mandated that inheritances that would have otherwise gone to an émigré not be passed on to the relatives who would normally have been next in line, but instead to the government. The government justified its right to appropriate such property partially by the fact that an émigré was civilly dead. Those who protested the confiscation of such property complained, as Mathieu was to do later, that it was not the "dead" outsider who was punished by the laws concerning inheritance, but innocent "widows" and "orphans." For example, one champion of the rights of the relatives of émigrés, Martin, had argued against the laws affecting the relatives of émigrés by claiming that

> a guilty man punished by civil death can no longer enjoy the advantages of society; he can possess nothing; it is as if he does not exist. If you confiscate his fortune, you are not punishing him, but his unfortunate heirs whom you despoil. You punish the widow and orphans more severely than the father, since you take away their fortune and their subsistence, to leave them only tears and disgrace.[43]

None of the legislators charged with creating the Civil Code openly addressed the connections between appropriating an émigré's property and that of a deceased foreigner, and it is unclear whether they considered the issue directly, in large part because émigrés were supposedly excluded from the Code.[44] However, they did endeavor to define the legal difference between foreigners—who were not French, but might become so—and those who were permanently deprived of all rights in France. Mathieu argued that confiscation might be justified for those condemned to civil death, but not for foreigners: "How you can you ascribe to the quality of foreigner . . . more rigorous consequences than to those declared to be civilly dead? It is frightful that an irreproachable foreigner could ever be affected, himself or his heirs, by penalties reserved only for criminals."[45]

Similarly, in his closing speech on the loss and acquisition of civil rights in France in March 1803, Alexandre Gary compared the confiscation of the property of a foreigner's family and the family of those deemed to be civilly dead. He argued that

> these rights can be more powerfully invoked by the relatives of a foreigner dead in France, who, it is true, lacked the title and rights of a French citizen, but who had the hope and ability to acquire them, than by an individual civilly dead who lost them by a crime, and was declared incapable and unworthy of regaining them.[46]

Such arguments initially triumphed when the Tribunate rejected the project of the section of the Code on *la jouissance et la perte des droits civils*. The makers of the Civil Code, however, eventually decided to maintain the *droit d'aubaine* on a reciprocal basis with other countries, largely for economic reasons.

Their decision was not revoked until 1819.[47] Opponents of the system continued to argue throughout the Napoleonic period that such restrictions on foreigners were based on an insufficient distinction between those who had been actively deprived of the *qualité de français*—the civilly dead—and those who might have become French and on outmoded equations of familial and citizenship rights. For example, several years after the promulgation of the Code, Louis Barnabé Cotèle, professor of law, carefully distinguished foreigners from enemies and the state of foreignness from civil death: "We have always felt that there was a real difference between someone condemned to civil death and a foreigner, despite the errors and confusion into which our practitioners have sometimes fallen. A foreigner has all the rights to civil life; a civilly dead person has lost them all."[48]

Like Chazal, Cotèle observed that in Roman law only full citizens could marry and decide how they would bequeath their property or avoid capital punishment. These "citizenship" rights depended on a particular understanding and application of *puissance paternelle*.

> The rights proper to a Roman citizen, which separated him from all other men, affected him throughout his life and in all his relations. Following *justae nuptiae*, *puissance paternelle* resulted from legitimate marriage, which only a citizen could contract, and which was clearly distinguished from a simple union between two sexes. It was the same for succession, which the *paterfamilias* regulated by a solemn testament.[49]

The special status of Roman citizens as fathers thus led to the creation of the *droit d'aubaine* for foreigners. But in France, *puissance paternelle* was not a right that belonged only to a small subset of the male population exercising full political citizenship. Since all male French citizens could theoretically control familial property regardless of whether they could vote or hold office, the laws that prevented foreign-born fathers in France from transmitting familial patrimony could no longer be justified.

The Civil Code's preservation of the *droit d'aubaine* accorded with Napoleonic legislators' approach to civil death. Men who had been stripped of the rights of French citizenship through civil death were legally cast out of their literal families as well as the "great family" of the nation; men who had not become part of the "great family" of citizens could marry and have legitimate offspring in France, but they could not fully act as fathers in control of their own familial property. In both cases, critics worried about the effects of such laws on a man's wife and children but did not want to accord them the independence—through divorce or formal procedures for treating their status separately from that of the head of the household—to dissociate themselves voluntarily and definitively from the *paterfamilias*.

Critics of the *droit d'aubaine* like Mathieu, Chazal, and Cotèle also argued that the law threatened families. Their solution—the continuing or renewed abolition of the *droit*—implicitly dissociated immediate family bonds from the metaphorical bonds linking men to the "great family" of the nation. The general preoccupation with the economic and political consequences of the *droit d'aubaine*, both in the making of the Code and during its abolition in 1819, meant that critics seldom debated the possible contradictions between this policy and ideas about civil death. When they did, the distinction between two different ways of lacking the *qualité de français*—in the case of foreigners, not having obtained it; in the case of the civilly dead, being permanently stripped of all titles of membership in the nation—allowed them to reconcile the importance they placed on paternal rights and familial integrity with the laws on national citizenship.

Conclusion

The combination of these trends meant that the integrity and internal hierarchy of the family often officially took priority over "individual" national citizenship—whether that "citizenship" entailed civil or political rights. Napoleonic laws on adoption provide further evidence of these changes. Napoleon had initially imagined adoption as a "new sacrament" and had wanted to reserve the power to ratify adoption to the legislature. His proposal echoed older notions of a father-king creating new children and citizens and the National Assembly as the "father of the nation." But this idea was abandoned in favor of adoption as a simple private contract between adults (meaning that a minor could not be adopted), a contract that was further limited to childless couples over fifty years old.[50] This policy marked the definitive abandonment of national adoption as anything other than an honorific act.

Moreover, the relevance of adoption for non-French citizens changed dramatically. In the Constitution of 1793, adoption was a means for a foreigner to become French (among other means, such as caring for the elderly or marriage to a French woman). In contrast, the Civil Code forbade foreigners to adopt or act as guardians in France; they would not have that right again until 1923.[51] Moreover, adoption of foreign children by French families was limited: only children who were natives of countries where adoption was legal or who had already become French through other means could be adopted in France.[52] Tronchet, the jurist who defended *jus sanguinis* on the grounds that membership in the nation should be determined by descent rather than by the accidents of birthplace, also defended limits on adoption by arguing that families should be biologically defined. Familial bonds were no longer a means of integrating foreigners into the "great French family"; instead, Napoleonic legislators sought to protect biological families from intruders and to protect French children from the loss of their rights under the authority of a foreign *paterfamilias*.

The decisions made by Napoleonic legislators—and particularly the restrictions on divorce in the Civil Code—also meant that the bond between husband and wife could be legally stronger than the bond between women and the state, at least while both partners were alive. Looking at immigration and naturalization policies in the United States—which were partially modeled on the Napoleonic Code—Virginia Sapiro has argued that "as modern ideas of citizenship took hold, especially after the French Revolution, consent on part of citizens became important. . . . the bond between husband and wife by default became stronger than the bond between citizen and state, particularly for women. Whereas expatriation was possible, divorce for the most part was not."[53] Sapiro summarizes the implications of this situation: "If women give consent to accept the patriarchal authority of an alien male they are bound to give consent to the consequent shift of their national allegiance." In the aftermath of the Civil Code in France, marriage could still represent a woman's decision to align herself with both a spouse and a national community. But it was a difficult decision to undo. Divorce might allow women to break marital bonds, but the mechanisms for divorce were now severely limited. Dependents were no longer required—nor potentially allowed—to choose between family and national bonds after marriage. While legislators believed that civil death should mandate the loss of *puissance paternelle* for men and argued about whether foreign men in France should also be deprived of such rights, they also established that marriage would no longer legally transform male foreigners into French citizens.

The Napoleonic Code thus officially fixed the relations between the *qualité de français* and the family. Yet the interpretation of the Code, combined with related measures and jurisprudence, would prove to be critical in determining how those relations were actually understood. The courts still had to face the legacy of earlier laws that had used terms like "citizen" far more ambiguously than the Napoleonic Code. Jurists and lawyers would confront not only abstract debates about the consequences of *mort civile* for those condemned of new crimes, but also the lasting effects of the revolutionary penalty. Returning émigrés, men who had ceased to be both French and citizens during their civil death, were now potentially restored to both qualities; they would demand the associated return of full power over their wives and children. The courts were also not the only site of contestation; indeed, putting the Code's definitions of foreigners and French into practice would prove even more challenging for subsequent applications of citizenship law to immigrants. As we will see, the formal separation of political and civil aspects of citizenship and the new definitions of marriage as a distinctive form of contract would have particularly dramatic implications for women's loss and acquisition of French national citizenship.

6 Looking Backward: The Consequences of Civil Death

Applying the Napoleonic Code was particularly difficult in wartime conditions and in conquered areas that had been governed by vastly different legal and social systems. A contemporary treatise on illegitimate and abandoned children gives a vivid indication of some of the conflicts between family and citizenship law provoked by the Napoleonic wars and the expansion of the empire. Jurists and administrators were called to decide whether an English prisoner of war in France could legitimate his children born out of wedlock. Could a French soldier in Spain adopt a child there? Was a child born on French territory considered to be the product of adultery if his parents—like Egyptians and other "Oriental refugees" in southern France—conserved their legal residence in countries that permitted polygamy?[1] But it was not simply that the Napoleonic solution to conflicts between family and national status was difficult to implement in the far-flung outposts of the empire. Making sense of family and citizenship rights and obligations in practice proved to be challenging even at the heart of the empire. Leading jurists struggled to come to terms with the legacies of the Revolution, especially the challenges of converting émigrés, who had lost all citizenship rights in their absence, back into full citizens entitled to rights as husbands and fathers over their French wives and daughters.

Fathers "Restored to All the Rights of Citizenship"?

As laws on emigration were relaxed in the late 1790s and especially after the amnesties of 1800 and 1802, émigré men returned to France in droves. Many were reunited with the families that they had left behind. Contemporary plays and novels depicted the return of such men as a smooth transition, a natural return to domestic order and hierarchy. For example, in *Les femmes politiques,* a play first produced in Year VII (1799), the playwright Etienne Gosse portrayed a woman whose mind was filled with dangerous ideas from reading newspapers and who wanted to "govern the cabinets of Europe." When her husband, a man who had been falsely accused of emigration, was finally able to return home, he took matters into his own hands. M. Gérard persuaded his gardener to masquerade as a gendarme and threaten to arrest his wife on the grounds that "the government demands the silence of women."[2] As the play unfolded, the Gérards discovered that a rogue had persuaded the women of the household to read about politics. Order was restored; Mme. Gérard recognized her mistakes, renounced any interest in politics, and promised to listen to her husband's superior wisdom.

Although the political role of women was sharply curtailed by the turn of the century, the return of émigrés or accused émigrés to France did not reestablish domestic order as neatly as the resolution of *Les femmes politiques* suggests. The amnesty officially restored "all the rights of citizenship" to those who had been civilly dead. Many of those who returned longed for the status and social position that had belonged to them before they left France. They were eager to reclaim property, the *biens nationaux* zealously commandeered by the state and often sold during the Revolution. Many men also wanted to regain a position of authority within their families. However, events that had taken place earlier during the Revolution—such as divorces initiated by their spouses, their wives' decisions to enter into contracts or to buy or sell property, and their children's legal emancipation or marriages—often made it difficult for them to exercise full control in the home. They contended that the "rights of citizenship" restored to them included the right to act as fathers and husbands and to contest challenges to their authority as heads of households.

The courts often initially supported such claims. In 1803 the Court of Appeals of Paris considered a disputed property case involving the Rohan-Guémenées, a prominent Old Regime family. It declared that a woman could not have acted as "mistress of her rights" during her husband's emigration if she had not obtained a divorce.[3] The court of Besançon came to a similar conclusion when it considered a property dispute within the Masson family. Madame Masson insisted that she was the sole proprietor of an estate that she had acquired while her husband was an émigré—despite the fact that she had not legally divorced him—and that she had not lost her rights to the estate upon his return. The court ruled against her, arguing that when returned émigrés were restored to all the civil and political rights of French citizens, they were also restored to their previous powers over their wives and children. On 28 Pluviôse Year XII (February 12, 1803), it proclaimed that

a French man who emigrated or who was accused of emigration is now fully reestablished in his civil and political rights. If a spouse recovers his marital authority, a father his paternal authority, they must enjoy all the advantages that are attached to these qualities and that derive from them. It is not a new right that a husband acquires, but a return to his original authority that he continues to exercise after a temporary suspension. New consent by his wife is unnecessary if she never freed herself by divorce; the dame Masson did not take this route, and is thus under the power of her husband.[4]

The Supreme Court, however, reversed these rulings. In 1804, when it considered the case of the dame Saffrey and her émigré husband, the sieur Joubert, the court concluded that "the fact of emigration deprives an émigré of his civil rights; it follows that the wife of an émigré could make contracts without his permission from the moment that her husband was placed on the list of émigrés."[5] If a woman had acquired or sold property during her émigré husband's absence, she had done so legally, regardless of whether her spouse approved of her actions. Furthermore, the Supreme Court ruled that dame Saffrey had originally been incapable of forming contracts and controlling her property not because she was a woman but only because she was a wife. Even though her marriage had not been formally ended by her husband's emigration, the civil effects of the marriage had been suspended; Saffrey, or any other woman in her position, had been free to act as she pleased.[6]

The court also reversed the specific decision affecting the Masson couple on June 10, 1806, proclaiming that a man's civil death meant that he had ceased to be *en communauté de biens* with his wife, and that such *communauté conjugale* was not automatically restored by his return.[7] Not only were property transactions made in his absence binding, but a woman also retained exclusive rights to the property that she had acquired during her husband's "death" and enforced ostracism from French society. When men had lost the rights of citizenship, they had lost all powers as fathers and husbands.

The MacMahon-Latour Trial, February 1804–March 1806

The most frequent cases on emigration that came before the courts in the early years of Napoleonic rule, however, addressed not the acts of women who had remained legally married to their ostracized spouses, but rather the validity of marriages or divorces involving émigrés. The government initially responded to the barrage of contested divorces with the law of 26 Germinal Year XI (April 13, 1803), which decreed that all divorces that had taken place before the institution of the Civil Code would have legal effects based on the laws in place at the time of the divorce. The Conseil d'Etat elaborated and interpreted the law further on 11 Prairial Year XII (May 30, 1804), proclaiming that the "reborn" civilly dead could not nullify divorces granted because of their emigration.[8] Its ruling primarily affected couples whose partnership had continued with or without official sanction during the Revolution.[9] However, the decree was also used by women who wanted to remain separate from their husbands. One celebrated court case from the early Napoleonic era, between Térence MacMahon and Caroline Latour, is particularly revealing of the stakes involved in determining the legitimacy of such divorces. MacMahon was an Irish-born man who had served in the French military from 1782 until he left France in 1792; his French-born wife, Latour, was granted a divorce in his absence in Year IX (1801). MacMahon challenged the divorce when he returned to France two years later; Latour insisted that the divorce was valid, drawing on the Conseil's decree to bolster her claims.

The conflict between Térence MacMahon and Caroline Latour played out in the courts from 1804 to 1806. It was repeatedly appealed and was judged twice by the Supreme Court.[10] Because the case touched on a series of issues involving nationality, emigration, and marriage law, it provoked a lively debate on what it meant for men and women to forfeit their citizenship voluntarily. Had Latour become a foreigner and had thus been prevented by Irish law from divorcing her spouse? Or had MacMahon become French, in which case the marriage was regulated by French law?

The case was extremely complicated, in part because it required judging the relevance and validity of a variety of routes for becoming a French citizen, from the Old Regime through 1792, when MacMahon left France. Since the divorce was based on MacMahon's absence or emigration, it also involved assessing the laws on emigration, including a measure from 9 Thermidor Year X (July 27, 1802), which decreed that foreigners could not be held responsible for emigration. French citizens were subject to the amnesty of April 26, 1802; they could safely return to France, but they could not reclaim property that had been sold in their absence. Foreigners, however, were now decreed to have been falsely inscribed on the list and could in theory reclaim property that had been taken from them.[11] If MacMahon was a foreigner and not an émigré, the divorce could be invalid even if French law regulated it. Finally, the trial presented an early opportunity for testing whether or how the principles of the Napoleonic Code on citizenship and family relations could be applied retrospectively.

A Conscious and Voluntary Marriage to a Foreigner?

Latour's champions attempted to demonstrate both that MacMahon had been French and that she believed him to have been so when they married and thus had not voluntarily forfeited her French citizenship. Echoing earlier arguments for women who claimed to have remained French despite their marriages, her lawyers asked if it was possible that she "who had believed that she was marrying a French man, who, without this belief, would never have accepted this union of which her family would never have dreamt, would find herself involuntarily and through no deed of her own, violently deprived of her civil rights in France, a subject of a foreign nation?"[12] Her opponents countered by arguing that she had wittingly allied her fate with that of a foreigner: "She and her family understood perfectly the nature and the effects of the union that she contracted; they thus knew that she would become a foreigner by her marriage, and would no longer have another country, other laws, or another domicile than the country, laws, and domicile of her husband."[13]

Such arguments conflated two issues: whether MacMahon was actually a foreigner, and whether Latour had known him to be so at the time of their marriage. There was no clear legal advantage if she could prove that she had believed him to be French when he was not; his actual status determined her fate. But in the logic of the Civil Code, a woman's marriage to foreigner entailed a legitimate loss of her citizenship status precisely because it was a voluntary and witting decision to ally her fate with that of her husband's, although it was also a decision that she could not undo after marriage. As we have seen, men and women had periodically emphasized the importance of individual will in determining whether marriage should or should not affect a woman's citizenship status, from the Old Regime court cases over inheritance to the pleas of women threatened by the decrees of the Terror who claimed that they had been forced to marry nobles as minors. But article 19 of the Civil Code made French women who married foreigners into foreigners themselves, in contrast to Old Regime practices, which had often treated such women as still legally French. This law meant that the voluntary nature of a woman's decision to renounce her citizenship status through marriage gained a new and more systematic importance. As the Napoleonic Code served as a model throughout the world, liberal political theorists in the nineteenth century, from the United States to Argentina, would justify the loss of a woman's independent citizenship status by emphasizing her deliberate decision to change her country.[14] Proving that Latour had wittingly married a foreigner would greatly strengthen the claim that she could not legitimately divorce him; conversely, if she had believed she was marrying a Frenchman, she held a moral high ground in calling for French law to be applied to their relationship.

The question of Latour's national status also depended on whether a married woman could indeed have a separate country, domicile, or laws from those of her husband. Caroline's opponents argued that she could not; however important her will in marrying a foreigner or alleged foreigner, dependents in the family could not make an independent decision about their national affiliation after marriage. As we have seen, article 214 of the Civil Code mandated that a married woman live with her husband. In drafting the article, legislators did not incorporate a proposed exception for residence in a foreign country, but neither did they explicitly state that the obligation persisted beyond France's borders. MacMahon's lawyer, Gaspart-Gilbert Delamalle, contended that because the article did not include any explicit exceptions, French law had changed irrevocably from Old Regime practices: "Do not argue that a French woman cannot be obliged to follow her husband into a foreign country. This was a former maxim of French jurisprudence that the Code did not adopt."[15] In this interpretation, the unity of the family took priority over a woman's connection to her homeland.

There was, however, one strong counterargument to the idea that a married woman was obliged to follow her husband in all circumstances: the case of the émigrés during the Revolution. Latour's lawyers quickly referred to the laws on emigration. In one important hearing of the case, in February 1805, her advocate Philippe-Antoine Merlin highlighted the year in which MacMahon had left France: 1792. He argued that the law at the time not only had obliged women with French spouses to remain in France but also had required women whose husbands were foreign to do so: "The principle that a woman changes domicile with her husband gave way at that epoch to political law, which forbade the wife of a foreigner domiciled until that point in France to follow him outside [French] territory."[16]

Merlin alluded to the precedent of Madame O-Mahoni or O-Mahoney, the French-born wife of an Irish officer who had been judged an émigrée because she had gone to England with her husband during the Revolution. O-Mahoney's case was actually a more controversial one than it first appeared. She had at one point been declared to be a foreigner because of her marriage and thus freed from the obligation to remain in France; she was later held guilty of emigration in part because her husband was ultimately judged to be French himself.[17] But although Latour's champions later downplayed O-Mahoney's case as they realized its complexity, they continually invoked the precedent of laws on emigration to interpret both Latour's status during the Revolution and the relevance of the Civil Code. As another one of Latour's lawyers, Bureau du Columbier, contended in May 1805, even though laws forbidding emigration were no longer in effect, Napoleon could not have endorsed the principle that a woman would be forced to move to an enemy country because of her husband's will:

> One cannot suppose that the Legislator of an Empire had the intention of damaging himself by making a law that would tend to favor emigration and diminish his force and glory, that he could have conceived of forcing a woman to abandon her laws and her country, to become the enemy of her family in going to reside in a strange country at war with the one in which she was born, where she has her fortune, her children, her dearest affections, while on the other hand it pursued émigrés and punished them by the confiscation of their goods and the loss of their civil status.[18]

Bureau du Columbier's rhetoric, however, also suggested that this was not a choice of country before family but rather that such a woman would be forced to abandon and "become the enemy" of her real family, which he implied was congruent with her native country, France. Even while emphasizing Latour's ability to choose, he implied that she did not really have to do so.

MacMahon's lawyers continued to argue that the Napoleonic Civil Code brooked no ambiguity. As Delamalle proclaimed in 1806, the authority of the head of the household was absolute and transcended other bonds: "Open the Code, open the *procès-verbal* of the beautiful discussions of the Conseil d'Etat, listen to the sovereign who reigns over us today. When asked if a French woman, the wife of a foreigner, will be obliged to follow her husband to his country, what is his [Napoleon's] response? I know of no law that dispenses with it [the obligation]."[19]

"Does Marriage Make Me a Citizen against My Will?"

Since Caroline Latour had not naturalized or left France, the only way she would have ceased to be French was through her marriage. The situation was more complicated for Térence MacMahon, who could have become French through a variety of routes. He had never formally proclaimed his desire to become a French citizen. However, certain of his acts suggested this desire, including possibly swearing a civic oath—whether he had actually done so was contested—and taking military service in France at a time when doing so risked permanent exile from Ireland and a death sentence if he returned to his native country. It was also possible that he had become a French citizen regardless of whether he had explicitly proclaimed his willingness to do so, either through Old Regime dictates or by meeting the requirements for automatic naturalization in the 1790 law or the 1791 Constitution.

MacMahon's marriage was nonetheless a key factor in determining his citizenship status and whether he had willingly become a French citizen. Jurists were concerned not only with his condition at the time of his marriage but also with the impact of marriage on his national status. Given the Napoleonic Code's emphasis on a married woman's subordination to her husband's status, concern about whether a French woman had knowingly married a foreigner was not surprising. But the same question—whether marriage voluntarily or inevitably transformed an individual's citizenship—also arose repeatedly in debates over MacMahon's national status. Latour's proponents contended that he was French, and that even if he had not been so before their marriage, he had become so with it. His marriage to a French woman had taken place on French territory, according to French law; its dissolution also had to follow the same procedures as the dissolution of a marriage between any French man and woman.

MacMahon's lawyer, Delamalle, violently opposed the idea that marriage might have naturalized his client: "It is impossible to say anything more false, or to proffer more monstrous heresy. It's a universally recognized principle that marriage does not naturalize. A foreign man loses his native country when he marries? Never would one have imagined it. On the contrary, all authorities have repeated that a woman acquires her husband's country and abdicates her own."[20] In subsequent pleas, Delamalle reiterated emphatically that "marriage in itself, by the nature of the contract, naturalizes only the woman."[21]

Delamalle and MacMahon's other lawyers objected to the idea that marriage naturalized men in part because it violated the principle that naturalization was a voluntary contract for a man, made directly between an immigrant and his sovereign. They described naturalization as adoption. But they did so in order to emphasize its deliberate nature: foreigners became citizens through a formal contract with the nation, not through "accidents" of marriage. Naturalization was "a true contract of adoption, a reciprocal contract that requires the declaration and formal acceptance of the adopted, who by consequence of naturalization requires legal title, a solemn title, a written title, which records and makes permanent and irrevocable both the adoption and the acceptance of the adoption."[22]

Such language echoed the Old Regime and revolutionary language of the adoption of foreigners, but added a new twist to it. Just as the Civil Code had mandated that literal adoption could take place only between adults capable of consenting to adoption, so too the political adoption of aliens had become less a relationship between parent and child than a contract between independent adults.

> Naturalization of a foreigner among us is a genuine bilateral contract between a foreigner and his adoptive country. As he wants to participate in the benefits of the Government that he preferred to that of his country, he must necessarily fulfill all the obligations of the subjects of this Government. Protection on one side, submission and loyalty on the other; those are the reciprocal engagements that create this august and sacred contract of political adoption.[23]

The case took a number of twists and turns before its resolution. The Parisian appeals court judged that MacMahon was a foreigner but subject to French law concerning his marriage; the Supreme Court initially supported this view, arguing that the divorce should stand as long as long as the procedures had been performed correctly. MacMahon appealed again. The Court of Appeals of Orléans accepted Delamalle's logic that naturalization was a voluntary and reciprocal contract, and judged that the former Irish soldier was a foreigner and not subject to French laws; the divorce was invalid. The Supreme Court finally judged the case conclusively in 1806, proclaiming that the divorce should stand.

In the final trial, Merlin, Latour's champion and *procureur général* for the Supreme Court, argued strongly that revolutionary jurisprudence, especially the 1790 law, could indeed have made foreigners into French citizens without their expressed desire to change their national status.[24] Drawing on Roman examples and the law of 5 Ventôse Year V, which decreed all the inhabitants of Belgium to be French, he contended that the government could proclaim anyone living in France to be French regardless of an individual's desire. But the judges of the Supreme Court supported the divorce not by establishing that MacMahon was legally French or ruling explicitly on what made family and citizenship contracts either voluntary or permanent.[25] Instead, the judges decided that they did not want to reopen challenges to divorces that taken place during the Revolution. Their decision thus validated implicit challenges to the authority of the head of household, but it also focused on ending discussion of the revolutionary period. On March 23, 1806, the Supreme Court invoked the law of 26 Germinal Year XI, which decreed that all divorces that had taken place before the institution of the Civil Code would have legal effects based on the laws in place at the time they were instituted. "Simultaneously moral and political considerations made this a true law of general police, which made no distinction between French individuals and foreigners residing on French territory."[26] MacMahon's citizenship status was thus irrelevant.

Adoption and the Paternal Power of the Sovereign

The language of naturalization as a reciprocal contract corresponded to contemporary changes in both standard and special procedures of adoption, and to the increased power of the state. The Civil Code, combined with the Constitution of Year VIII, made naturalization dependent on ten years' residence in France, but it was no longer automatic. The *senatus consulte* of 26 Vendémiaire Year XI (September 4, 1802) rewarded "foreigners who will render or who have rendered important services to the Republic, who will bring talents, inventions, or useful industries to its breast, or who will form great establishments." It empowered the first consul to naturalize any foreigner he believed useful to the state, as long as the newcomer had lived in France for at least a year and expressed a desire to naturalize. On February 19, 1808, Napoleon's government renewed the decree, with minor alterations designed to acknowledge the emperor's authority.[27] The two decrees echoed the article in the 1791 Constitution that had allowed the revolutionary government to grant exceptional naturalizations to foreigners who for "important considerations" were to be welcomed immediately into the state. But because naturalization was no longer automatic for those who had met the residence and other requirements stipulated by the Constitution, the procedures for exceptional naturalization took on a new importance.

While naturalization was a "reciprocal contract" in Delamalle's summation, it was not an equal one. As Michael Rapport has noted, new measures on naturalization reinforced the authority of the state.[28] Indeed, Napoleon revived the term "subject" in 1806.[29] In 1809 he went a step further, reintroducing Old Regime *lettres de naturalité* and making naturalization once again a discretionary act of the head of state. As Marie-Hélène Varnier and Karin Dietrich-Chénel have observed, naturalization thus resulted from a double engagement, that of a foreigner who desired to become a French citizen and that of the government that pronounced his naturalization.[30]

Changes in naturalization also coincided with certain uses of the old metaphors of the sovereign as a father who adopted foreign "children," and the portrayal of Napoleon as the father of the Grand Empire. Such language appears frequently in the petitions of immigrants asking to be granted citizenship rights in France. For example, in 1811 a young man in Rouen, Alexis Vincent, pleaded for a certificate of naturalization by portraying himself as a supplicant child: "Permit a young orphan, without parents, without a name, without a state, to throw himself at the feet of the imperial throne to ask for the title of honor to continue his service in your majesty's navy. . . . he calls upon the common father of the French."[31] An 1813 petition on behalf of the Norwegian-born businessman Sollberg similarly declared his desire to become a part of the "great French family," "this immense and fortunate family that lives peacefully and gloriously under the laws of a hero and a father."[32]

The rhetoric of "national adoption" may have appeared most explicitly in the trial of a certain Saint-Simon, a French-born man accused in 1809 of carrying arms against the Napoleonic empire.[33] Saint-Simon contended that he had been made a foreigner when he acquired the title of "grand d'Espagne" long before the Revolution, and was therefore not subject to the laws affecting French citizens. French authorities ruled that only his civil death in France—and not his supposed naturalization—had stripped of him of French citizenship: "He ceased to be French only by the penalty of civil death attached to his emigration, a penalty that was lifted by the government when it pronounced his definitive removal from the list of émigrés and reintegrated him, with the literal qualification of *citizen* Saint-Simon, and granted him control of all the goods he possessed before his desertion." For him to make war against France was literally "parricide":

> For is it not the cry of sentiment, that political and civil adoption are both equally incapable of freeing someone from the primitive duties toward the true country and the true father? The penalty and name of parricide should be attached both to the denatured son who, after his emancipation, brings an impious hand against the author of his days, and to the wicked man who

wants to use a political adoption to authorize himself to bring a sacrilegious arm against the country that gave him birth.[34]

Saint-Simon was condemned to death by a military commission for having carried arms against his country, but received a reprieve from the emperor.

However, the revalorization of the metaphor of the sovereign as father and the use of the term "parricide" to describe attacks on France and France's leader did not equate with a simple return to Old Regime principles or practices concerning national citizenship. This becomes especially clear if we turn back to a last appearance of the idea of national adoption in the courts, in yet another case involving emigration.

The Voyneau Affair and "National Adoption" Revisited

The courts considered the relationship between national adoption and parental authority once more in 1808, after the resolution of most emigration cases in 1806. The Voyneau case was trumpeted to the public as a modern-day version of the case of Martin Guerre; like its famous sixteenth-century predecessor, the case centered on the contested identity of a young man who had resurfaced after years of absence. But it also led jurists, as well as the public that followed the ins and outs of the *cause célèbre*, to reconsider the impact of civil death on family relations and the possibility for the state to act as a metaphorical and literal father of its "adopted children."[35]

The roots of the affair lay in 1792, when Voyneau *père* had fled France. His son, a small boy, Auguste, was entrusted to the care of a peasant family in the Vendée. At this point the story becomes murky; either Auguste was killed during the chaos of the Terror, or he was found living among the corpses of a destroyed village and taken under the wing of a merchant woman. In 1796 a former servant of the Voyneaus traveling in the area encountered the boy by chance and recognized him, or at least claimed to recognize him, from a telltale scar near his hairline. Madame Voyneau, however, refused to accept that the boy was her son. She insisted that the child was actually the son of a poverty-stricken miller and the center of an elaborate plot to introduce an "intruder" into her family and thus deprive them of the money that Auguste or the would-be Auguste would eventually inherit from his parents.

Madame Voyneau initially lost her case; the courts ruled that Auguste was indeed her lost son. However, she still refused to recognize the boy as her own. When the former émigré Monsieur Voyneau returned to France, he launched an appeal based on the fundamental importance of paternal rights and authority. Voyneau portrayed himself as "reborn" to his country and his family, only to be prevented from exercising one of the central rights of a citizen and father, that of being able to acknowledge or deny that children were his own. He argued, through the intermediary of his lawyer, M. Boncenne, that

> I finally leave the tomb, I return to life, the doors of my country are open to me; I run, I fly to receive the tender embrace of my wife and children—and the first object that presents itself to me is a thief introduced into my house. . . . I am restored to all the rights of *puissance paternelle,* and it is doubtless one that derives essentially from this *puissance* to reject a vile impostor from one's breast.[36]

Voyneau continued to maintain that paternal rights, being natural and inalienable, took precedence over the formal penalties that had been imposed on émigrés. What could the government do "against the sacred rights of a father? Is it in the power of men to destroy natural order? Could one, even during my absence, deprive me of imprescriptible and inalienable rights, those of paternity?"[37]

The Court of Appeals in Poitiers ruled on July 23, 1806, that Voyneau's "rebirth" as a French citizen did not restore him to the position of a *père de famille* with complete power over his family, since "the rights acquired by a wife or children of an amnestied man during his civil death belong to them irrevocably." Furthermore, all the rights of *puissance paternelle* had rested with his "widow" during his absence. She had definitively lost her—and, by extension, his—case; the ex-émigré was powerless to change the decision.[38]

The thwarted *père* then took his case to the Supreme Court, where the case was tried in 1808. Jean Simon Loiseau, one of the chief compilers and editors of the jurisprudence of the Civil Code, represented Voyneau's ostensible son Auguste. He argued that before the amnesty, M. Voyneau, émigré, had been neither a father nor a French citizen: "In the eyes of the law, he was not a father, a husband, or a citizen; he was dead for his children, for his family, as for his country."[39] Loiseau's argument directly echoed the rationale presented by the makers of the Civil Code for dissolving the marriages of those proclaimed to be civilly dead; in the tribune Alexandre Gary's concluding words, a man who had been deservedly ejected from society "was no longer a citizen, a father, or a husband."[40]

In response to such arguments, Monsieur Voyneau and his lawyers invoked the specter of national adoption. They contended that if he had been stripped of his rights as father and citizen, then as an émigré he "should have been represented by the nation that put itself in the place of émigrés." In other words, he should have been represented not by his wife, but by the state itself, since the Republic had "adopted" his son during his absence. If he could not act as a father, then the state as Auguste's surrogate father should have acted in his stead.[41]

But despite the common use of the metaphor of "public adoption" and of the French nation as a family headed by a father to whom the inhabitants of France owed primal loyalty, the idea that the state could and should literally behave as the father of its adopted children was quickly dismissed in 1808. Loiseau, the lawyer for the young Auguste Voyneau, ridiculed the idea—floated and rejected in the Suzanne Lepeletier case several years earlier—that the state really could act as a literal parent of a individual citizen:

> Since when has one imagined, and what law can one find to show, that the Republic took upon itself the purely personal rights of émigrés, that it adopted their wives, their husbands, their children; in a word, that it became husband, wife, son, and daughter? The Nation, it is true, took on all the rights of émigrés, but only in what concerned their property. . . . When the wife of an émigré filed for divorce, did she call the Nation before the police? Did she cite it in the courts? Did she ask for its authorization to appear as a witness or to make a contract? Did children require its consent to marry when they were minors?[42]

The response to these questions was clearly negative. The French legislature may have seriously considered whether Suzanne Lepeletier required the consent of the nation to marry, but by 1808 such a proposition appeared ludicrous, proof only that it was ridiculous to pretend that the nation could act as a literal parent over its "adopted" children. The judges agreed with Loiseau that the state had not, and could not have, adopted the children of émigrés or any other French subjects.

Voyneau *père* nonetheless ultimately won the day. The Supreme Court reversed the lower court's ruling on December 7, 1808, declaring that Voyneau retained the right to "defend the condition of a child born of his marriage," and thus to reject a child believed to be an impostor: "This right cannot be excluded from the class of rights restored to a former émigré by the amnesty."[43] In concluding that Voyneau could not disown a child he did not recognize as his son, the lower court had falsely applied the *senatus consulte* of 6 Floréal Year X, which granted an amnesty to returned émigrés. In one of the presentations of the case as a *cause célèbre*, the publicist Maurice Méjan explained that "in virtue of the amnesty they [émigrés] are able to exercise all the rights of *puissance paternelle* that had been only temporarily suspended; first among these rights is incontestably that to examine and contest the titles by which a child has been introduced into their family."[44] The case was ultimately sent back to the Court of Appeals in Orléans, where it was judged in 1810. After rehashing extensive testimony about the boy's physical appearance, especially his eye color and the exact placement of his scar, the court ruled that the evidence did indeed indicate a plot to introduce an intruder into the Voyneaus' home. The supposed Auguste was not their child.[45]

The final victory of Voyneau *père* suggests the limits to the concept of civil death. The courts of the early nineteenth century generally applied the principles that had guided the makers of the Civil Code in establishing the consequences of *mort civile*. When men were condemned to civil death, their loss of French citizenship had also meant their loss of rights as husbands and *pères de famille* in France. They could not challenge contracts made by their spouses, divorces, the emancipation of their children, the marriages of their daughters, or other acts that their wives and children had performed in their absence. The limits placed on the ability of returned émigré men to overturn property transactions by their "widows" and the final recognition of the validity of divorces like that of Térence MacMahon and Caroline Latour show the seriousness with which legislators took the consequences of civil death. But lawmakers' and jurists' desire to preserve paternal authority within the household and to protect the family from intrusions of the state could lead even the Supreme Court to decide that civil death had temporarily suspended, rather than ended, an émigré's position and rights as the head of a household.

The Voyneau case also reveals the evolution and limits of the relationship between literal families and the metaphorical "great family" of the nation. The implicit equation of "French citizen" and *père de famille* meant that the expulsion of a criminal from the *grande famille* had also necessitated his expulsion from a position of power within his immediate family. But this did not mean that the state was also expected to act as a parent. As we have seen in the Suzanne Lepeletier affair, the idea that the state could, and should, act as a literal father had already been discredited during the Directory. Napoleon and the Restoration kings who followed him were able to use the rhetoric of the sovereign as the father of the French people and naturalization as the "adoption" of new citizens by the French nation in part precisely because—as Voyneau's experience demonstrated—such "adoption" would not be taken literally in the postrevolutionary state.

Conclusion

In general, the courts' rulings on emigration upheld the need to close the books on legal decisions made during the revolutionary era. The juridical consequences of civil death overrode the authority of a male head of household. Wives and children had been free to act as they chose during the absence of an émigré head of household; his return as a citizen did not allow him to overturn decisions made in his absence. Yet, as cases like the Voyneau one show, there was often a tension between the desire to bury the juridical morass inherited from the Revolution and the desire to promote paternal authority. Such tensions were not simply a matter of legal formality; they were shaped by the new limits of the model of great family, and by changing views about the determination and relevance of women's citizenship. Indeed, in cases like the MacMahon-Latour trial, lawyers and commentators debated at length what made foreigners into citizens and the relationship between marriage and citizenship for men and women.

If the courts could ultimately set aside such questions, administrators and officials in other arenas could not. Immigrants and local authorities demanded to know how laws on gender and citizenship affected them. Indeed, if we turn to the application of citizenship law during the Napoleonic era, we will see more clearly the ways in which the return to a model of a powerful individual sovereign and the rhetoric of "father-ruler" disguised real changes. The separation of political and civil aspects of Frenchness and nationality in the Civil Code meant that laws concerning both the loss and acquisition of citizenship rights in France would be applied differently to men and women even though both were considered "children of the nation." At the same time, the social practices of integration would present lasting challenges to the order established by the Napoleonic Civil Code.

7   Looking Forward: Women and the Application of Citizenship Law

Napoleonic legislators, jurists, and litigants struggled to make sense of the chaos of statutes inherited from the Revolution when they looked backward. The application of citizenship law in the future promised to be more straightforward; the Napoleonic Code laid out a comprehensive series of laws, which clearly separated the *qualité de français* from that of citizen, and rigorously subordinated both women's and children's national status and associated rights and duties to those of the *paterfamilias*.

But real innovations actually came in the wake of the Code. Forced by queries and petitions to clarify the implications of the Civil Code and other new laws concerning loss and acquisition of national citizenship, Napoleonic officials argued that such citizenship did not concern women. While Old Regime laws forbidding expatriation and revolutionary laws on emigration had affected both sexes, now both single and married women were exempted from new laws that stripped those who left France without "permission" of the titles and rights of citizenship. Women were told that they could no longer naturalize in France because naturalization conferred political rights for which they were ineligible. Married women were further removed from the procedures of *admission à domicile* that conferred civil rights but not political citizenship in France. Foreign women who wished to marry French men—a class of women who had initially been subject to the same procedures for the intermediary stage of *admission à domicile* as men, at least in certain areas in France—were now automatically subsumed under their fiancés' or husbands' status.

The Mechanisms of Citizenship

Scholars have often assumed that immigrants during the early nineteenth century were predominantly men or families whose immigration can be

158

traced only through male heads of household. Certainly, the statistics on naturalization bear out this impression. Scarcely one percent of the acts granting naturalization or civil rights to foreigners recorded in the central list, the *Bulletin des lois*, from 1790 to May 1871 directly concern women, and the majority of these acts date from after 1848.[1]

But although the majority of immigrants in France during the early nineteenth century were men, the records are misleading. They conceal the deliberate exclusion of women from the records of both loss and acquisition of French citizenship after the Revolution. Officials during the Napoleonic period proclaimed that French women did not need the approval of the sovereign in order to forfeit their *qualité de français* without suffering further penalties. Both married and single women who petitioned for naturalization were told that it pertained only to those capable of exercising political rights, and thus was irrelevant to their sex. Even the intermediary form of citizenship, *admission à domicile,* which granted civil but not political rights, came to be seen as unnecessary for married women, whose national status was determined by their husbands' *qualité.*

The disappearance of individual women from the formal mechanisms of national citizenship ironically took place during the period in which the title "French" was granted collectively to—or, more often, imposed upon—hundreds of thousands of people. As Napoleon's armies plowed through Europe, France annexed vast parts of the continent. Some territories were ruled by French men appointed by Napoleon and were nominally distinct from the empire, and other states in the Napoleonic orbit continued to be governed by native sovereigns allied with the empire. Large areas, however, were officially incorporated into France. Following the example set up by the earlier revolutionary conquest of Belgium, inhabitants of such conquered areas were collectively declared to be "French citizens," with all the accompanying rights and, especially, duties.

The idea that laws regulating acquisition and loss of national citizenship pertained only to men also represented a real rupture with both Old Regime and revolutionary practices. As we have seen, both men and women petitioned for and obtained *lettres de naturalité* during the Old Regime. Only men obtained naturalizations through article 4 of the Constitution of 1791, which allowed the government to naturalize exceptional foreigners who had come to France and taken the civic oath. However, few men were formally naturalized through this exceptional mechanism; a decree of August 26, 1792, naturalized eighteen men, and the National Convention issued only three other individual naturalization decrees.[2] The Constitutions of 1791 and 1793, as well as certain other measures and decrees, automatically naturalized foreigners who met the stipulated conditions without necessarily recording their naturalizations individually.[3] These measures potentially applied the same criteria to both men and women. While some immigrants, like Térénce MacMahon, protested the possibility of such automatic naturalization, others reclaimed their status as new French subjects, like Suzanne Néau, whose grandmother had fled France for England after the revocation of the Edict of Nantes. She returned to France and claimed a disputed inheritance on the grounds that the 1790 law on returned *religionnaires fugitifs* had made her French. Memoires on her behalf described her as "naturalized French by the law of December 15, 1790, domiciled in France for fifteen years, and having taken the civic oath."[4]

Mechanisms regulating the loss of citizenship status also applied to both sexes. Like Old Regime measures that forbade men and women to leave the kingdom without the king's permission, the measures against émigrés penalized all who had left France during the Revolution, explicitly including both sexes. Both men and women were declared civilly dead, stripped of their titles of membership in the revolutionary community of citizens as well as all rights in France.

By the late 1790s legislators had begun to apply laws on the acquisition and loss of national citizenship differently to men and women. The most notable example is that of the partial amnesty that allowed all émigré women to return to France, regardless of their husbands' status. The makers of the Code rigorously subordinated both women's and children's national status and associated rights and duties to those of the *paterfamilias*. Lawmakers proclaimed that a woman assumed her husband's nationality at marriage, and that her husband could force her to reside with him wherever he chose.[5] These trends represent a change that Anne McClintock has formulated with particular lucidity:

> In post-French Revolution Europe, women were incorporated into the nation-state not directly as citizens, but only indirectly, through men, as dependent members of the family in private and public law. The Code Napoleon was the first modern statute to decree that the wife's nationality should follow her husband's, an example other European countries briskly followed. A woman's political relation to the nation was submerged as a social relation to a man through marriage. For women, citizenship in the nation was mediated by the marriage relation within the family.[6]

However, the proclamation of the Civil Code did not immediately transform how men and women became, or ceased to be, French citizens. Instead, both administrators and ordinary men and women throughout the Napoleonic era were forced to consider whether women should, or could, be incorporated into or excluded from the nation directly as citizens when they tried to apply the new laws that turned French into foreigners or granted political and civil rights to foreigners in the French empire.

Gender, Territory, and the Loss of Citizenship

The question of whether women could lose their citizenship by leaving French territory without official permission seemed to have been resolved when the revolutionary laws against emigration were lifted and when the partial amnesty of 28 Vendémiaire Year IX (October 20, 1800) excused women émigrés regardless of the status of their husbands. The Civil Code confirmed this principle: a woman's marriage to a foreigner made her into a foreigner herself, since she was theoretically obliged to follow her husband wherever he chose to live. As we have seen, the Code was ambiguous about whether this obligation applied outside France, an ambiguity, which in cases like the MacMahon-Latour trial, could have serious consequences. However, a French woman was, at least in theory, free to marry as she pleased, and she could recover the *qualité de français* after her husband's death. Moreover, although the makers of the Code concentrated on civil death as a penalty for criminal acts, rather than for the political crime of leaving France, they assumed that it was a punishment that would henceforward be applied to men and not to women.

Yet the issue of responsibility for emigration reappeared when Napoleon revived certain penalties aimed at émigrés and applied them to those who left the empire. On August 26, 1811, Napoleon forbade French subjects to naturalize in foreign countries or to enter into the service of foreign powers without permission from the sovereign.[7] Unless they took up arms against France, such new French emigrants did not face the death penalty that had threatened émigrés. But, like émigrés, their property in France would be confiscated, and like foreigners subject to the *droit d'aubaine*, they would be deprived of the right to inherit from French relatives in France. Moreover, if they were found in the territory of the empire after the law went into effect, they faced deportation; if they returned, they could be imprisoned for up to ten years.

In applying the law, the definition of "French" was stretched to include such extremes as Florentine natives serving as valets and cooks in the court of the grand duke of Würtzburg, day workers who had crossed recently created French borders in formerly German territories, and Jewish diplomats employed by the Ottoman government in Turkey.[8] However, there was no initial consideration of whether the law could, or should, be applied to women, unlike earlier laws on émigrés, which from March 1793 through the Terror had specified that they applied to both sexes. Indeed, women appeared in the decree only indirectly; article 9 specified that the titles and goods of a French man naturalized without permission would devolve onto those who remained French, except for his wife's rights, which would be regulated as in a case of widowhood.[9] The jurist B. J. Legat would later use this article to bolster his case that a French woman could not become a foreigner involuntarily. In an unorthodox interpretation of the Civil Code, he contended that "although a woman, according to the dispositions of article 214 of the Civil Code, must follow her husband wherever he judges fit to reside, she is not required, if she is French, to follow him to a foreign country. If marital authority does not extend to forcing a woman to leave French soil, with even greater cause it cannot give her another country against her will." This fact was "corroborated by the dispositions of article 9 of the decree of August 26, 1811, which preserves the rights of women in the case of their husbands' naturalization in foreign countries."[10]

However, when administrators attempted to apply the 1811 decree they were besieged by petitions and letters from women who were afraid of losing property and inheritance rights in France. Such questions arose frequently in border areas, especially in the Swiss and German frontiers of the empire, where intermarriages were common. A number of letters from puzzled local officials are preserved in the archives, and they give some indication of the concerns both of such women and of the administrators attempting to make sense of the decree. For example, on November 11, 1811, the plenipotentiary minister at Basel wrote to the central government, noting that

> the law does not mention women, leaving doubts about whether or not they are subject to the same formalities. Since they do not carry arms, the motive for the law would appear not to apply to them, and if these formalities had to be fulfilled by women, they would put serious obstacles to the frequent marriages that the neighboring status of the two states makes inevitable between reciprocal subjects.[11]

Similarly, on January 20, 1812, the imperial prosecutor at the court of first jurisdiction in the Department of Mont Tonnerre observed that he had received many letters from anxious women and did not know how to respond to them:

> Since the publication of the August 26 imperial decree concerning French naturalized in foreign countries, I have received a large number of letters from Germany, written by women born in this country and who married former functionaries or followed their husbands to the courts of their respective princes. These women, whose families are still in this country and who expect inheritances, are worried that if not authorized according to the first two articles of the decree, they will lose their rights [within the French empire].[12]

In such cases, it was possible that a woman could be considered a foreigner because of her husband's status, as well as because of her own decision to leave France. But the 1811 documents also reveal single women who petitioned the government to be allowed to remain abroad while retaining their civil rights and their ability to return eventually to France. Such women include those who had left the empire with male relatives, like Marie

Françoise Truchesse, who cared for her ninety-year-old blind uncle, and Françoise Louise Barth-Barthenheim, a forty-year-old woman who had kept her father's household for years.[13] Other women had left France on their own, like Euphrasie Ardighetti, a twenty-seven-year-old who taught French in Baden and claimed that she could not leave her school there because the instruction of the youth would suffer.[14]

For the imperial government, the most problematic cases were single women who served directly in a foreign court or government, like Constantie Françoise de Bodeck, who, after the family fortune was lost in the Revolution, took a position as lady-in-waiting for the princess of Hohenloh.[15] Men who served a foreign power were considered not only to have left French territory without permission, but also to have actively given their allegiance to a foreign power. This was true even if they were only personal servants or aides to family members of the sovereign.[16]

The French ambassador to the court of Baden thus wrote to the central government on March 6, 1812, asking about single women who had left France, and especially those in the service of a foreign power. Should they be penalized like men for serving a foreign government without Napoleon's permission?

> There are French women placed near S. A. J. M. the Grande Duchesse of Baden, among others Mme. de Walsh, the Grande Maitresse. My opinion is that a woman under her husband's *puissance* follows his condition, but that widows and single women are in a different category. Don't they need to ask for authorization in order to remain in the service of a foreign power or be naturalized?[17]

The central government initially responded uncertainly to such queries. The rough draft of a reply to the plenipotentiary minister at Basel suggests that the minister was told that the law should apply to both men and women: "Since this decree makes no distinction between the sexes, I believe that women are included in its dispositions, and required to follow the formalities that it prescribes."[18] The Conseil d'Etat finally addressed the question systematically on May 22, 1812, and concluded that "given the aforementioned decree and the motives that dictated it," the measure did not apply to women, whether married or unmarried.[19] The minister of justice then wrote to administrators throughout the empire telling them to remove names of women from the lists of subjects who were to be penalized for having left France without permission.[20]

The "motives" that dictated the decree do partially explain why women were exempted from it. The law was presumably designed to increase the pool of soldiers who could be conscripted into the fodder-hungry armies of the expanding empire, and women were not eligible to serve in the military.[21] This justification echoed the rationales for pardoning women for the crime of emigration; apologists for the *émigrées* had contended that women, by definition, were not soldiers and should not lose their rights in France because they had left a country that they could neither defend nor oppose with arms. The plenipotentiary minister at Basel reproduced such logic directly: "Since they [women] do not carry arms, the motive for the law would appear not to apply to them."[22]

But the elimination of women from the 1811 decree was not simply a question of their inability to serve in the military. Instead, the judgment of the Conseil d'Etat reflected an emerging consensus that naturalization in a foreign country did not function in the same way for men as it did for women, and that evidence proving that men had definitively transferred their allegiance to another sovereign did not have the same meaning for women. For example, on July 28, 1811, the imperial law court of Brussels debated whether women who received pensions from foreign governments should be considered to have lost the *qualité de citoyen français*, as were men who accepted posts or pensions from other powers.[23] Generalizing from the case of Despiennes *vs.* the *heritiers* Dechot, the court ruled that the law mandating the loss of the *qualité de français* for anyone who received such a pension did not apply to women: "A French woman who, having married a foreigner, returns to France as a widow recovers the *qualité de français* that her marriage made her lose, even if she continues to receive a pension from a foreign government."[24]

To a certain extent, the elimination of women from the 1811 decree paralleled the *Bureau des lois*'s tolerance of marriages between members of the *grande nation* and subjects of allied or neutral countries in the late 1790s. But marriage and naturalization appeared to be functionally equivalent in the judgments of the *Bureau des lois,* as they proclaimed that a "French woman married to a foreigner before the Revolution thus has the right to invoke the principles of common law; she follows the condition of her husband, she is thus only a foreigner, and is at least in the same position as individuals naturalized or established in foreign countries before July 15, 1789."[25] Both naturalization and marriage served as proof that a French man or woman had legally become a foreigner before the Revolution or that one had forfeited the *droits de citoyen français* through ordinary channels, without incurring further penalties for the crime of emigration.

By 1811 naturalization and service to a foreign power had been differentiated from the transformations in national status implied by marriage. The first two were seen as changes in allegiance and status likely to represent a permanent choice. In contrast, marriage brought a potentially transitory change—not because a woman was expected to divorce her foreign husband, but because she might "recover" her original status if she became a widow. The late nineteenth-century jurist Isadore Alauzet summarized the situation:

> The extreme ease with which the law returns a woman to a nationality that it took from her previously—completely in contrast to the situation of the other

sex—showing so few scruples for the most legitimate act—demonstrates that it considers nationality to be without importance for her. The Conseil d'Etat thus decided without hesitating that the decree of August 26, 1811, did not apply to women.[26]

Alauzet was writing at a moment when there was considerable public discussion about what importance nationality, to use the Third Republic term, had for women. But he captures the reasoning of the 1811 decree. It was a view that would leave its mark on the whole of the nineteenth century. The 1811 decree, however, was also part of a peculiarly Napoleonic combination of laws and edicts that grafted the Old Regime definition of "Frenchness" as allegiance and service to the sovereign onto postrevolutionary concepts of citizenship. The requirement that "native" French citizens obtain the emperor's permission to settle permanently outside France revealed Napoleon's strategic use of certain Old Regime concepts. It echoed prerevolutionary laws, beginning with the 1669 ordinance mandating that French subjects obtain the king's permission before leaving their native country. But women ceased to be included in such edicts when this definition of Frenchness was combined with one of the ideas ultimately consecrated by the Revolution—that all men were potentially entitled to the rights of political citizenship, but that women were not.

"Naturalization Does Not Concern Her Sex"

This emerging emphasis on political and military service to the sovereign, combined with the Civil Code's distinction between civil and political components of Frenchness, also transformed the meaning of naturalization within France. While inhabitants of lands conquered by the French were often declared to be French en masse—whether or not they wanted to be—those from allied, neutral, or enemy countries had to petition the government individually for naturalization. In contrast to Old Regime practices, which had automatically granted *lettres de naturalité* to both men and women as long as their dossiers were procedurally correct, women were now told that naturalization did not apply to them. It conferred political rights—the *droits de citoyen*—for which women as a class were declared to be ineligible.

Such categorial exclusions resulted in part from the changes in naturalization during the Napoleonic era.[27] The Napoleonic Code set up a two-tiered system of access to French citizenship: *admission à domicile* and full-fledged naturalization. As we have seen, the Code preserved the *droit d'aubaine*, granting foreigners only the civil rights in France that French men and women enjoyed in immigrants' respective home countries. However, article 13 of the Code proclaimed that foreigners authorized by the government to establish their domicile in France would enjoy all civil rights as long as they remained in the country.[28] The Conseil d'Etat further decided that a foreigner who wanted to become French was obliged to obtain permission from the government to establish himself in France. As a result of these changes, *admission à domicile* became a step toward acquiring the *qualité de français* and the full rights of citizenship.[29]

However, the rights and obligations associated with naturalization were unclear. The Civil Code distinguished naturalization, which conferred political rights, from *admission à domicile*, which granted only civil rights. But naturalization traditionally conferred a variety of advantages that were not necessarily accorded by *admission à domicile*, including a statute that was clearly recognized by other countries, potential protection as a French citizen, and a more trustworthy means to protect personal and commercial property and inheritances than *admission à domicile*.

In theory, it was possible to obtain naturalization on simple request after having been *admis à domicile*. But legislation after the Civil Code modified these procedures and the significance of different steps of citizenship. The decree of March 17, 1809, definitively established naturalization as one of the powers of the *chef d'état*. It specified that even if a foreigner had requested citizenship and lived in France for the requisite period, he did not automatically acquire the *qualité de français*. His naturalization depended instead on a special decree, issued by the *chef d'état* or the minster of justice, depending on the period in question.[30] The 1809 law, like the 1811 edict mandating that French citizens acquire formal permission in order to naturalize in another country or serve another sovereign, stressed the contract between sovereign and subject.

However, unlike edicts and laws on the loss of French citizenship, laws concerning individual naturalization were rarely applied during the hubristic expansion of the Napoleonic empire. Those few people who petitioned for naturalization often attempted to do so not under ordinary law but under the auspices of the two *senatus consultes* that awarded citizenship after a year's residence instead of the usual ten. The *senatus consulte* of 26 Vendémiaire Year XI (September 4, 1802) rewarded "foreigners who will render or who have rendered important services to the Republic, will bring talents, inventions, or useful industries to its breast, or who will form great establishments." The *senatus consulte* of February 19, 1808, repeated the formula, simply replacing "services to the Republic" with "services to the State."[31]

Men and women from a variety of walks of life cast their life stories to fit the constraints of the *senatus consulte*. Most were from enemy or neutral countries. Naturalization in the French empire promised them rewards for their loyalty to the Napoleonic state. It could give them the assurance that they could protect their property and run a business freely, allow them to move about France without risk of expulsion, or simply accord them a clear and safe status in time of war. Politicians and soldiers—particularly those who had thrown in their lot with the French only to have their political fortunes in their homelands change—thus claimed that they had rendered important services to the French state. Such men included Ange Canaliolly, a former officer in the Venetian navy who had supported the French and had his property destroyed as a result; the Prussian diplomat Schmerz, who had helped broker the Peace of Basel; and Robert Hollingsworth, who declared that he had rendered vital services to the French in Guadeloupe by providing famine relief.[32] Other petitioners, particularly British manufacturers and entrepreneurs in the far-flung reaches of the empire, were quick to seize the financial opportunities and security that French citizenship promised, and contended that they had brought "useful industries" or would "form great establishments." Many were associated with the burgeoning cloth industry in some form or another.[33] But their ranks also included men like Jacques Dowling, an Irish-born merchant in Bordeaux, who claimed that his distillery was one of the first in France based on the English model; or another Irish-born man, Francis Jordan, living in Brussels, who vaunted his leathermaking skills.[34] Still other petitioners emphasized their intellectual accomplishments to claim that they were bringing "talents, inventions, or useful industry" to France. For example, Ferdinand Messia proudly chronicled his accomplishments as professor of astronomy and navigation in Naples. "Because of his attachment to the French nation," Messa had lost not only his chair but also his books and manuscripts; he had been able to recoup his fortune to some extent by teaching advanced mathematics in France but hoped that naturalization would ensure his future livelihood.[35] Bureaucrats charged with assessing the petitions often appeared particularly skeptical of would-be language teachers' and interpreters' claims to bring exceptional talents to France.[36]

When women applied for naturalization under the auspices of the *senatus consultes* or under the other laws regulating naturalization in the French Empire, they were told that naturalization granted political rights, not civil rights, and thus did not apply to them. In some cases, they or the intermediaries who often drafted their requests seemed to sense that their petitions for French citizenship were different from those for men. For example, Rachel Ratcliff, a single woman who had been born in England, petitioned for French citizenship in 1809. She declared that "she left England in 1802 with the family of Robert Beeby, who came to France with the intention of establishing himself here and obtaining the rights of citizenship, an intention that the undersigned shares in what may concern a person of her sex."[37]

Rachel Ratcliff was inspired to apply for naturalization because of her association with the household of Robert Beeby, an Englishman living in western France. Beeby had already naturalized in France, but he wanted to ensure that his daughters—then aged sixteen and thirteen—would be able to inherit familial property before transferring all of his fortune to France and buying a large rural domain; presumably his concerns for his daughters inspired Rachel to inquire into her own situation. But other women petitioned for full naturalization on the explicit grounds of their own service to the state or that of family members—and were reminded that naturalization did not in fact "concern a person of their sex."

Thus the petition of a rich widow, Dame Lawless, was rejected in Floréal Year XII (May 6, 1804) because she had no husband to intervene in her stead. In the eyes of the officials she encountered, she was wasting both her time and theirs; naturalization granted only political rights, for which women were ineligible.[38] However, her son was enthusiastically welcomed soon afterward as a new member of the French nation. His naturalization indirectly acknowledged his mother's claims to membership in the French polity; he was naturalized not because of his own merit or services to the state, but because Dame Lawless had turned a large swamp into fertile fields, and the youth was beginning to aid her in this venture.[39]

Similarly, Mathilde Wolfe-Tone petitioned for naturalization for herself and her son, a student in the military school of St.-Germain-en-Laye. She was the widow of the prominent Irish republican Théobold Wolfe-Tone and had already been granted a pension from the French government for her husband's services to the French revolutionary state. She noted that the National Assembly had expressed interest in her and her son. Her petition indirectly testified to the end of the idea of "national adoption"; she observed that following her husband's death in a Dublin prison, "a famous orator of the Council of Five Hundred (Lucien Bonaparte, session of 9 Brumaire Year VII), regretted that no form of public adoption existed."[40]

French naturalization was now imperative for her son, who was about to enter military service; otherwise, if captured in battle by English ships, he would be treated as a traitor to Britain rather than as a prisoner of war. The state readily granted him naturalization. However, it ruled explicitly in 1812 that "Mme. Wolfe-Tone, his mother, is not included in the degree, because women cannot be allowed to exercise the rights of citizenship."[41]

No woman was naturalized in France or the French empire during the Napoleonic period; or at least, no naturalizations appear in the central registry of such acts, the *Bulletin des lois*.[42] This policy was shaped by the separation of civil and civic rights consecrated by the Civil Code, combined with both the revolutionary exclusion of women from the exercise of political citizenship and Napoleon's renewed definition of "French citizenship" as service to the sovereign. Not only the obligations, but also the titles of full national citizenship, had ceased to appear relevant for women.

The Civil Rights of *Etrangères*

Women like Dame Lawless and Mathilde Wolfe-Tome were told that although they could not naturalize, they could "obtain permission to establish their domicile in France in order to exercise civil rights." Yet the institutionalization of the Napoleonic Code also led to the disappearance of many immigrant women from the supposedly intermediary stage of *admission à domicile*. The Code's insistence on the strict subordination of a woman's national status to that of her husband's changed the way that local administrators applied laws affecting even these stages of national citizenship.

Admission à domicile as an intermediary stage toward full French citizenship inherently combined local integration and a nationally defined status. It is thus illuminating to look closely at the ways this status was accorded in a particular locality. Strasbourg was the site where the procedures of *admission à domicile* were most commonly applied and perhaps most commonly disputed. As Marie-Hélène Varnier and Karin Dietrich-Chénel have demonstrated, Germans formed by far the largest community of immigrants *admis à domicile* in France between 1791 and 1848, and Strasbourg was at the center of such settlements.[43]

Contemporaries suggested that there were actually more foreign women than men living in Strasbourg and the surrounding area. For example, in January 1814 local authorities were asked to report on the foreigners living in Strasbourg, so that they could be expelled if the siege of the city continued.[44] One administrator responded to his superior's request with the disclaimer "I am only presenting you with a careful list of over 3,000 male individuals, not including women or girls, who are perhaps even more numerous."[45] This may have been an exaggeration. One of the rare documents that record the names and professions of all "foreigners of both sexes" (*étrangers non régnicoles de tout sexe*) in Strasbourg suggests that the proportion of women was somewhat smaller. The census, prompted by the mayor's order of June 12, 1815, was a response to a second siege of the city. Since it focused on outsiders whose means of subsistence were precarious and who could thus be expected or compelled to leave the city during times of crisis, it probably overrepresents working-class foreigners. About 20 percent of the names recorded were those of women, although the proportion varied with the district being surveyed.[46] However, the fact that most of these women were single—either unmarried or widows—suggests that the total population of women in Strasbourg who came from across the Rhine was considerably greater.

The profession of most of these women suggests one of the reasons why there would be many fewer women than men visible in the records of formal procedures of admission to French citizenship, despite their relative prominence in the working-class population of the city. Although the records list a few workers (*ouvrières*), seamstresses, wet-nurses, and prostitutes or abandoned women, the majority of women were servants.[47] Servants traditionally worked for a while in the nearest town or city to gain their dowry, and then often returned to their home regions to marry, rather than establishing themselves permanently where they had worked.[48] Presumably, Strasbourg's domestic servants were no exception.

But more important, French women were deliberately excluded from the procedures of citizenship. In the years before the Napoleonic Code was fully institutionalized, women were *admises à domicile* in the same way as men. Both men's and women's petitions were judged by mayors, subprefects, prefects of the department in question, and, at least officially, central authorities.[49] Women's dossiers were usually sketchier than men's, often recording only brief biographical information and, usually, the petitioner's intent to marry. For example, the dossier for Marie Josephe Sculere, *admise à domicile* in Year XI, noted that she had been in domestic service in Strasbourg since 1791, wanted to marry, and had sufficient savings not to be a burden on her adopted community. Similarly, the dossier for Anne Marie Wannesdeutch, daughter of a butcher in Kehl, recorded that she planned to marry a French chicken merchant and settle in Strasbourg.[50]

However, if their records were often shorter than those for men, the procedures were essentially the same for both sexes; authorities consistently sought to verify that immigrants' papers were in order and that newcomers were not, and would not become, a burden on the community. Moreover, petitions for *admission à domicile* for both men and women often proclaimed that they intended to become "French citizens," and thus at least potentially to acquire the full rights of citizenship. Variations on the formula during the early Napoleonic period proclaimed an immigrant's "intention to obtain the rights of a French citizen," desire to "acquire the rights of citizenship after the term prescribed by the constitution," or request to be allowed to establish domicile in France "to enjoy all civil rights and political ones after ten years."[51] Petitions for women sometimes dispensed with the controversial terms concerning citizenship, like *droits de cité* and *citoyen français*. Both Sculere and Wannedeutsch's petitions referred simply to their desire to become French.[52] But in other cases, the language was identical for men and women. For example, the petition for Marie Madeline Henninger, a baker's widow who planned to remarry a shoemaker in Strasbourg, proclaimed that she "intended to establish herself in this city and acquire the quality of a French citizen."[53]

This practice began to change with the institutionalization of the Civil Code. The first section of the Code, on the *jouissance et la perte des droit civils*, was promulgated on 27 Ventôse Year XI (March 18, 1803). It prompted an exchange between the mayor of Strasbourg and the prefect of the Bas Rhin about how to reconcile the Civil Code and the Constitution of Year VIII, and particularly how to interpret, or reinterpret, article 3 of the Constitution, which specified that "a foreigner becomes a French citizen, after having reached the age of twenty-one, declared his intention to settle in France, and resided there for ten consecutive years."[54]

The mayor wrote to the prefect on 12 Fructidor Year XI (August 29, 1803) that "before your *arrêt* of last 15 Thermidor, foreign women who applied for authorization to establish themselves in France were assimilated to foreign men, in the mode of admission." New laws, however, "give foreign women the same rights as French women, given that neither exercise political rights, and the former are encompassed under their husbands' condition."[55] He contended that the government should consider women's requests to establish themselves in France and marry Frenchmen as simple police matters, which could be regulated by local authorities, not as issues of citizenship.

Henri Shée, the prefect of Bas Rhin, confirmed that the constitutional procedures for access to French citizenship appeared to apply only to "foreigners capable of becoming full French citizens, and in consequence, only to the masculine sex, since the exercise of political rights does not belong to women."[56] Such logic directly echoed that used by officials opposed to women's naturalization, as in the response to Dame Lawless: "Her application pertains only to political rights, which a woman cannot acquire."[57]

Shée went on to warn against the idea that this policy should be interpreted to mean that the government should not keep track of such women, or that it should blithely allow them to establish themselves wherever they chose: "It does not follow that non-French women can settle in France without the authorization of the government." Since a French-born woman who married a foreigner needed governmental authorization to recover her *qualité de français* even after her husband's death, authorities should not be more lenient with real foreigners.

> It is clear, moreover, that the denomination "foreigner," like that of "French," in this law is generic. Women are specifically mentioned, in two articles, in order to determine the effects of marriage that a woman contracts with an individual of a different condition from hers before marriage, effects that are so specific to women that they can, in no case, be made common to men.[58]

In subsequent years, local authorities and police kept track of working-class women, particularly servants and vagabonds, but ceased to apply the procedures of *admission à domicile* to them on any systematic basis. A few women do appear in the records of *admission à domicile* during the late Napoleonic period and the Restoration. For example, the registers from 1821 show a thirty-two-year-old Swiss woman, Pauline Louise Françoise Carey, who wanted to establish a school for *demoiselles;* those from 1824 record the admission of the sixty-one-year-old Dorothée Branckehaffer, from Bavaria, who made bone buttons; while those from 1827 accord *admission à domicile* to the Swiss-born Lieu sisters, both cooks in Strasbourg.[59] But there are relatively few such women, and considerably fewer than before the Civil Code. In their statistical study of *admission à domicile* of German immigrants, Varnier and Dietrich-Chénel found only eleven such women in the forty-five years from 1803 to 1848, whereas the Strasbourg register from Year XII (September 1803–04) alone lists nine women.[60] Moreover, those women who formally applied for and were granted *admission à domicile* after the Napoleonic Code were either widows or single women with no immediate intention of marrying, unlike earlier women applicants for civil rights in France, who had usually been engaged to be married.

Conclusion

When the Bourbons returned to power in 1814—and definitively in 1815—they preserved certain key elements of the revolutionary and Napoleonic definitions and apparatus of national citizenship. The Restoration government maintained the distinction between *admission à domicile* and full naturalization, and the same residence requirements—five and ten years in France, respectively—for eligibility for each stage. The lower house of the legislature, the Chamber of Deputies, emphasized service to the sovereign when it debated the status of inhabitants of areas that had been part of the French empire and were not part of post-Napoleonic France. Echoing many of the ideas institutionalized by the Napoleonic *senatus consultes* on naturalization as well as Old Regime ideas about service, the legislators lauded soldiers, administrators, and businessmen who had served France well and argued that these groups deserved special treatment.[61]

But the Restoration government transformed both the practical implications of naturalization and the meaning of national citizenship in France. The majority of those who applied for and received naturalization after 1814 were no longer subjects of powers that had been opposed to Napoleonic rule or had been neutral or allied with the empire, but rather those who had been part of the French empire. Their reasons for requesting French citizenship often differed substantially from those of their predecessors.[62] Perhaps even more important, one of the first acts of the restored monarchy, on June 3, 1814, was to create a special procedure of *grande naturalisation*. A foreigner who had performed important services for France could be rewarded with *grandes lettres de naturalisation,* which would be verified in both the Chamber of Peers and the Chamber of Deputies. A foreigner naturalized through ordinary channels could vote—if he met the property and other requirements for eligibility for suffrage—but could not be elected to the legislature.[63]

This new category of naturalization, combined with the general limitations on the exercise of political rights during the Restoration, in which a minuscule portion of the populace was eligible to vote, meant that naturalization was less rigorously associated with the exercise of political rights.[64] Women did occasionally petition for and receive naturalizations during the early nineteenth century. Eight women naturalized during the Restoration: three Belgian natives, two from Luxembourg, two Dutch women, and one

English woman.[65] Several of these women were caught up in the general wave of naturalizations following the return of the Bourbon government. Others, like the two Luxembourg women, were presumably motivated by a campaign in the 1820s to make immigrants in several departments naturalize if they wanted to continue enjoying key local rights, like the right to gather firewood or graze their animals on the common grounds.[66]

However, such cases remained very rare. Like women's requests for civil rights in Restoration France, they concerned single women; and even more often than the acts of *admission à domicile*, they concerned widows.[67] Married women's petitions for naturalization were quickly dismissed. For example, Marie Heyrtz's attempt in 1825 to request naturalization for herself and her Luxembourg-born husband was met with a stern response. The Keeper of the Seals (*garde des sceaux*) declared that this was not her affair and that her husband should be dealing with anything concerning their citizenship status.[68]

But the fact that foreign women who married Frenchmen automatically became French in the post-Napoleonic years had unexpected consequences. It increased the perceived importance of liaisons between immigrant men and French women. In theory, such marriages transformed French women into foreigners—as the Napoleonic Code dictated. In practice, they were perceived to turn foreign men into Frenchmen. This was especially the case during the Restoration and in the frontiers of the kingdom, as we will see in the next chapter.

8 Immigration, Marriage, and Citizenship in the Restoration

Legal categories of national citizenship and social practices for incorporating foreigners into the nation operated on potentially contradictory levels in Restoration France. As we have seen, women often disappeared from the records of national citizenship in the aftermath of revolutionary changes and the institution of the Napoleonic Civil Code. As women, they were often told that laws on French citizenship did not apply to their sex; as wives, they were legally subsumed under their spouses' statuses and dissuaded from applying for naturalization or even civil rights on their own. But the very disappearance of foreign-born women from the formal mechanisms of citizenship increased the visibility of relationships between immigrant men and French women. Both administrators and ordinary men and women believed that, contrary to the principles of the Napoleonic Code, these marriages effectively bestowed the rights of French citizenship on foreign men.

Archival records from Strasbourg concerning *admission à domicile* dramatically reveal these contradictions. In the early nineteenth century, and especially during the Restoration, city officials and local elites proclaimed that the most important attribute of citizenship was the right to work for oneself. They tried to limit this right to native French citizens and to foreigners who actively sought to become French. But immigrant workers continually circumvented official procedures. To the frustration of authorities and formerly powerful master artisans, foreigners were able to acquire the right to settle and set up shop independently in Strasbourg precisely because of their relationships with native French women.

Beginning in the 1820s, conflicting international regulations made marriages between foreign-born men and native French women increasingly difficult. Nonetheless, immigrants continued to believe that they could acquire both the titles and the rights of French citizenship through their liaisons with French women, especially if they succeeded in marrying. In more rural frontier areas than Strasbourg, *avantages* or *biens communaux*—rights that were often essential to daily existence, such as grazing animals on common lands or gathering firewood from the local forest—became key sites of contention. Representatives of the state tried to limit these to native-born French and to naturalized foreigners, while immigrants contended that they were entitled to the "rights of citizenship" because of their long residence on French territory, and especially because of their marriages to French women. In both rural and urban areas, even the right to live on French territory was controversial; fighting popular perceptions, authorities endlessly reiterated that marriages to French women did not make foreigners into French men entitled to live in the kingdom, but instead, following the Napoleonic Code, made such women *étrangères*, themselves subject to expulsion from their native country.

The "Most Beautiful Attribute of a Citizen"

Shortly before the Chamber of Deputies voted for the abolition of the *droit d'aubaine* in 1819, one Paris-based legislator proclaimed that

> the only civil rights that have any real value, and which, separately from political rights, are attached to the *qualité de français*, are the capacities to receive and transmit inheritances. In giving foreigners the ability to bequeath property and inherit it, they are assimilated to French [citizens], and except for political rights there will remain scarcely any difference between the two.[1]

But on France's frontiers there were other civil rights that were closely associated with French citizenship, especially during the Restoration. This association was particularly clear in Strasbourg, where immigrants simultaneously sought membership in several different communities: the city itself; the network of artisans and employers who could provide jobs and social support; and, at least in the rhetoric of their petitions and the vision of central administrators, the French nation as a whole. The process of *admission à domicile*, which legally granted foreigners civil rights in France, often conflated the formal procedures for becoming a member of these different communities.

This situation represented a radical break with Old Regime traditions. Before the Revolution, Strasbourg city authorities zealously controlled who, man or woman, could become a "bourgeois de Strasbourg" or even obtain the subordinate status of *manants*, residents of the city who had certain rights, but lacked political rights and other privileges.[2] If men and women from outside France became bourgeois of the city, they were legally accepted as French in the kingdom as a whole. As the Strasbourg municipal council explained in 1790, since the incorporation of Strasbourg into France in 1691 the city had maintained the privilege "to be governed by its particular customs and laws." It sufficed to be "received as a bourgeois and inhabitant of Strasbourg under the authority of its magistrates to be recognized as French."[3]

The right to become a master artisan had also been determined locally, and under strict constraints, before the Revolution. Throughout France, would-be master artisans served first as apprentices and journeymen, or *compagnons;* after they had completed their training, they were required to produce a masterwork and gain approval from their guild before they could set up shop independently. Journeymen workers often contested the control of master artisans over different trades, while the Controller-General Turgot attempted and failed to abolish guilds in 1776; but the corporate structure of industry persisted until the eve of the Revolution. Indeed, Strasbourg had a particularly strong tradition of corporate life, one linked intimately to the city's social and political structure. Only bourgeois of the city could exercise a profession independently, while all bourgeois were members of one of the city's twenty guilds, or *Zünfte.*[4] The famous 1791 Le Chapelier law abruptly abolished the Old Regime structure of apprenticeships and masterships and allowed anyone to purchase a patent (*patente*) to exercise his or her profession. Like their counterparts elsewhere in France, Strasbourg master artisans tried to resurrect aspects of the corporate system in the aftermath of the Revolution.[5] City elites also attempted to control the labor market by limiting the right to work independently to French citizens. In Year VII (1798) the mayor declared that only French citizens could obtain a patent to work as master artisans: "As a general principle, it is necessary to be a French citizen in order to obtain a patent and legitimately exercise one's industry in France."[6] This principle was quickly linked to postrevolutionary procedures for making foreigners into French citizens.

Procedures both for allotting patents and for granting foreigners the status of *admis à domicile* often worked smoothly. Officials laconically noted the resources of migrants, the dates and places of their birth, and the formal papers that they had acquired. Potential in-laws, fellow artisans or employers, and neighbors provided supporting testimony. The fact that German immigrants often spoke the same dialect and shared many elements of the culture of native "French" inhabitants in Strasbourg partially accounted for the large number of foreigners in the area. As we have seen, Germans formed by far the largest community of immigrants *admis à domicile* in France between 1791 and 1848, and Strasbourg was at the center of such settlements.

But such statistics do not indicate a process of conflict-free integration. Hostility to Jews was especially marked. Native Alsatian Jews were often treated as unwelcome "foreigners" by anti-Semitic Christians, who resented the fact that men and women whom they believed to be degenerate usurers had formally become French citizens.[7] Jews who were literally foreigners to France were often subject to further restrictions. The "Infamous Decree" of March 17, 1808, not only restricted the movements and employment of Jews but also forbade foreign Jews to settle in France unless they owned property, established a business, or performed military service.[8]

Various non-Jewish immigrants also met with hostility. Groups of master artisans resented foreign artisans who competed with them by setting up shop, and workers sometimes opposed the establishment of specific immigrants during the Napoleonic period.[9] Their complaints reached a crescendo during the early years of the Restoration. The problem of absorbing foreigners suddenly became pressing, since the native French Alsatian population was no longer suffering the ravages of the Napoleonic wars.[10] At the same time, the restoration of the monarchy promised the restoration of certain aspects of the Old Regime. Local officials hoped that Strasbourg would be able to return to its previous independence. They longed to control who could settle and obtain civil rights in the city, rather than relinquishing such authority to the central government. Master artisans hoped that the royal regime would be sympathetic to a return to a corporate spirit and hierarchy.

In this context, marriage between foreign men and native French women suddenly became deeply controversial. Marriage had been a stepping-stone to obtaining rights and privileges during the Old Regime, but not a guarantee of it. In the kingdom as a whole, marriage to a French citizen did not make an immigrant French. Spouses of bourgeois in Strasbourg were likely, but not guaranteed, to become bourgeois themselves, and the government had to approve their requests individually.[11] Similarly, marriage to the daughter or widow of a master artisan expedited the process of becoming a master but did not ensure it. Now immigrants appeared to be able to gain key rights of citizenship in France not by submitting to either old or new procedures for becoming citizens, but simply by courting French women. Local elites and authorities frantically denounced the fact that foreign men were able to gain the *droits de cité* by marrying French women. They reiterated endlessly that foreigners did not and neither could nor should become French through their marriages; instead, their wives became foreign.

Their complaints were colored by an ever-increasing emphasis on the unity and internal hierarchy of the family. The Restoration government abolished divorce in 1816, in part to restore the Catholic order it saw as intimately related to the successful return of the monarchy.[12] But by making it impossible to end marriage, the government made the marital bond prominently and undeniably different from other kinds of contracts, going one step beyond the Napoleonic Civil Code in redefining familial relations as qualitatively distinct from other social bonds. To an even greater extent than the Napoleonic legislators, Restoration authorities celebrated the importance of paternal authority. Writers like J. P. Chrestien de Poly and

Esquiron de Saint-Agnan extolled the virtues of paternal power in the 1820s, while the Bourbon government cultivated its own dynastic images.[13]

In this context, references to the usurpation of the "natural" hierarchy of the family—in which citizenship rights were determined by women, not by men—were particularly effective ways of dramatizing social and political disorder. Their laments echoed the protests by Térence MacMahon's lawyers in the MacMahon-Latour divorce case that it was a "monstrous heresy" and an "unimaginable reversal" to contend that "marriage naturalized a man." But concern over relationships between foreign men and French women also reflected social realities. Strasbourg was flooded with immigrant workers whose ability to provide for themselves and their potential families was tenuous; such newcomers readily became acquainted with native French Alsatians, and they seemed eager to marry.

A variety of officials, local elites, and artisans—especially the municipal council of Strasbourg, the mayor, and the Conseil des Prud'hommes, an industrial tribunal of master artisans and merchants whose fifteen members were drawn from the spectrum of trades in Strasbourg—presented potential solutions to the problems of unregulated industrial production and immigration.[14] During the early days of the First Restoration, local elites complained about marriages between foreigners and French women, but they concentrated their hopes for solving the city's problems on restoring guild regulations and the city's prerevolutionary independence. They sought to institutionalize ways in which the "most beautiful attribute of a citizen" (*le plus bel attribut du citoyen*)—that of working for oneself—could be limited to virtuous French citizens. As authorities discovered that their hopes for a return to the old order would go unfulfilled, they protested the ability of immigrants to gain civil rights in France by marriage. They increasingly emphasized the principle articulated several years earlier by a Strasbourg police commissioner in his report on foreigners and the patent: "Marriage is an act not simply of natural law but also of civil law, and one to which the state must attach maximum importance; one cannot deviate from this principle without attacking the rights of the sovereign."[15]

The Strasbourg municipal council presented one of the first calls for far-reaching changes in the mechanisms controlling labor, citizenship, and marriage relations in the city. On June 3, 1814, the council proposed a series of changes that would effectively restore the city to much of its prerevolutionary independence. It asked that "former rights of the city [*droits de cité*] be reestablished, with appropriate modifications for current times and the progress of civilization." The council focused on restoring guild regulations to industry, proposing that all artisans should serve as apprentices and then journeymen before they could become masters, that patents should be a mark of skill—evaluated by a jury for each profession—and that labor needs should be coordinated. They demanded that no "étranger non-français" be *admis à domicile* unless he had sufficient proof of his fortune, industry, and morals. It also suggested that social disorder was due not only to the lack of guild structures and local controls on immigration into the city, but also to frequent marriages between French women and foreigners who lacked any formal rights in France. The council proposed that "marriages between a foreign man and a French woman should not be allowed unless they have everything completely in order for their temporary admission or naturalization in France."[16]

The Conseil des Prud'hommes expressed many of the same concerns and proposed many of the same solutions as the city council. On January 16, 1815, the Conseil complained about the "vicious" system of the patent, which made no distinction between newcomers and those who had been masters under the Old Regime, and which generally conflated the deserving with the unworthy. Such problems had been exacerbated in Strasbourg, which as a frontier town was subject to a flood of foreigners who

> come to exercise and spoil all trades, simply by purchasing a patent, without making other contributions, without taking part in the National Guard, which has been so constantly onerous to our citizens, without giving their children for the defense of a country [*patrie*] to which they belong only by the ill they do to it.[17]

The Conseil proposed a series of remedies to this crisis. In general, it insisted that all those who wished to receive the patent must work for three years after receiving an apprenticeship. Requirements for foreigners were more stringent: immigrants should have to work for six years in the same profession in France, with a two-year hiatus between their initial declaration that they would like to stay in the country and the judgment of local authorities that such newcomers should be accepted. Moreover, they should be required to pay ten times the price of the patent in order to purchase it.

The deputy mayor of Strasbourg quickly confirmed the situation reported by the municipal council and the Conseil des Prud'hommes.[18] Like the latter, the adjunct bewailed abuses that resulted from the proliferation of foreigners in Strasbourg and "the immense harm that these admissions do to national industry." Ignoring the formal procedures for acquiring the rights of French citizens, particularly that of the patent, immigrants courted French women and then presented their relationships, and often their children, as incontrovertible reasons for granting them civil rights in France:

> For a long time, you have noticed with sorrow the considerable augmentation of requests made by foreigners to obtain permission to marry French women and settle in this city. The great majority, I would say almost the totality, of petitioners are Germans who work as assistant laborers in each craft or profession for masters established here. Most come from the Grand Duchy of Baden, the Kingdom of Württemburg, and Saxony. The ease with which these people

find others who speak their language when they arrive allows them to get to know girls of this country; intimacy is established, promises of marriage follow, and often they have lived in concubinage and produced children before they have received permission from you to marry. They count on your indulgence and readiness to be moved by pity and commiseration for an unmarried mother of children who would be declared illegitimate, to grant what in all other cases you would not do.[19]

His solution was to draw on the Napoleonic Civil Code, particularly article 11, which established that foreigners enjoyed the same civil rights in France that French men and women enjoyed in their home countries. But in his view, "civil rights" were not primarily those concerning property and inheritance, but rather the right to form business establishments. He contended that these rights should be limited to French and naturalized foreigners:

> Article 13 of the Code allows the exercise of civil rights only to foreigners naturalized in France by the government. These civil rights, beyond the right to inherit . . . must necessarily include, among others, the ability to form commercial and industrial establishments in France, an ability that everywhere is one of the principal civil rights in a state.[20]

Brackenhoffer, the mayor of Strasbourg, promptly issued an *arrêt* in response to his subordinate's report and the "numerous complaints that he has received from heads of workshops and master artisans established in this city against the admission of foreigners who intend to establish a business, exercise a profession, or enjoy the civil rights accorded to the French." He proclaimed that foreign artisans were worming their way into French households, upsetting social and political order in the process. The ability to speak the same version of Alsatian German as local French residents "too easily paves the way for them to introduce themselves in the homes of inhabitants of Strasbourg exercising the same profession or similar ones, where they form liaisons, often clandestine ones without the knowledge of parents, but often also with their knowledge, their trust captured by a promise of marriage." Such liaisons opened the door to a "torrent of foreigners" and threatened "national industry"; the only solution was to apply article 11 of the Civil Code.[21]

The new government's attempts to work out a viable way of dealing with foreign artisans were temporarily halted by the chaos of the Napoleonic Hundred Days and a renewed siege of the city. With the start of the second Restoration, the central government definitively rejected the Conseil de Prud'hommes's and city government's plans for restoring Strasbourg's prerevolutionary independence and guild system. On November 28, 1815, the minister of the interior wrote to the new prefect of Bas Rhin and informed his subordinate of the responses that should be given to the Conseil. The minister correctly perceived that the latter's goal was a return to the structures of the

Old Regime: "In making the patent conditional on apprenticeship and even a stage as journeyman, in giving the name of 'master' to the patented crafts-man, the intention of the authors is clearly to demand the reestablishment of the old system of masterships."[22] In the eyes of the central authorities, such a policy was both undesirable and impossible.

Local authorities nonetheless continued to clamor both for stricter labor regulations in general and for the patent to be limited to French citizens. They now argued explicitly that foreigners were able to challenge the "rights of the sovereign" because they flouted the gendered logic of citizen-ship. In April 1816 the new mayor of Strasbourg, de Kentziger, issued an *arrêt* concerning *admission à domicile* and the extension of civil rights to foreigners. He contended that allowing foreigners to purchase the patent was a fundamental attack on French sovereignty: "Until now, they have been delivered patents and accorded civil rights, thus usurping the rights of the sovereign."[23]

Central authorities soon chastened the mayor for his presumption in try-ing to dictate the way the mechanisms of access to French citizenship should be applied in Strasbourg. De Kentziger responded apologetically in Decem-ber 1816 that "I did not claim to accord or refuse, on my private authority, the right of naturalization, which belongs only to the sovereign and which should not be confused with residence." But he reiterated the same argu-ments: immigrants were forming "a nation superimposed in the adopted nation" and were illegally enjoying civil rights in France. Such rights funda-mentally concerned the ability to work independently, an ability that could be delegated to outsiders only through permission from the sovereign:

> The ability to run a shop or a profession as a boss and other than as a journey-man or laborer, or what amounts to the same thing in effect, to use a patent, is essentially part of the exercise of civil rights, which obliges a foreigner to cease to be a foreigner among us by making the necessary declaration, or to renounce these rights, which can only be exercised with the permission of the king.[24]

De Kentziger then contended that foreigners were gaining the rights that should be limited to French citizens because the laws of citizenship were not functioning as they should. In practice, the ways in which the *droits de cité* were accorded to foreign men contradicted fundamental laws about the relationship between family and national citizenship. He proclaimed that "contrary to the jurisprudence of all people, it was the woman who estab-lished the residence or domicile of her husband, since it seemed to suffice here that he marry a Strasbourg or French woman in order to receive all the rights of citizenship [*droits de la cité*]."[25]

The mayor's April 1816 *arrêt*, combined with the end of the wartime siege of Strasbourg, provoked a wave of *admissions à domicile*. Only five people were granted civil rights in the Department of the Bas Rhin during

1815, whereas 102 were granted civil rights in 1816. The numbers continued to rise steadily over the next few years: only 33 people were *admis à
domicile* during the economic crisis of 1817, but 64 were granted rights the
following year, and 74 the subsequent year.[26] But despite the mayor's rejection of the principle that it sufficed for a foreigner to marry a French
woman to obtain citizenship rights in Strasbourg, Restoration authorities
themselves were soon forced to use such marriages to determine which
immigrants should obtain the *droits de cité* in Strasbourg.

For example, the Conseil des Prud'hommes reviewed a list of candidates
for *admission à domicile* in Strasbourg in the following year, 1817, and presented its judgment about the financial resources and morality of each
applicant.[27] Strasbourg was in a period of severe economic crisis, which the
Conseil blamed largely on uncontrolled immigration: "We repeat on all
possible occasions that the suppression of workshops, however deplorable
it was, has not done as much harm to the city as the willy-nilly, unre-
strained admission of foreigners to the number of its citizens."[28] The
Prud'hommes thus sought to reject a large number of demands for *admission à domicile*. More prosperous trades, such as jewelers, presented no
problems. But joiners, shoemakers, weavers, tailors, and locksmiths were
all overcrowded occupations.[29] While it was easy to dismiss applicants like
the mason Denzel, who "has no money, has a very bad reputation, and has
been guilty of numerous acts of disloyalty to master masons," reputation
and skill did not suffice to separate deserving candidates from those whose
requests had to be rejected.[30]

Nor, perhaps surprisingly, did the Conseil favor particular national origins; indeed its report made no mention of applicants' ethnicity, even
though several were natives of Prussia, a nation that had been at war with
France during much of the Napoleonic era.[31] Instead, the Prud'hommes
concluded that the deciding factor often had to be an immigrant's marriage
to a native French woman, especially if she was also a native of Strasbourg.
Its list of acceptable candidates regularly noted that petitioners had married
"une strasbourgeoise" or "une française," while those rejected were often
unmarried or married to a foreign woman—although sometimes the Conseil added further disqualifications. Thus, the buttonmaker Hack was
described as a "foreigner, married to a foreign woman, and a servant who
never exercised his profession and who, since receiving a patent, has never
paid the charges of his profession." In a few cases the Conseil did reject
men whose wives were French but not from Strasbourg, but its judgments
in these cases were often overridden by city government. For example, the
locksmith Spitzbart, rejected by the Prud'hommes because he "has little
money and his wife is not from Strasbourg," was granted civil rights in
France the next year.[32]

However, the Conseil de Prud'hommes referred to petitioners' marriages
with reluctance even when it considered them favorably. The case of an

impoverished tailor who had obtained a patent in 1815 against the Conseil's wishes because his wife was from Strasbourg led it to a more general proclamation. The Conseil condemned the prevailing belief that marriage to a French woman—particularly but not exclusively a locally born woman—transformed a foreigner's status by giving him civil rights in the kingdom:

> Almost all foreigners who intend to settle in Strasbourg begin by marrying, or sometimes also by having children before marriage in the hopes of using them as a title for their *admission* [*à domicile*]. It would undoubtedly be desirable to prevent such unions from being contracted legally, but since the laws do not allow that, it would at least be useful and necessary to announce with maximum publicity that marriage gives no right to admission or to the patent, that a woman follows her husband's condition, and that a French woman and even a native of Strasbourg, far from transferring a right to be a bourgeois [of Strasbourg] and patentholder to her husband, risks being obliged to leave the city with her husband.[33]

The Conseil also noted that the law that a woman followed her husband's citizenship status meant that not only did French women run the risk of being deported with their foreign husbands, but that even women who were allowed to remain in France could no longer purchase a patent themselves or exercise the civil rights belonging to French citizens. The Prud'hommes spelled out this logic when considering the case of the blacksmith Fiala; it proclaimed that he would "do very well to continue to work as a journeyman; his wife is not a native of Strasbourg and has no more right than he does to take a patent, because in marrying a foreigner she must follow the condition of her husband."[34]

The registers of those *admis à domicile* in Strasbourg during the Restoration reveal that the vast majority were men married to French women.[35] But although local elites and authorities themselves accorded certain rights of French citizenship to foreigners on the basis of their marriages, they remained profoundly frustrated with being forced to use this criterion. Master artisans and city officials continued to complain that foreigners gained practical and legal citizenship rights through their alliances with French women. The Strasbourg Conseil des Prud'hommes phrased this view bluntly in an 1820 letter to the prefect of the department. The Conseil complained again about "clandestine" industry and argued that because article 13 of the Civil Code established that only foreigners *admis à domicile* were entitled to civil rights in France, no immigrant who was not formally granted *admission à domicile* could "exercise an industry or acquire a patent, since these are civil rights." But foreigners, "most often fathers of families before marriage, introduce themselves into French families by seduction, and imagine that they acquire the *droits de cité* by dishonoring our daughters."[36]

Local authorities in Strasbourg were not the only ones to bewail the fact that foreign workers acquired the right to work for themselves and potential citizenship status in France through their liaisons with native French women. Master artisans in nearby towns lodged similar complaints. For example, in 1826 the master knitters and bonnetmakers of Barr complained about six immigrants in their town—two from Baden and four from Württemburg—and, more generally, about a "crowd of foreigners" who "ruin the industry of fathers of French families." They linked this new invasion to wartime intrusions, partly rewriting Napoleonic history in the process: "After so many sacrifices to their country [*la patrie*], the French will be reduced to seeing their industry ruined by natives of Baden, Württemburg, Bavaria, and Austria, who have shot us, bombarded our cities, pillaged and set fire to our countryside."[37]

The knitters complained that French men and women were prevented from living in German territories, while German immigrants settled blithely in France. Their petition reveals both a general perception that a "foreigner" ceased to be one in marrying a French woman and their awareness that this policy contradicted the laws on national citizenship. They explicitly drew upon the Civil Code to refute the idea that foreigners could gain citizenship rights in France through marrying French women:

> If someone said that a foreigner ceases to be one in marrying a French woman, we would respond with article 13 of the Civil Code, *that a foreigner can establish his domicile in France only with the authorization of the government,* and article 19 of the same code, which states that a French woman who marries a foreigner follows her husband's condition, which means that instead of conferring the quality of French citizen on him, she herself becomes a foreigner.[38]

Unlike many of their contemporaries, who depicted French women as virtuous beings seduced—and usually abandoned—by their "foreign" lovers, the knitters also cast aspersions on the loyalties of women who would stoop to marrying immigrants: "And what kind of women would marry these foreigners lacking in everything? Their choice can fall on only the last class of people, who have left their homelands [*pays*] only because they had no other means of existence or even because they were chased out; they are drawn to France only because of the lure of communal advantages and the absence of corporations."[39]

The mayor of Barr responded to the knitters' petition by condemning the personal animosity behind their protest. He insisted that it was necessary to distinguish recent immigrants from those who had been established in France for decades. However, if the latter did not regulate their situation within three months, they should be allowed to work not as masters, but only as journeymen in the employ of others. The mayor further suggested temporarily suspending the celebration of marriages between foreigners and French citizens, emphasizing the practical problems of conflicting international policies:

a French woman who marries a foreigner follows the condition of her husband. It is clear from certificates delivered by the authorities of foreign countries that young men who settle in France will not be allowed to return to their native countries and exercise the *droits de cité* there, unless they return alone and without wives; these latter can never hope to obtain the same favor. In this light, it is in the interest of French families not to attach themselves to a foreigner until he has his papers in order.[40]

Citizenship, Concubinage, and *Avantages Communaux*

Such practical complications were widespread. Beginning in the 1820s, immigrants throughout France, especially those from Switzerland and various German states, were often caught between the policies and whims of two governments, as Katherine Lynch and others have shown.[41] Immigrant men often lost their rights in their home countries if they married in France without formal permission from the governments of their native countries; their children were also deprived of the possibility of citizenship rights in their fathers' homelands. But as representatives of the state relentlessly, if often ineffectively, proclaimed, immigrant men did not gain French citizenship in France by marrying, even if they wed a native French woman. Moreover, the governments of France and of an immigrant's home country often sought different papers before approving requests either for marriage or for citizenship rights. The result was sometimes a vicious circle in which men and women had to get documents from one side in order to get papers from the second side in order to get the first set of papers.

Conflicting international regulations frustrated both authorities and workers in Strasbourg and elsewhere in the Department of Bas Rhin. But they were far more problematic in the neighboring Department of Haut Rhin. During the Napoleonic period, the department was primarily rural and easily capable of absorbing migrants; by the late 1820s, it was industrializing rapidly and being flooded with thousands of German and Swiss workers.[42] Controlling this new class of industrial workers created major problems for local authorities, especially as Alsatian localities were required to provide for the poor who settled there. In this context, the practical and legal relationships between family and national citizenship relations became especially controversial in three situations: "concubinage," or relationships between unmarried couples; the distribution of key rural privileges, or *avantages communaux;* and threats of expulsion.

Couples for whom marriage was difficult or expensive to arrange often lived together in "concubinage," often with the hope of marrying and becoming French citizens. Such liaisons were not a new phenomenon in Alsace, and in the first few years of the nineteenth century administrators often responded favorably to such requests. For example, in Year IX (1800–01), the tailor Sauer presented his desire to legitimize his two children as one of the strongest reasons why the mayor of Strasbourg should grant him civil rights in France; he was in fact *admis*. Indeed, local authorities sometimes made marriage a prerequisite for the *admission à domicile* of foreigners with children born out of wedlock in France. Thus, in the same year the municipal council of Molsheim, a town on the outskirts of Strasbourg, declared that it would approve the petition of an Austrian deserter, employed as a servant to a local haberdasher, only on the condition that he marry a fellow servant whom he had made pregnant.[43]

Authorities throughout Alsace became frustrated with this situation, even as they found themselves granting rights to newcomers with French partners and French-born children. By the later 1820s, calling attention to children born out of wedlock was a dangerous strategy for immigrants, especially in Haut Rhin. Living with someone outside of marriage was anathema to the moralizing Catholic regime of the Restoration. Local officials, priests, and neighbors sought to discredit men and women living together with constant references to the "scandal" they caused.[44] The complaint of the mayor of the small town of Ottensheim was typical; he railed against one immigrant who "lives publicly in concubinage and causes so much scandal that the curé of the parish has great difficulty in calming the deep impressions that this vicious man has made in the hearts of children, who recount in public what they have seen him commit with his accomplice. . . . In a word, he is the terror of all the inhabitants."[45] Immigrant workers accused of immorality were regularly driven out of France, especially the newly industrializing center of Mulhouse. References to their French partners and children were at least as likely to result in their expulsion as in their legal integration into France.[46]

Nonetheless, immigrants continued to believe that they could acquire both the titles and rights of French citizenship through their liaisons with French women, especially if they succeeded in marrying. Many local administrators shared this belief. For example, when the prefect of Haut Rhin demanded an accounting of all foreigners in his department in 1821, the mayor of Rouffbach responded with a list of "thirty-five fathers of family, who believed themselves *admis à domicile* in France, who have long supposed themselves able to exercise the rights of French citizen, and whose children were born in France." These men now feared that they might be considered "still to be foreigners in all the force of the term." The mayor presented a comprehensive list of the dates of their marriages to French women. The prefect responded impatiently that "it is not the date of their marriage but of their residence and declaration that serves to fix the position of the foreigners in relation to civil and political rights."[47]

Whether women could transfer any of the rights—if not the formal title—of French citizenship to their foreign-born spouses or companions was particularly disputed in two cases: entitlement to *avantages communaux* and the right or obligation to remain on French territory. In areas that traditionally had few artisans, like the Department of Haut Rhin, entitlement to the patent was not a particularly important point of controversy.[48] Instead, authorities tried to link French citizenship to *avantages communaux*, local rights often essential to everyday existence, such as gathering firewood and grazing animals on common lands. During the 1820s such rights became an important site of contention not only in Alsace, but also in other northern and eastern frontier departments, like Moselle, which bordered Luxembourg, and Ain, near Switzerland.[49]

Linking *avantages communaux* to national citizenship was not a new strategy. Men and women had done so periodically throughout the Revolution. For example, Henry, *électeur du district de Montmédy*, proposed in 1793 that those who did not marry or adopt children within a certain time frame should be legally stripped of the "quality of citizen," including both political rights, such as the right to vote and hold office, and civil rights, such as *avantages communaux*.[50] Conversely, the law of June 10, 1793, which gave an equal right to *biens communaux* to all inhabitants of a commune regardless of their sex, may have contributed to the sense that women had a political voice in contemporary debates over the new Constitution.

Napoleonic administrators had also tried to limit entitlement to *avantages communaux*, but had done so not by linking them to citizenship, but rather by separating them from the procedures concerning French citizenship. For example, in Year XII (1803) the subprefect of Porrentruie contended that the status of French citizen and the enjoyment of local rights—particularly those of access to *forêts* and *pâturage*—had been traditionally conflated: "entitlement to these properties was confused with that of the rights of citizen or bourgeois." He argued that the Revolution had changed the meaning of "citizen," politicizing the term and making it dependent on national laws rather than on a status that could be locally inherited or purchased. Local property rights were separate from those of French citizenship. The subprefect insisted that he would not propose financial or similar qualifications "for political rights in France, but such rights can easily be separated from those that concern *biens communaux*, and nothing interferes with the possibility that a person be deprived of these goods and still enjoy all the advantages attached to the quality of citizen." The minister of the interior ultimately rejected his proposal, contending that "the Constitution has fixed the conditions to be fulfilled to become a French citizen and to exercise the rights of citizenship."[51]

By the 1820s, prefects in frontier departments had adopted a strategy opposite to that of the Porrentruie subprefect: they led several campaigns to limit *avantages communaux* to French citizens or foreigners who had not only been granted civil rights in France but had been fully naturalized in France. They argued that because an 1818 law on conscription freed non-naturalized foreigners from military service in France—a special status that many immigrants welcomed—immigrants who shirked the duties of French citizenship should not be entitled to the privileges of citizenship, the most concrete forms of which were local rights. They thus tried to institute measures that not only would prevent new immigrants from being able to enjoy *avantages communaux,* but would also be applied retroactively.[52]

In Haut Rhin, the prefect Puymaigre decreed in July 1821 that only naturalized foreigners should be allowed to enjoy *avantages communaux.* Immigrant men and their families living in the department protested the loss of rights that they had often enjoyed for years. They pointed to long residence in France and their integration into the social and economic life of the commune in which they resided, the taxes and other charges that they had dutifully paid, and their deeply held conviction that they were "French." In a few cases, they pleaded that they had been kept ignorant of the laws regulating national citizenship in France and sincerely believed that they done all required of them. The petition for the day worker Schruck thus proclaimed that "today he had the misfortune to lose his portion [of communal rights] for not having naturalized; he did not know he needed to do so, since he could not read or write and was left alone in his ineptitude."[53]

But immigrants also protested their deprivation on the grounds that *avantages communaux* were rights that their wives held as native citizens of a commune and of France, or that foreign men had legitimately acquired through their marriages to French women. For example, Rusch, a Bavarian-born carpenter, complained in 1817 that the mayor of his town wanted to deprive him of *avantages communaux* and referred to his marriage as proof of his rights: "The petitioner does not believe that, having married a French woman, he can be considered as lacking rights to gather firewood in the common."[54] Similarly, Eberwein, master shoemaker in Hautmanschwiller, protested the possibility that he and his wife might be stripped of the right to gather firewood because of his foreign origins. He contended that marriage had led him to participate in the rights and obligations shared by all inhabitants of the village: "During the eight years that he has been married to the widow Zoller, he has constantly shared in the advantages that other bourgeois and property owners of this commune have enjoyed; as such he was continually required to pay all the costs of war, and ordinary and extraordinary levies on the commune," as well as all taxes. Eberwein went on to argue that, regardless of his own status, his wife was a native of the village who was entitled to rights through her birth and through her first marriage to a native Frenchman. He pleaded for the prefect to "order the mayor of Hautmaschwiller to give him or his wife, under whatever denomination he likes, the right to gather firewood in 1822, as has been attributed to other inhabitants of the commune."[55]

Rusch was eventually granted formal *admission à domicile,* probably because his request predated the department-wide campaign in the 1820s to limit *avantages communaux* to naturalized foreigners. But the response given to Eberheim was the more common one. He was told that as a foreigner, he was not entitled to the rights of French citizenship, and that his wife had lost her own titles to such rights when she married him. In a variation of the familiar refrain, the prefect of Haut Rhin proclaimed:

> Considering that in principle the right to share in *biens communaux* in France and to participate in the distribution of firewood belongs only to French citizens . . . neither his residence of twenty years nor his marriage to a French woman gives him this quality [of French citizen] . . . and on the contrary, following the terms of article 17 of the Code Civil stating that a woman who marries a foreigner follows the condition of her husband, she herself has lost civil rights in France in marrying the petitioner, whose request is not founded.[56]

Even when native French spouses of immigrant men became widows, their status remained in question. The Napoleonic Code allowed widows to "recover" their original status, but local and regional authorities often believed that such women had permanently forfeited their rights in France. For example, on July 20, 1821, the mayor of Niederhangau asked the prefect of Haut Rhin what to do about two such women in his community. The prefect contended that the women were still technically foreigners. However, he decided that they were entitled to some consideration because they had originally been French. He advocated allowing them to continue in the rights they had held, but "in continuing to allow them to enjoy the rights that they have held until now, you should tell them that have been granted an exception and that if the law were applied strictly, they could be deprived of *avantages communaux*."[57]

The relationships between foreign-born men and native French women were controversial in their effects not only on citizenship rights in France, but also on deciding who could, and should, remain on French territory. Unlike revolutionary laws on emigration or the 1811 Napoleonic laws on naturalizing outside France or serving a foreign sovereign, many Restoration decrees were more concerned with clarifying who could be expelled from the kingdom than with compelling French men and women to remain in their native land.

However, expelling immigrants often risked undermining family bonds. As the mayor of Barr noted, German and Swiss regulations stipulated that young men who settled in France could return as citizens to their homeland only if they left their wives in France. Restoration authorities argued that the fact that a foreign man could abandon his family in France or that his family could be legally prevented from following him into his home country was one of the strongest reasons for preventing marriages between foreign men and French women. In 1828 the chief prosecutor of the royal court of Colmar warned local administrators against approving marriages between French women and German or Swiss immigrants because "officials risk giving an uncertain status to a French woman and her children. In every case, these bonds can be broken by the sole will of the husband, since in returning to his country he would have them pronounced null by the judges of the conjugal domicile."[58]

The prosecutor's circular responded not only to a practical problem but also to an ideological one. The contract between spouses was supposedly inviolable. Following the abolition of divorce in 1816, neither men nor women were to be able to break the legal bonds of marriage except by death, while the Napoleonic Code obligated a woman to follow her husband wherever he chose to live. The discrepancy between postrevolutionary French laws on citizenship and those of Swiss and German countries, which were still governed by older definitions of local citizenship rights and obligations, gave one partner the freedom to place national bonds before familial ones after marriage. But this was an ability now repudiated by the French state. However much early revolutionary laws may have obliged men and women to choose duty to the country over loyalty to the family, the possibility that a man could break familial ties merely by crossing a frontier now appeared reprehensible.

Marriage was a factor in debating not only whether immigrant men would or could voluntarily abandon their families in French territory, but also whether they could be forced to leave France against their will. Foreigners could be expelled from the kingdom for a variety of causes, such as concubinage, vagabondage, or simply not having their papers in order.[59] Besides protesting their innocence of specific crimes or misdemeanors, immigrants often referred to their French families. Thus the tailor Heydorffer proclaimed that "the petitioner is father of two children born in France; he is the husband of a French woman, and you want to expel him from French soil! What would become of his wife and children?"[60] Such bonds could in fact help them. As the mayor of a small town in Haut Rhin wrote to the subprefect in 1825, "usually married to French women, they [immigrants] hold on to their families by this line. . . . it is hard to propose the expulsion of an individual who believes himself to be a French citizen and who may not be received in his country."[61]

Indeed, French-born women repeatedly emphasized their own "Frenchness" over their spouse's official "foreignness." They contended that their membership in the French nation had not disappeared with their marriages to immigrants, and should instead affect their husbands' status. The case of Monsieur and Madame Vigezzy demonstrates this phenomenon particularly vividly. M. Vigezzy was a Lyonnais printer who came to trial in the early 1820s for selling obscene books and publicly displaying seditious objects. Acquitted of the charges, he was nonetheless expelled as a foreigner who did not have his papers in order. His French-born wife was tried soon afterward on the same charge of selling subversive images and texts.

She was similarly acquitted but was nevertheless ordered to follow her husband to Lombardy.

Mme. Vigezzy then pleaded with the authorities to rescind these orders. She presented herself as deeply rooted in France, implying that her familial and social standing should override the fact that her husband was foreign-born. She explained her position thus: "My husband, as an Italian, was ordered to leave France, and for having married a foreigner, I find myself enveloped in his exile, forced to abandon my country, my father, my mother, a considerable establishment that is my fortune, and the future of my child." A few lines later she reiterated that "all my relatives are French; in their name and that of my daughter, I ask you to consider my request."[62]

Mme. Vigezzy's request was taken seriously. Neighbors and local authorities not only collaborated to allow her to stay but also permitted her husband to return clandestinely and intervened on her behalf with the Haute Police. Her story clearly indicates that laws regarding French national citizenship were in fact flexible in practice, and that examining formal political and legal structures reveals only a part of the story. Although citizenship was formally defined by the status of the *paterfamilias*, a woman's lived familial connections could be as important as the legal status her husband passed on to his children.

Conclusion

The specific circumstances of Restoration Alsace made marriages between natives and "foreigners" particularly common and controversial, especially in the eyes of officials trying to negotiate both the consequences of industrialization and the growing discrepancies between French practices and those of neighboring Swiss and German states. Authorities who lauded the reinforced rights of the *paterfamilias* in other circumstances were often wary of immigrant fathers who came primarily from working classes and seemed to threaten political and social order. Yet their complaints point to a more widespread tension. In the wake of Revolution and empire, women were largely excluded from the legal categories of national citizenship, while for men, citizenship bonds had been made qualitatively different from family bonds. The social practices of integration implicitly undermined and challenged both of these developments. The postrevolutionary order was far less coherent than many of the legislators and politicians of the new regime wanted to believe.

Conclusion: Reversals and Lasting Contradictions

A Return to the Old Regime?

On first glance, structures of family and national belonging during the Restoration monarchy look remarkably similar to those of the Old Regime. Contending that there were fundamental links between the authority of the *paterfamilias* and the authority of the king, the Bourbons resurrected old metaphors of the king as "father" of the French nation. Legislators went beyond the Napoleonic Civil Code to limit dependents' ability to challenge the head of the household, and they prevented both men and women from easily dissolving or changing familial bonds. They revived prerevolutionary terms to distinguish French from foreigners and shaped laws on national citizenship according to Old Regime models of sovereign and subject.

Louis XVIII and Charles X regularly portrayed themselves as the fathers of the French people, contrasting the familial nature of their reign to Napoleon's illegitimate rule.[1] The favorite hymn of official ceremonies was "Where can one be better than in the breast of one's family?"[2] References to the *grande famille* of the nation and the paternal nature of the monarchy resonated throughout Restoration discourse, including that on national citizenship. When the legislators of the First Restoration debated what status should be accorded to people who had been part of the Napoleonic empire but had been born or lived in territories that were no longer part of France after 1814, they emphasized the king's paternal concern.[3] Groups and individuals petitioning for membership in the French nation adopted similar language. Proponents of the reunion of Belgium and France in 1814 declared their "love for their ancient mother country, their respect for your virtues, their faith in your paternal administration."[4] Individuals seeking naturalization similarly proclaimed their loyalties to the "Father of the French" throughout the Restoration, as certain of their predecessors had done during the Old Regime and the later Napoleonic era. The 1814 petition of Paul Francesony, an Italian immigrant in Marseilles, was typical in this respect: he proclaimed that he wanted to "end his days in the service of France, under a legitimate and paternal regime . . . [he] is an orphan and nothing now attaches him to Italy; with all his heart he desires to possess the title of French and of loyal subject of a just and benevolent king."[5]

Both the mechanisms and the language controlling national citizenship also echoed prerevolutionary structures. As we have seen, the edict of June 3, 1814, created *grande naturalisation,* a procedure that not only made naturalization through ordinary channels an insufficient qualification for holding office in France but also emphasized service to the French state—and particularly, as before the Revolution, service to the royal family.[6] The other major law of the Restoration on national citizenship—that of October 14, 1814—also drew on Old Regime principles. The government resolved the question of what status to accord to those who had been considered French during the Napoleonic empire by using essentially the same solution that had been applied to territories taken from France by prerevolutionary fortunes of war. Inhabitants of formerly French territories were not considered French if they remained in their homelands after 1814. However, if they had come to France during the time that their homeland was united to France, or moved promptly after its severance to the territory of "ancienne France," their integration as French citizens would be expedited.[7] Varnier and Dietrich-Chénel have contended that "these two laws mark a partial return to the law of the Old Regime, both in spirit, by making new French citizens ineligible [for office], and in its letter, by recourse to the term 'lettres de déclaration de naturalité.'"[8] Indeed, the Restoration government revived not only this expression but also other Old Regime terms for distinguishing "French" from "foreign," including *naturel français,* or *naturel du pays,* and *régnicole.* Men and women had occasionally continued to use such expressions even during the height of the radical Revolution, but they had often substituted the revolutionary neologism *républicole* or, more commonly, used *citoyen* as both a political and a juridical term. Napoleonic administrators gradually revived *régnicole.* But Restoration legislators, administrators, and politicians employed the expression constantly, especially when they sought to contrast the rights of ordinary French citizens—*régnicoles*—to those of foreigners, or *étrangers.*

In many ways, the legal basis of family bonds during the Restoration resembled that of the Old Regime. Napoleonic legislators had reversed many of the dramatic changes in family law introduced during the Revolution; the Restoration government sought to go further and to discredit the idea consecrated in revolutionary law that voluntary, individual, and dissoluble contracts formed the basis of family relationships.[9] Authorities and propagandists emphasized that marriage was not only a civil contract, as the 1791 constitution had proclaimed, but also a religious bond. The makers of the Civil Code had limited divorce, making it especially difficult for women to obtain; the Restoration government abolished it completely in 1816. As before the Revolution, physical separation and separation of property (*séparation de corps* and *séparation de biens*) were the only ways for women and men to distance themselves legally from their spouses.[10] Napoleonic legislators had overturned the right of illegitimate children to inherit equally with those born to married couples, curtailed the circumstances in which people could adopt, and bolstered paternal and marital authority in the home. Restoration leaders built on these changes, and attempted to go beyond the Civil Code in restoring paternal authority to its previous glory. In short, the Bourbon kings appeared to preside over a polity that had succeeded in restoring national and domestic bonds as they had existed before the upheavals of the Revolution.

A Limited Restoration

But on closer inspection, things look very different. The mechanisms for becoming or ceasing to be a French citizen had changed dramatically. During the Old Regime, naturalization was automatic if petitioners followed procedures correctly; now men and women had to petition first for *admission à domicile,* then for naturalization, and were scarcely assured that the government would approve their requests. While women naturalized regularly during the Old Regime, they did so rarely in the new order. In frontier regions like Alsace, Restoration authorities refused localities the possibility of returning to prerevolutionary independence in regulating *admission à domicile,* just as they blocked the revival of the eighteenth-century system of artisanal guilds.

Similarly, despite the resurgence of the term *régnicole,* both *citoyen* and *citoyenne* remained potent words, and ones that could sometimes still conflate civic and civil aspects of national belonging. At the same time, a new word, "nationality" (*nationalité*), appeared on the political scene.[11] Even when reviving Old Regime policies and formulas, Restoration leaders themselves often used new terms and ideas. In debating the October 1814 law, for example, legislators considered not only how certain foreigners could obtain *lettres de déclaration de naturalité* but also when they would exercise the rights of French citizens (*jouir des droits de citoyen français*). They invoked not only royal precedents but also revolutionary concepts of territorial and political belonging and ideas about collective "social contracts," debating whether inhabitants of certain countries incorporated into the Empire might have legitimately expressed their desire to be part of France instead of simply submitting to conquest.[12]

Indeed, changes were not limited to the formal procedures regulating citizenship or the vocabulary for discussing membership in the nation. The apparent similarities in the pre- and postrevolutionary states mask both the immense upheavals that took place between the destruction of one monarchy and the consolidation of another, and a series of enduring contradictions.

Upheavals and Lasting Changes

The celebration of the king as father of the nation concealed a new sense that domestic bonds were qualitatively different from other social contracts, a distinction that fully emerged only over the course of the Revolution and early nineteenth century. Though early revolutionaries attempted to restructure society and politics on very different grounds from their predecessors in the Old Regime, they still saw family and nation as fundamentally intertwined. The Jacobin government of 1793 and 1794 brought this model of interconnected domestic and political relationships to its zenith as it mandated personal relationships with the state and extolled the great family of the nation. In the wake of the Terror, those in authority slowly began to portray families, rather than abstract rights-bearing individuals, as the fundamental units of the nation. They did so partly in an effort to rebuild social order after a period of chaos and violence, associating the abuses of the Terror with the domestic disruption it had caused. They also sought to remove the ambiguities of earlier measures, defining the citizen both more clearly and more narrowly. The Restoration metaphor of the nation as a great family corresponded more to this emerging model of the nation as a loose conglomeration of separate families than to one of a large family connected by the sovereign's recognition of subjects as children or by family bonds between newcomers and outsiders.

Both the relative importance of familial and citizenship bonds and the specific significance of national citizenship for each sex also changed. Beginning in 1789, men, and especially women, faced unprecedented conflicts between family and *patrie*. These conflicts were particularly pronounced when individuals risked losing rights in France because of someone else's actions or status or when duty to the nation directly contradicted duty to the family. Revolutionaries initially resolved such conflicts by emphasizing the power and centrality of the state. Gender differences, legal subordination in the family, and marriage to a foreigner were all inadequate excuses for disloyalty to the nation. Yet as authorities increasingly emphasized the legitimacy of *puissance paternelle* and *puissance maritale* in the late revolutionary and Napoleonic periods, they also became increasingly wary of requiring either dependents within the household or those deemed incapable of full citizenship to choose between family and *patrie*. Most Napoleonic legislators opposed forcing—or even permitting—married women to decide between the ties that bound them to a spouse and their rights or obligations as French women. This was one of the reasons why lawmakers agonized over the consequences of the civil death of the head of the household and dismissed the solution of allowing a woman to decide whether to remain with her condemned husband or divorce him.

Legislators' growing wariness of such choices did not completely preclude the possibility that both women and men could make critical decisions about their familial and national identities. Indeed, nineteenth-century law-makers and administrators—as well as ordinary men and women—viewed a woman's marriage as a voluntary allegiance with the national community represented by her spouse. For example, the liberal jurist B. J. Legat proclaimed in 1832 that

> a French woman who marries a foreigner, and who must therefore follow him outside of France, consents to abandon her own country and adopt her husband's country that also becomes that of her children. She knew that she would follow her husband's condition; how can she protest? She voluntarily preferred individual affection to that of her country.[13]

But if a woman could choose between "individual affection" and "her country," there was now only one moment of choice: that of marriage itself. Once made, it could not be undone. Marriage, moreover, was assumed to be a free contract, even when made under parental influence. Women had had some hope of persuading the Jacobin state to see their marriages as invalid social contracts because their alliances had been coerced. By the Napoleonic period, and especially by the Restoration, such pleas often fell on deaf ears. This is particularly clear in the case of couples who had married during the Napoleonic era so that the man might avoid conscription, and who found themselves faced with the prospect of permanent union following the 1816 abolition of divorce. They begged the Restoration state to see their marriages not only as religiously invalid, but also as dictated by circumstances and parental folly.[14] The government refused to allow them to end their unions. Marriage was a permanent bond, as it had been during the Old Regime. But unlike during the Old Regime, it was a bond that determined citizenship status—for women, but, at least officially, not for men.

The title of "French citizen" and its variants also had different implications and consequences for men and women. One of the most volatile aspects of defining national citizenship for both sexes was the infusion of prerevolutionary categories of the *qualité de français* with revolutionary concepts of political citizenship. This infusion was often unintentional; lawmakers did not anticipate the possible consequences or contested interpretations of their measures, and they often tried to eliminate controversial ambiguities when they became apparent. Yet it was nonetheless a powerful combination. As many historians have noted, it could imply far more rights for women than had Old Regime titles of membership in the French kingdom. It also implied more obligations. The radical Revolution took certain aspects of both to unprecedented heights. Its champions proclaimed the contractual logic of liberty and equality for both sexes and mandated both men's and women's devotion to the state even as the violence of the Terror curtailed political rights, particularly for women.

Authorities after 1794 increasingly attempted to separate legal nationality from political citizenship and to limit the term "citizen" to men. In so doing, lawmakers and officials confronted the legacies of earlier measures and categories but could not completely control them. Indeed, nineteenth- and twentieth-century activists for women's rights would continue to seize upon the terms *citoyenne* and *citoyenne française* precisely because of their sustained potency. Even in very different revolutionary and postrevolutionary regimes, membership in a national community could suggest a connection to the political basis of that community. But as few historians have noted, the persistent conflation of national and political citizenship was double-edged. Whereas some argued for rights or obligations for women on the basis of their implicit participation in the national polity, others sought to defend specific women's rights on the grounds that Frenchness and citizenship were separate. The latter argument was especially common in debates over certain civil rights, such as the ability of émigrée women to return home or the ability of women abroad to retain property in France because of their political "nullity."

The Napoleonic regime codified a formal distinction between civil rights associated with the *qualité de français* and political rights. Yet in making naturalization separate from *admission à domicile* and associating it with political rights, it also reintroduced a certain confusion between juridical nationality and political citizenship. This combination could function to distance women not only from political rights but also from the very mechanisms of becoming or ceasing to be a member of the French nation. However, while this exclusion was clearly shaped by the events of the Revolution, it took place primarily not during the Revolution itself, but during the Napoleonic era. The makers of the Civil Code forced a woman to adopt her husband's national status and place of residence. During the Napoleonic empire, women were explicitly excluded from laws pertaining to the loss of French citizenship, told that they could not naturalize because naturalization conferred political rights that did not belong to women, and, if engaged to marry French men, distanced them even from intermediary stages of citizenship that granted civil but not political rights in France. Their relationship with the state was officially no longer a direct relationship as citizens or would-be citizens, but was instead limited because of their sex and mediated through their marriages.

For men, an identity as actual or potential head of household was also bound up with evolutions in the nature of national citizenship. From the Old Regime through the most radical stages of the Revolution and into the Restoration, men and women praised marriage and parenthood as institutions for encouraging civic virtue. The moderate revolutionary Nicolas de Bonneville expressed a common sentiment in 1792: "the law intends that the citizen should be a father." The Declaration of the Rights of Man in Year III (1795) proclaimed that "no one is a good citizen if he is not also a good son, father, and husband." In the opening discourse of the Civil Code, Portalis echoed this claim directly, declaring that "it is by the small country [*patrie*] that one becomes attached to the large one; it is good fathers, husbands, and sons who make good citizens."[15]

Yet the motives behind the equation of good fathers and good citizens changed by the later 1790s and early nineteenth century. In part, the equation of citizen and father became more rigid. Bonneville may have identified the two, but he also contended that "marriage is a social bond that unites the citizen to the *Patrie* and the *Patrie* to the citizen," proposed identical marriage vows for each partner, and championed divorce.[16] Hostility to celibacy during the radical Revolution was motivated in part by the belief that both bachelors and spinsters were parasitic outsiders in the great family of the nation. In contrast, later paeans to the family and the *père de famille* were often motivated by the conviction that social order depended on reinforcing family bonds.

The equation of father and political citizen implied the equation of "father" and "French." Yet if the relationships between juridical and political citizenship were vexed for women, the connection between Frenchness and citizenship was also complicated for men. Legislators and administrators repeatedly debated whether only individual French citizens—as opposed to the state or to men without full national citizenship in France—could exercise rights over dependents in the family. Authorities faced a quandary when relating paternal and marital rights to national citizenship. If an immigrant could provide for a family, his marriage to a French woman was often highly desirable; it transformed him from a wanderer into a respectable *père de famille*. But marriage to a French woman could not legally help a foreign man to become French, because it threatened the primacy of the head of the household. The difficulties of authorities, especially during the Restoration, were compounded because the men who prevailed upon their liaisons with French women to procure themselves civil rights in France, rather than on their personal connections to the state, were often from the working class and thus dangerous in the eyes of the monarchy. Such men, caught between the bureaucratic demands of different national governments, often became fathers before becoming husbands—a situation that scarcely endeared them to the moralistic Restoration state. The government was torn between accepting that marriages should or at least did procure outsiders rights in France and reasserting the principles of the Civil Code.

Embedded Contradictions

In all the cases that we have examined, the application of the laws on national citizenship presented the state with dilemmas that might have been solved logically. But in many cases, enforcing one standard meant violating another principle that other representatives of the state—often even the same people—held dear. Thus, in purging the body politic of nobles and enemy foreigners, the government of the radical Revolution was caught between its desire to establish clear social divisions, in which families formed unchanging social units, and a belief in the importance of voluntary, active adhesion in the contracts both of kinship and of citizenship. Similarly, the difficulties of applying laws on emigration led officials and contemporary observers to confront their conflicting beliefs that emigration was a crime for all who left French territory, that membership in the French nation had a different significance for men and women, and that a married woman's status was, and should be, subordinated to her husband's. Despite their goal of establishing a systematic law code that would end the contradictions between citizenship and family that the Revolution had bequeathed them, even the makers of the Civil Code found themselves struggling with competing convictions that the *qualité de français* was an individual title and that the status of the *père de famille* should determine the legal condition of dependents.

None of the governments of the revolutionary and postrevolutionary eras could establish permanent solutions to conflicts between family and citizenship rights. Although evolutions in family and citizenship rights were intimately bound with the tumultuous series of political regimes in the late eighteenth and early nineteenth centuries, competing models of family and citizenship rights cannot be mapped simply onto specific regimes. Nor do they correspond neatly to particular political persuasions or specific groups within the state. Instead, representatives of the state struggled to understand and cope with the transformations wrought by earlier governments—including earlier laws on family and national citizenship. Authorities thus found themselves responding to the often unintentional or unforeseen consequences of their own categories. Contradictions between the rights and duties associated with the titles of "French citizen" and those associated with men's and women's legal status within the family often became apparent only when laws were applied, or when ordinary people pushed the state to clarify how new categories and laws actually pertained to them. But perhaps most important, contradictions between individual national citizenship and family status were built into the very fabric of the New Regime.

Long-Term Repercussions

Conflicts between individual titles of national citizenship and men's and women's status in the family would punctuate the nineteenth century, becoming subjects of great public debate in the Third Republic. In the decades immediately following 1830, they were often overshadowed by the issue of immigrants' military service. Immigrants often sought the status of *admis à domicile* in France but balked at becoming full French citizens, since, following an 1818 law, naturalization would make them subject to conscription. Local authorities responded to this situation in the 1820s by attempting to limit key local rights to native French men and women and to naturalized foreigners. They would try this solution in different forms until the central legislature extended the principle of *jus soli* in 1851 and in the 1880s to encompass children born on French soil of foreign parents.[17]

Indeed, contradictions between family and citizenship rights during the July Monarchy and Second Republic and Empire were often of pressing concern only to immigrants themselves, to border officials concerned with the nightmarish complexity of conflicting international laws on marriage, and to employers and administrators intent on managing working-class populations of immigrants and ending the "scourge" of concubinage.[18] The problem of a woman's national and citizenship status was more urgent in the colonies throughout the nineteenth century, since racial hierarchies explicitly overlaid—and sometimes opposed—"national" differences. Moreover, the status of "subject" survived in the colonies even under a republic; being technically French often guaranteed neither political rights nor full civil rights.[19] The idea that the head of the household should determine a family's national citizenship status was often modified in the colonial context. Colonial leaders often sought to avoid potential conflict by preventing marriages between white Europeans and people of color. The most famous example is Napoleon's edict of Nivôse Year XI (January 1803) forbidding marriages between whites and blacks, shortly before the May 1803 reinstitution of slavery. Even after the second abolition of slavery in 1848, colonial authorities often tried to discourage liaisons between Europeans and subjects.[20] In other cases, colonial governments created anomalies that became increasingly problematic as France's colonial enterprise grew during the Third Republic. For example, in 1848 the French government granted the privileges of French citizens to all Senegalese living in the towns of St.-Louis and Gorée but allowed them to retain customary law in matters of land, inheritance, marriage, and divorce. By the late nineteenth and early twentieth centuries, many Frenchmen objected to the idea that an African with four wives could be a citizen.[21] Similarly, as Ann Stoler points out, the Dutch West Indies adopted a law code based on the Napoleonic Civil Code in 1848 but consciously ignored the principle that a married woman's national status followed that of her husband's. By the late

1880s, however, the authorities there had adopted a patriarchal principle, contending that European women who married natives were not true Europeans and deserved to be deprived of Dutch citizenship.[22]

By the Third Republic, the relationship between family bonds and national citizenship rights would again become a topic of widespread debate in both colonial and metropolitan France. This was in part a practical issue, inspired by specific situations and problems. For example, in the late 1870s the *affaire célèbre* of the Princess Bibesco drew public attention as the courts and press debated whether a woman *separée de corps* from her French husband could naturalize in England without her husband's permission.[23] At the same time the government sought to determine the status of Alsatian women after the 1870 Prussian conquest of Alsace-Lorraine, debating whether a woman necessarily followed her husband's status if he became French or German, and whether she was required to formally declare her choice of nationality.[24] But more general factors contributed to the revival and escalation of public debate. Some of these were specific to the social and political context of the late nineteenth and early twentieth centuries. Waves of immigrants settled in France, while the country's perceived demographic crisis and growing colonial enterprise brought questions of French national citizenship to the forefront of public attention. Amid considerable public fanfare, the government began a major overhaul of the legislation on naturalization; legislative debate on the topic continued episodically from the 1880s through the interwar period.[25] At the same time, feminist activism reemerged as a strong force, and legislators reinstituted divorce in 1884, albeit in a more restricted form than during the Revolution.[26] Debate on nationality had also become international; governments throughout the world considered whether a woman could have a nationality separate from that of her husband, and their decisions influenced discussion in France. In one particularly influential example, the U.S. government reversed its policy on September 22, 1922. Although the United States, like many governments throughout the world, had adopted principles of gender-based nationality based on the Napoleonic Code, now it decided to grant women the right to an independent nationality.[27]

But debates over family and citizenship rights would continue to use many of the same terms and confront many of the conflicting principles first articulated and shaped during the Revolution and in the early nineteenth century. In establishing the welfare state, the Third Republic government struggled with the metaphor of the state as "father" and with the task of defining appropriate relationships along the state, individuals, and families. As Sylvia Schafer has shown, competing impulses were clear when the National Assembly proclaimed in 1889 that civil courts could deprive "morally dangerous" parents of custody of their children. Supporters of the law drew in part on revolutionary ideas of the state as a paternalistic "great family" to justify government intervention in the home. But, like the men and women of the late Revolution and early nineteenth century, they also wanted to build a republic based upon self-regulating "private" families, governed by "respectable fathers."[28]

Like those who stressed the rights and duties of French *citoyennes* during the Revolution, champions of the idea that married women could have a separate citizenship emphasized the nature of membership in the polity. They invoked the possibility, especially after the Naquet Law reinstitutionalized divorce in 1884, that women could, and potentially should, choose between their spouse and their duty to the nation. In response, their opponents would revive arguments emphasizing women's dependency in the household and the dangers of conflict between marital and national authority. As one polemicist wrote, "If a woman could affirm a nationality and an autonomy distinct from her husband, it would threaten marital power; the struggle between the duties that a woman owes to her country with those that she owes her husband would destroy the good harmony of the household."[29]

Proponents of paternal power would initially prevail. In 1889 the National Assembly declared that an individual born in France whose father or mother had been born in France was automatically French. Contemporaries, especially foreigners anxious to preserve their status, protested the threat to *puissance paternelle* implicit in the idea that mothers and fathers could have equal power in determining a child's nationality; the law was changed accordingly in 1893.[30] On August 10, 1927, the French legislature finally proclaimed that a woman could have a nationality independent of her husband's. But not until 1973 would the French government decree that marriage should be considered separately from nationality.[31]

By looking concurrently at changes in national citizenship and family law and examining both law and practice, we can see a series of dramatic evolutions between the fall of the Bastille and the consolidation of a postrevolutionary monarchy. Revolutionaries created unprecedented contradictions between the rights and duties associated with the titles of "French citizen" and those associated with men's and women's legal status within the family. These contradictions were initially resolved by placing duty to the nation above familial bonds; by the time of the Napoleonic Code, this priority was reversed. Even the patriarchal Code, however, could not completely nullify the potential power of women's identity as French citizens or establish an unassailable definition of men's relation to the national community.

In the long run, the upheavals of the revolutionary era had a profound effect in changing the relationships between family and polity and in redefining the relevance of not only political, but also national, citizenship, for both men and women. At the same time, however, women's membership in the French nation remained a potent challenge to hierarchical family relations. This challenge would endure and resonate long after the closing salvos of the French Revolution.

Notes

Introduction

1. Archives Nationales (henceforth A.N.) DIII 238, pièce 82.
2. H. Duveyrier, *Réponse à la consultation faite par M. Hoppé hambourgeois, et signée Portalis, Tronson du Coudray, Muraire, et Cambacérès* (Paris, n.d.).
3. Archives Communales (henceforth A.C.), Strasbourg, Police 48.
4. Rogers Brubaker, *Citizenship and Nationhood in France and Germany* (Cambridge, 1992). An earlier version of Brubaker's arguments appeared in idem, "The French Revolution and the Invention of Citizenship," *French Politics and Society* 7 (1989): 30–9.
5. Gérard Noiriel, "Socio-histoire d'un concept: Les usages du mot nationalité au XIX siècle," *Genèses* 20 (1995): 4–23.
6. Dominique Godineau did not locate a single instance of the word in the electronic collection "Frantext" or in the extensive archives that she consulted; "Femmes en citoyenneté: Pratique et politique," *Annales historiques de la révolution française* no. 300 (1995): 197–207. I have also never encountered the term in contemporary archives.
7. Both Peter Sahlins and Charlotte Wells have argued that "citoyen"—as the opposite of "étranger"—had more significance in early modern France than had been previously acknowledged. See Sahlins, "Fictions of a Catholic France: The Naturalization of Foreigners, 1685–1787," *Representations* 47 (1994): 85–110; idem, *Unnaturally French: Foreign Citizens in the Old Regime and After* (Ithaca, 2004); and Wells, *Law and Citizenship in Early Modern France* (Baltimore, 1995). But Sahlins also emphasizes that no single statute or privilege defined the status of a citizen during the Old Regime, and that the Revolution profoundly transformed the meaning of French citizenship.
8. Gail Bossenga, "Rights and Citizens in the Old Regime," *French Historical Studies* 29, no. 2 (1997): 217–243.
9. See Peter Sahlins, *Boundaries: The Making of France and Spain in the Pyrenees* (Berkeley, 1989).
10. On the growing importance of the idea of the nation in the years leading up to the Revolution, see David Bell, *The Cult of the Nation in France: Inventing Nationalism, 1680–1800* (Cambridge, Mass., 2001).
11. Gérard Noiriel, "French and Foreigners," in *Rethinking the French Past: Realms of Memory*, ed. Pierre Nora (New York, 1996), 145–179.
12. See especially Carole Pateman, *The Sexual Contract* (Stanford, 1988).
13. William Sewell, "Le citoyen/la citoyenne: Activity, Passivity, and the Revolutionary Concept of Citizenship," in *The French Revolution and the Creation of Modern Political Culture*, ed. Colin Lucas (Oxford, 1987), 105–123.

14. Including Dominique Godineau, *The Women of Paris and Their French Revolution*, trans. Katherine Streip (Berkeley, 1998); Darline Gay Levy, Harriet Branson Applewhite, and Mary Durham Johnson, *Women in Revolutionary Paris, 1789–1795* (Urbana, 1980); Darline Levy and Harriet Applewhite, "A Political Revolution for Women? The Case of Paris," in *Becoming Visible: Women in European History*, ed. Renate Bridenthal, Susan Mosher Stuard, and Merry Wiesner (Boston, 1998), 265–294; and Anne Soprani, *La révolution et les femmes de 1789 à 1796* (Paris, 1988).

15. Olwen Hufton, *Women and the Limits of Citizenship in the French Revolution* (Toronto, 1992).

16. Joan Landes, *Women and the Public Sphere in the Age of the French Revolution* (Ithaca, 1988); Geneviève Fraisse, "Rupture révolutionnaire et l'histoire des femmes," in *Femmes et pouvoirs sous l'ancien régime*, ed. Danielle Haase-Dubosc and Eliane Viennot (Paris, 1991), 291–305; and Lynn Hunt, *The Family Romance of the French Revolution* (Berkeley, 1992). In one influential recent exception, Carla Hesse, in *The Other Enlightenment: How French Women Became Modern* (Princeton, 2001), has argued that an increasing number of women actually published in the revolutionary era, and that novels offered an important arena for women to reflect on and intervene in determining moral and social issues. More generally, Suzanne Desan provides a powerful critique of interpretations of gender in the Revolution framed in dichotomous terms of the empowerment or exclusion of women; *The Family on Trial in Revolutionary France* (Berkeley, 2004), 20–24.

17. For an influential comparative look at how the obligations as well as the rights of citizenship could be gendered, see Linda Kerber, *No Constitutional Right to Be Ladies: Women and the Obligations of Citizenship* (New York, 1998).

18. Landes, *Women and the Public Sphere*, 147.

19. This is beginning to change. Among other works that examine the late Revolution, see Hesse, *The Other Enlightenment;* Suzanne Desan, "Reconstituting the Social after the Terror: Family, Property, and the Law in Popular Politics," *Past and Present*, no. 164 (1999): 81–121; idem, "Marriage, Religion, and Moral Order: The Catholic Critique of Divorce during the Directory," in *The French Revolution and the Meaning of Citizenship*, ed. Renée Waldinger, Philip Dawson, and Isser Woloch (Westport, Conn., 1993), 201–210; and Elizabeth Colwill, "Transforming Women's Empire and the Sovereignty of Man in *La Décade Philosophique*, 1794–1807," *Eighteenth-Century Studies* 29, no. 3 (1996): 265–285. But the majority of work on gender in the Revolution still focuses on the earlier period, ending at latest in 1795 or 1796.

20. See especially Patrick Weil, *Qu'est-ce qu'un Français? Histoire de la nationalité française depuis la Révolution* (Paris, 2002); and Sahlins, *Unnaturally French*.

21. Michael Rapport, *Nationality and Citizenship in Revolutionary France: The Treatment of Foreigners, 1789–1799* (Oxford, 2000).

22. This is less true of work on the policing of foreigners, like Rapport's work, or Sophie Wahnich, *L'impossible citoyen: L'étranger dans le discours de la révolution française* (Paris, 1997), than it is of studies of the development of nationality law.

23. In addition to the works cited above, see Charles Tilly, "The Emergence of Citizenship in France and Elsewhere," *International Review of Social History* 40 (suppl. 3) (1995): 223–236; and Gérard Noiriel, *The French Melting Pot: Immigration, Citizenship, and National Identity* (Minneapolis, 1996).

24. Lora Wildenthal, "Race, Gender, and Citizenship in the German Colonial Empire," in *Tensions of Empire: Colonial Cultures in a Bourgeois World*, ed. Frederick Cooper and Ann Laura Stoler (Berkeley, 1997), 265.

25. Weil, *Qu'est-ce qu'un Français?*, provides one recent exception, but he focuses on the whole of the nineteenth and twentieth centuries. In contrast, Wahnich's overview of the place of the "foreigner" in the Revolution is based on the *Archives Parlementaires*, while Brubaker's influential comparison of French and German models of citizenship draws primarily from nineteenth- and twentieth-century legislative debates: Wahnich, *L'impossible citoyen;* and Brubaker, *Citizenship and Nationhood*. Other works specifically on nationality and citizenship in revolutionary and early nineteenth-century France tend to focus on laws rather than their application; see especially Christian Bruschi, "Droit de la nationalité et égalité des droits de 1789 à la fin du XIXe siècle," in *Questions de nationalité: Histoire et enjeux d'un code*, ed. Smain Laacher (Paris, 1987), 21–59.

26. Hunt, *The Family Romance;* Jean-Louis Halperin, *L'impossible code civil* (Paris, 1992); and Desan, *The Family on Trial.* Some legal and family historians, however, do emphasize continuities between the Code and the Revolution. Jean Bart argues for a "juridical individualism" in both "L'individu et ses droits," in *La famille, la loi, l'état de la Révolution au Code civil,* ed. Irène Théry and Christian Biet (Paris: Imprimerie Nationale, 1989), 351–362; and "La famille bourgeoise, héritière de la Révolution?," in *L'enfant, la famille, et la révolution française,* ed. Marie Françoise Lévy (Paris, 1990), 357–372. For another argument for continuity, see Michèle Bordeaux, "L'universalisme juridique ou l'impasse de l'égalité," in *Les femmes et la Révolution française,* ed. Marie-France Brive, 3 volumes (Toulouse, 1989–1991), 1: 426–440.

27. Elisabeth Sledziewski, *Révolutions du sujet* (Paris 1989), 85. See also her "Postface: Une idée neuve de la femme," in Annette Rosa, *Citoyennes: Les femmes et la révolution française* (Paris, 1988). Joan Scott, drawing on Sledziewski's analysis, similarly contends that the combined recognition of women as civil agents and their exclusion from politics during the Revolution ultimately engendered feminism. Scott, *Only Paradoxes to Offer: French Feminists and the Rights of Man* (Cambridge, Mass., 1996), 19–20.

28. Desan attributes this partially to a "wariness of subsuming women's actions and identity to 'family history.'" Desan, "'War between Brothers and Sisters': Inheritance Law and Gender Politics in Revolutionary France," *French Historical Studies* 20, no. 4 (1997): 597–635.

29. The most extended investigation of this dynamic is Hunt, *The Family Romance.*

30. On the political culture of the late 1790s, see especially Bernard Gainot, *1799, un nouveau Jacobinisme? La démocratie représentative, une alternative à brumaire* (Paris, 2001); and James Livesey, *Making Democracy in the French Revolution* (Cambridge, Mass., 2001). For the Napoleonic period, Natalie Petiteau, ed., *Voies nouvelles pour l'histoire du premier empire: Territoires, pouvoirs, identités* (Paris, 2003); and on the Restoration, Sheryl Kroen, *Politics and Theater: The Crisis of Legitimacy in Restoration France, 1815–1830* (Berkeley, 2000).

31. See especially Isser Woloch, *The New Regime: Transformations of the French Civic Order, 1789–1820s* (New York, 1994).

32. The penalty of *mort civile* was abolished in 1854. Antoine Toussaint Desquiron de Saint-Agnan, *Traité de la mort civile en France* (Paris, 1822), provides a detailed explanation of its history and implications in French law.

33. François Richer, *Traité de la mort civile: Tant que celle qui résulte des condamnations pour cause de crime que celle qui résulte des voeux en religion* (Paris, 1755), 25.

34. *AP* 1, 63: 352.

35. "Procès-verbal de la séance du 16 thermidor an IX–4 août 1801," in Pierre-Antoine Fenet, *Recueil complet des travaux préparatoires du code civil,* 15 vols. (Paris, 1827), 7: 55–56. Philippe-Antoine Merlin, *Répertoire universel et raisonné de jurisprudence,* 5th ed., 36 vols. (Brussels, 1825–1828), 12: 361.

Part I. The Family of the Nation

1. Michel Borgetto, "Métaphore de la famille et idéologies," in *Le droit non civil de la famille,* ed. Michel Borgetto et al. (Paris, 1983), 1–21; Jeffrey Merrick, "Fathers and Kings: Patriarchalism and Absolutism in Eighteenth-Century French Politics," *Studies on Voltaire and the Eighteenth Century* 308 (1993): 281–303; Christian Bruschi, "Essai sur un jeu de miroir: Famille/Etat dans l'histoire des idées politiques," in *L'état, la révolution française et l'Italie. Actes du colloque de Milan (14–15–16 septembre 1989),* ed. Association Française des Historiens des Idées Politiques (Aix-en-Provence, 1990), 49–65.

2. François André Isambert, Athanase Jean-Léger Jourdan, and M. Decrasy, *Recueil des anciennes lois françaises depuis l'an 420 jusqu'à la révolution de 1789,* 29 vols. (Paris, 1829–1833), 20: 296. See also Sue Peabody, "Colonialism's Challenge to French and English Marriage and Citizenship Law: The Case of Mary Anne Raworth," *Eighteenth-Century Life* 18 (1994): 79.

3. Sahlins, *Unnaturally French,* 73–75 and 120–130; idem, "Fictions of a Catholic France"; and idem, "La nationalité avant la lettre: Les pratiques de naturalisation en France sous l'ancien régime," *Annales Histoire, Sciences Sociales,* no. 5 (2000): 1081–1108.

4. The edict first appeared on May 15, 1669; it was officially approved on August 13, 1669. *Edict du Roy, pour empescher les sujets de sa Majesté, de s'habituer dans les pays étrangers, et faire retourner en France ceux qui y sont établis* (Paris, 1669). See also Isambert, *Recueil des anciennes lois*, 18: 367.

5. In 1685, 1698, 1699, 1704, and 1713. Isadore Alauzet, *De la qualité de français, de naturalisation et du statut personnel des étrangers*, 2nd ed. (Paris, 1880), 28.

6. *Mémoire sur le partage pour Marie Anne de James, veuve de Phillipes Tourton, mère et héritière de Claude Tourton* (Paris, 1733), 9.

7. On the *droit d'aubaine*, see especially Sahlins, *Unnaturally French*; Wells, *Law and Citizenship*; and Michael Rapport, "'A Languishing Branch of the Old Tree of Feudalism': The Death, Resurrection, and Final Burial of the Droit d'Aubaine in France," *French History* 14, no. 1 (2000): 13–40.

8. Jacques Mulliez, "Pater is est . . . la source juridique de la puissance paternelle du droit révolutionnaire au Code Civil," in Théry and Biet, *La famille, la loi, l'état*, 412–431.

9. Colette Joutard Danjou, *La condition civile de l'étranger dans les trois derniers siècles de la monarchie* (Paris, 1939), 38.

10. Sahlins, *Unnaturally French*, 136; Jean-François Dubost and Peter Sahlins, *Et si on faisait payer les étrangers? Louis XIV, les immigrés, et quelques autres* (Paris, 1999), 129; and Françoise Bayard, "Naturalization in Lyon during the Ancien Regime," *French History* 4, no. 3 (1990): 277–316.

11. Joan Gundersen, "Independence, Citizenship, and the American Revolution," *Signs* 13, no. 1 (1987): 61. Gundersen draws her conclusions primarily from records of Huguenot refugees.

12. Sahlins, *Unnaturally French*, 136; Tamar Herzog, *Defining Nations: Immigrants and Citizens in Early Modern Spain and Spanish America* (New Haven, 2003), 25–26.

13. For a particularly explicit example, see *Mémoire pour Marguerite Doucet, veuve et donataire par son contrat de mariage de Barthélemy Tourton* (Paris, 1733), 6.

14. Sephardic Jews were accorded the *droit de cité* in January 1790; citizenship was extended to all Jews, including Ashkenazis, in September 1791. Key studies include Gary Kates, "Jews into Frenchmen: Nationality and Representation in Revolutionary France," in *The French Revolution and the Birth of Modernity*, ed. Ferenc Feher (Berkeley, 1990); Robert Badinter, *Libres et égaux: L'émancipation des Juifs, 1789–1791* (Paris, 1989); and Frances Malino, *A Jew in the French Revolution: The Life of Zalkind Hourwitz* (Oxford, 1996).

15. Julien Bonnecase, *La philosophie du Code Napoléon appliqué au droit de la famille: Ses destinées dans le droit civil contemporain* (Paris, 1928), 84.

16. *AP*1, 24:598.

17. Hunt, *The Family Romance*; Marcel David, *Fraternité et la révolution française, 1789–1799* (Paris, 1987).

Chapter 1. New Contracts of Kinship and Citizenship, 1789–1793

1. A.N. DIII 361, pièce 64.

2. A.N. DIII 236, dossier 10, pièce 6.

3. For parallel narratives of husbandly constraints on women seeking naturalization, see Sahlins, *Unnaturally French*, 129–130. Jurists periodically reiterated that a woman following her husband's household could not be judged to have renounced her country; as in one influential case from 1630 in *Journal des principales audiences du Parlement, depuis l'année mil six cens vingt-trois jusques à present avec les arrests intervenus en icelles* (Paris, 1646), 222–223.

4. *Mémoire pour dame Marie-Elisabeth de Belleney, veuve de Me Jean Jannon* (Paris, 1728).

5. Bernard Vogler, "La vie économique et les hiérarchies sociales," in *Histoire de Strasbourg des origines à nos jours*, vol. 3: *Strasbourg de la Guerre de Trente ans à Napoléon*, ed. Georges Livet and Francis Rapp (Strasbourg, 1980–82), 191; and France (Parlement de Metz), *Arrêt du parlement qui a jugé que Me. Luc de Craye* (Metz, 1685), 9.

6. *Recueil des anciennes lois françaises,* 18: 208. Other possible qualifications for being considered as a *naturel français* and bourgeois of Marseilles included purchasing a house above a certain price and various lengths of residence.

7. Dubost and Sahlins, *Et si on faisait payer les étrangers?,* 129 and 149; Sahlins, "La nationalité," 1103; and idem, *Unnaturally French,* 136. This was also the case in the United States, where courts ruled repeatedly in the early 1800s that a female alien married to an American citizen remained an alien unable to inherit property. Kif Augustine-Adams, "'With Notice of the Consequences': Liberal Political Theory, Marriage, and Women's Citizenship in the United States," *Citizenship Studies* 6, no. 1 (2002): 5–20.

8. Gayle Brunelle, "Dangerous Liaisons: Mésalliance and Early Modern French Noblewomen," *French Historical Studies* 19, no. 1 (1995): 75–104.

9. The institution of *mort civile* did, however, limit its civil effects. See Richer, *Traité de la mort civile.*

10. Kristen Gager contends that some adoptions took place, but they were not officially part of French law; *Blood Ties and Fictive Ties: Adoption and Family Life in Early Modern France* (Princeton, 1996).

11. Jurisprudence was nonetheless divided about whether the children of Huguenots could inherit in the kingdom; Sahlins, *Unnaturally French,* 62 and 362 n. 154.

12. Roderick Phillips, "Remaking the Family: The Reception of Family Law and Policy during the French Revolution," in *The French Revolution: Paris and the Provinces,* ed. Clarke Garrett et al. (Arlington, Tex., 1992), 64–89; and James Traer, "The French Family Court," *History: The Journal of the Historical Association* 59 (1974): 211–225.

13. Desan, "'War between Brothers and Sisters.'"

14. Bernard Schnapper, "L'autorité domestique et les hommes politiques de la Révolution," in Théry and Biet, *La famille, la loi, l'état,* 222 and 229.

15. On divorce during the Revolution, see James Traer, *Marriage and the Family in Eighteenth-Century France* (Ithaca, 1980); Francis Ronsin, *Le contrat sentimental: Débats sur le mariage, le divorce de l'Ancien Régime à la Restauration* (Paris, 1990); Roderick Phillips, *Family Breakdown in Late Eighteenth-Century France: Divorces in Rouen, 1792–1803* (Oxford, 1981); and Dominique Dessertine, *Divorcer à Lyon sous la Révolution et l'Empire* (Lyon, 1981).

16. A.N. BB30–34.

17. France (Ministère de Justice), *La nationalité française: Textes et documents* (Paris, 1985), 53.

18. A.N. BB11 2. Both Hobe and Priestley were under twenty-five, the age of majority; the issue of parental permission was thus especially critical. Sahlins, *Unnaturally French,* 277. Both were naturalized in August 1792, along with Thomas Paine, Anarchis Cloots, and several other well-known figures.

19. For an example of such claims, see Guérard, *Mémoire à la Convention Nationale pour Jean Pratbernon et Susanne Néau son épouse contre Nicolas Costard* (Paris, 1795).

20. For example, in Phillipe Egalité's plea to have his daughter exempted from the laws on emigration, he referred briefly to her companion as the "citoyenne Pamela Seymour, naturalisée Française depuis plusieurs ans"; *AP*1, 53: 501.

21. There is considerable debate on contemporary interpretation of these articles. For some competing views, see Pierre Rosanvallon, *Le sacre du citoyen: Histoire du suffrage universel en France* (Paris, 1992), 72–75; Weil, *Qu'est-ce qu'un Français?,* 20; Sahlins, *Unnaturally French,* 274.

22. When the laws on emigration were applied to territories conquered during the Revolution, different dates were used depending on the particular situation of the area "reunited" with France. Marcel Ragon, *La législation sur les émigrés, 1789–1825* (Paris, 1904).

23. For some exceptions, see Ladan Boroumand, "Emigration and the Rights of Man: French Revolutionaries Equivocate," *Journal of Modern History* 72, no. 1 (2000): 67–108; and Jean-Jacques Clère, "L'émigration dans les débats de l'assemblée nationale constituante," in *Les droits de l'homme et la conquête des libertés, des Lumières aux révolutions de 1848. Actes du Colloque de Grenoble-Vizille 1986* (Grenoble-Vizille, 1988), 156–162.

24. Especially under the auspices of the count of Provence in Koblentz and in the army of the prince of Condé.

25. Donald Greer has estimated that 51 percent of émigrés were members of the Third Estate, 25 percent were clergy, and 17 percent nobles. Although the inherently incomplete nature of his data and the slipperiness of the term "Third Estate" mean that such figures cannot be regarded as absolute, large numbers of émigrés were commoners. Greer, *The Incidence of the Emigration during the French Revolution* (Cambridge, 1951), 65.

26. A.N. AD XII 1, pièce 10, Réflexions et autorités qui peuvent déterminer une loi contre les emigrans, 4.

27. A.N. AD XVIIIc 192, pièce 27, Opinion de M. S** Député du département de l'Aube à Lassemblée nationale sur les emigrans.

28. A.N. ADXII 5.

29. A.N. DIII 237, pièce 8.

30. Richer, *Traité de la mort civile.*

31. A.N. AD XII 1, pièce 10, Réflexions et autorités qui peuvent déterminer une loi contre les émigrans, 7.

32. A.N. ADXVIIc 192. This translation is Boroumand's, from "Emigration and the Rights of Man," 97.

33. *Observations sur le projet de résolution relatif au partage des biens des parens d'émigrés* (Paris, [1797]), 2.

34. A.N. F7 3330.

35. A.N. DIII 376.

36. Pierre Robin discusses how the seizure of the property of enemy foreigners compared with that of émigrés and the criteria used to distinguish the two groups. Robin, *Le séquestre des biens ennemis sous la révolution française* (Paris, 1929).

37. For analyses of how one could be juridically a foreigner, but politically a French citizen in the early Revolution, see Jean Portemer, "L'étranger dans le droit de la révolution française," in *L'étranger-foreigner,* Recueils de la société Jean-Bodin pour l'histoire comparative des institutions (Paris, 1984), 533–552; Noiriel, "French and Foreigners"; Wahnich, *L'impossible citoyen;* and especially Rapport, *Nationality and Citizenship,* 138–144 and 158.

38. Greer, *The Incidence of the Emigration,* 100.

39. Ibid., 27.

40. A.N. F7 3329.

41. A.N. DIII 236, dossier 2, pièce 14.

42. *Observations d'une femme sur la loi contre les émigrés* (Paris, n.d.). The pamphlet seems to have enjoyed some popularity. It exists in at least three versions: the one cited above, another printed in Paris by the Imprimerie de la Feulle du Jour, and a third cited by Patrice Higonnet in *Class, Ideology and the Rights of Nobles during the French Revolution* (Oxford, 1981), 162. The pamphlet is undated, but internal evidence suggests that it dates from late 1792.

43. *Observations d'une femme.*

44. A.N. DIII 237, dossier 18, pièce 11.

45. A.N. DIII 212.

46. A.N. DIII 236, dossier 2, pièce 33. The pièce is undated but appears to have been written soon after the October 1792 measure.

47. Charles-Pierre Ducanel, *Justice, humanité, Les femmes absentes et les enfants appelans de la Convention nationale à elle-même* (Paris, n.d.), 7, 11.

48. A.N. DIII 362. Other exceptions considered at the same time included servants, those who left because of illness, and children pursuing their education.

49. AP1, 53: 456.

50. *Observations sur les exceptions à faire à la qualification d'émigrés* (Paris, n.d.), 2.

51. At least under the 1791 Constitution; the June 1793 one technically allowed servants to vote, but it required that they be domiciled separately from their masters in order to exercise this right. On the rationales for excluding servants, see Claude Petitfrère, "Liberté, égalité, domesticité," in *Les droits de l'homme et la conquête des libertés,* 181–188; François Hincker, "La citoyenneté révolutionnaire saisie à travers ses exclus," in *Le citoyen fou,* ed. Nathalie Robatel (Paris, 1991), 7–28; and Rosanvallon, *Le sacre du citoyen.* On the importance of domicile, see Anne Verjus, *Le cens de la famille: Le sexe des individus politiques de la révolution de 1789 à celle de 1848* (Paris, 2002), 36.

52. AP1, 53: 458.

53. *Réclamations pour l'interprétation de la loi du 12 novembre concernant les émigres* ([Paris], n.d.), 3.

54. A.N. F7 4324, 3rd series, dossier 93.

55. Linda Kerber, *Women of the Republic: Intellect and Ideology in Revolutionary America* (New York, 1980), 123. Kerber notes that this policy freed American revolutionaries from the task of providing for economic dependents and allowed them to gain abandoned property without a struggle—especially as there were often severe restrictions on the supplies and household goods a woman could take with her—but also sanctioned the idea that women had no political obligations to the state.

56. The age at which children were held responsible for emigration varied. The March 1793 law officially exempted children under age fourteen if they returned to France within three months of the decree; for children under ten, the time requirement went into effect only when they reached their tenth birthday. The amnesty of vendémiaire an IX (October 1800) allowed children under sixteen to return to France. Ragon, *La législation sur les émigrés*, 226, 287.

57. A.N. DIII 136, dossier 41, pièce 31.

58. AP1, 97: 397. The language is from the popular society of Wassy, which clearly believed that the latter applied.

59. A.N. DIII 236, dossier 1, pièce 6.

60. A.N. DIII 236, dossier 11, pièce 10.

61. A.N. DIII 237, dossier 2, pièce 16.

62. A.N. DIII 236, Aisne, pièce 6.

63. A.N. BB16 122.

64. A.N. DIII 361.

65. Traer, *Marriage and the Family*, 132–133. The relevant exchanges between the minister of the interior and the minister of justice are in A.N. BB16 (Cantal).

66. A.N. F7 3330.

67. Ibid.

68. Albert Joseph Hennet, *Du divorce* (Paris, 1789), 73 and 122.

69. A.N. F7 3330.

70. A *séparation de biens* assured a woman material rights. However, divorce often preserved more property, since it was followed by a return not only of a wife's contribution to the marriage but also of a life annuity on the property of her husband. Phillips, *Family Breakdown*, 148.

71. The statistics are from Francis Ronsin's synthesis of case studies in *Le contrat sentimental*, 272.

72. For particular examples, see Jean Lhote, "Les divorces d'émigrés et de suspects à Metz sous la Révolution," in Brive, *Les femmes et la révolution*, 191–195; and Joseph Bouland, *Douze femmes d'émigrés divorcées à Limoges sous la Terreur, 1793–1794* (Limoges, 1913).

Chapter 2. *"Duty to the Patrie above All"*

1. A.N. DIII 375.

2. Hunt, *The Family Romance*, 74.

3. The original decree is in A.N. AD II 30.

4. Lucien Dejob, *Le rétablissement de l'adoption en France* (Paris, 1911), 83; Rey, *Observations sur l'adoption* (Paris, n.d.), 13.

5. However, not all were convinced of the parallels between "national adoption" and adoption within families; the deputy Berlier argued in 1793 that the mode and effect of adoption for "adopted children of the Republic" was sufficiently different from literal adoption that it should be treated separately. Théophile Berlier, *Exposé sommaire des motifs qui ont déterminé les bases qui renferme le projet du code civil, sur l'adoption* (Paris, 1793).

6. Michel Azéma, *Rapport et projet de loi sur l'adoption, présenté à la Convention Nationale, au nom du comité de législation* (Paris [1793]), 26.

7. Dejob, *Le rétablissement de l'adoption*, 83.

8. Eric Andrew Goodheart, "Adoption in the Discourses of the French Revolution" (Ph.D. diss., Harvard University, 1997).

9. *AP*1, 72: 126.

10. *AP*1, 91: 213.

11. A.N. DIII 375 and DIII 136, dossier 18, pièce 20.

12. A.N. DIII 147, "Pétition de Josephine Letellier aux citoyens législateurs, 26 pluviôse an II" (February 14, 1794); quoted in Desan, "'War between Brothers and Sisters,'" 631.

13. For some examples, see A.N. *DIII 3, register no. 3724; A.N. DIII 361, pièce 258.

14. *AP*1, 89: 41.

15. *AP*1, 90: 44.

16. A.N. DIII 361, pièce 257, Abolition indirecte et modifiée du célibat, motifs général.

17. Roderick Phillips, "The Attack on Celibacy in Eighteenth-Century France," *Proceedings of the Annual Meeting of the Western Society for French History* 17 (1990): 165–171; Jacques Godechot, *Les institutions de la France sous la Révolution et l'Empire* (Paris, 1951), 135.

18. A.N. AD II 30.

19. Pierre Murat, "La puissance paternelle et la révolution française: Essai de régénération de l'autorité des pères," in Théry and Biet, *La famille, la loi, l'état*, 403.

20. This measure was particularly controversial because it could be applied retroactively.

21. Quoted in Bernard Schnapper, "Liberté, égalité, autorité: La famille devant les assemblées révolutionnaires, 1790–1800," in Lévy, *L'enfant, la famille et la révolution*, 331.

22. Cambacérès, "Rapport sur le premier projet de Code civil devant la Convention au nom du Comité de législation civile et criminelle," in Fenet, *Recueil complet*, 1:4, 5.

23. *AP*1, 70: 638.

24. A.N. DIII 361, pièce 121, Epoux Emigrés, Observations sur la loi du 20 7bre 1792 relative au divorce (2 nivôse an II).

25. Sewell, "Le citoyen/la citoyenne."

26. Dominique Godineau, "Masculine and Feminine Political Practice during the French Revolution, 1793–Year III," in *Women and Politics in the Age of Democratic Revolution*, ed. Harriet Applewhite and Darline G. Levy (Ann Arbor, 1990), 61–81.

27. A.N. *DIII 3, No. 3640, Seine et Oise. See also No. 3250, Lot et Garonne.

28. Levy, Applewhite, and Johnson, *Women in Revolutionary Paris*.

29. Quoted in Serge Aberdam, "L'élargissement du droit de vote entre 1792 et 1795 au travers du dénombrement du Comité de division et des votes populaires sur les Constitutions de 1793 et 1795" (Thèse de doctorat, Université de Paris 1 Panthéon-Sorbonne, UFR d'Histoire, Paris, 2001), 761.

30. Godineau, "Femmes en citoyenneté."

31. Aberdam, "L'élargissement du droit de vote," 766–770.

32. A.D. de l'Oise, liasse cotée provisoirement 2 Lp 9048; Baron, chef-lieu de Canton, réponses au questionnaire de l'été 1793. Quoted in Aberdam, "L'élargissement du droit de vote," 745.

33. A.D. de l'Orne, L 593–595; district d'Argentan. Quoted in Aberdam, "L'élargissement du droit de vote," 744.

34. For analyses of this clash, see especially Godineau, *Women of Paris*, 158–174; and Hufton, *Women and the Limits of Citizenship*.

35. The most influential formulation of this view is Landes, *Women and the Public Sphere*, 147.

36. Godineau, *Women of Paris*, "Masculine and Feminine Political Practice," and "Femmes en citoyenneté."

37. Stephanie A. Brown, "Women on Trial: The Revolutionary Tribunal and Gender" (Ph.D. diss., Stanford University, 1996).

38. On December 17, 1791, nobles were forbidden to join primary assemblies; on March 19, 1793, they—along with foreigners—were singled out for particular punishment if they took part in rebellions; on March 21 they were barred from membership in *comités de surveillance;* on April 17 they were declared ineligible to receive passports; and in September 1793 the Convention declared that any noble could be arrested for not having been an active supporter of the Revolution. See Higonnet, *Class, Ideology and Rights of Nobles*, 127–128; and Alain Texier, "Le régime politique applicable aux nobles pendant la révolution ou la dialectique de l'égalité et de la répression," in *Noblesse et Révolution*, Institut de recherches européennes sur les noblesses et aristocraties (Les Eyzies, 1991), 107–119.

39. Alphonse-Honoré Taillandier and Sylvian-Charles Théodore Mongalvy, *Recueil général des lois et des arrêts concernant les émigrés, déportés, condamnés, leurs héritiers, créanciers et ayants-cause, depuis 1791 jusqu'en 1825*, 2 vols. (Paris, 1825), 1: 182. The publication of this exception was nonetheless limited.

40. Wahnich, *L'impossible citoyen*, 7–8 and 128–130; and Rapport, *Nationality and Citizenship*, 140–141.

41. Rapport emphasizes political motives for this, rather than the growing distrust of cosmopolitanism that Wahnich addresses; ibid., 191.

42. See A.N. AD I 87 for the original texts of various decrees, and, for discussions of laws concerning foreigners, Albert Mathiez, *La révolution et les étrangers: Cosmopolitisme et défense nationale* (Paris, 1918); Wahnich, *L'impossible citoyen*; Portemer, "L'étranger dans le droit"; and Michael Rapport, "Robespierre and the Universal Rights of Man, 1789–1794," *French Historical Studies* 10, no. 3 (1996): 303–333.

43. Mathiez, *La révolution et les étrangers*, 161.

44. *AP*1, 73: 463.

45. *AP*1, 76: 638, 641.

46. *AP*1, 76: 613, 641.

47. Dillon, *Pétition de la citoyenne veuve Dillon à la convention nationale* (Paris, Year II).

48. It built on the Law of Suspects of September 17, 1793, and on other laws centralizing the administration of revolutionary justice. On the institutional apparatus of the Terror, see Colin Lucas, *The Structure of the Terror: The Example of Javogues and the Loire* (Oxford, 1975); and the articles collected in Keith Baker, ed., *The French Revolution and the Creation of Modern Political Culture*, vol. 4: *The Terror* (Oxford 1994).

49. Most documents are in A.N. DIII 373–377; a few more are scattered throughout the DIII series. A.N. AFII 61–62 contain the texts of supplementary decrees and exceptions, judgments on some individual cases, and some additional petitions and reports. It is impossible to give a definite total for the number of cases, both because of the way the documents are preserved and because the uncertain orthography of eighteenth-century names could mean that petitions from the same individual or family were filed separately.

50. Wahnich, *L'impossible citoyen*, 231–232.

51. On ennoblement, see Guy Chaussinand-Nogaret, *The French Nobility in the Eighteenth Century: From Feudalism to Enlightenment* (Cambridge, 1985); Jay Michael Smith, *The Culture of Merit: Nobility, Royal Service and the Making of Absolute Monarchy in France, 1600–1789* (Ann Arbor, 1996); and David Bien, "Manufacturing Nobles: The Chancelleries in France until 1789," *Journal of Modern History* 61, no. 3 (1989): 445–486.

52. *AP*1, 88: 648.

53. Wahnich also observes that women's marital choices were supposedly motivated by pride or virtue, not chance; *L'impossible citoyen*, 226. However, she has not examined how the men and women affected by the decree responded to this prescriptive vision or the possibility that such decisions could be reversed.

54. On some of the sites of tension, see Arlette Farge and Michel Foucault, *Le désordre des familles: Lettres de cachet des Archives de la Bastille au XVIIIe siècle* (Paris, 1982).

55. Higonnet, *Class, Ideology and Rights of Nobles*, 155.

56. *Noblesse concédée* refers to the fact that her husband was not born noble, but had obtained *lettres de noblesse* from the former Polish king; A.N. DIII 373. Higonnet also mentions that these petitions contain cases involving non-noble women who claimed to have been forced into marriage as minors; *Class, Ideology and Rights of Nobles*, 155.

57. Dossiers for Daminous, Bougainville, and Rhaimbault in A.N. DIII 374, 373, and 377.

58. Brunelle, "Dangerous Liaisons." Brunelle looks at letters of relief of derogation in Rouen and argues that such noble-born women were often resentful of the loss of status that they had suffered.

59. Farge and Foucault, *Le désordre des familles*.

60. A.N. DIII 375.

61. Brunelle points out that few widows tried to argue that their *roturier* husband was actually a noble, and that only a handful expressed regret for their husbands; "Dangerous Liaisons," 89.

62. A.N. DIII 374.

63. Ibid.

64. At least, such women were not exempted on the grounds that their marriages had been coerced. Many petitioners who decried the role of parental despotism in their marriages were widows and were eventually encompassed in the exception for childless widows born *roturières*.

65. A.N. DIII 373.

66. Ibid.

67. Charles-François Oudot, *Rapport et projets d'articles additionnels sur le divorce, présentés au nom du Comité de législation, le 27 germinal, l'an II de la République* (Paris, Year II), 2.

68. *AP*1, 87:316.

69. A.N. AFII 61, dossier 445.

70. Higonnet, *Class, Ideology and Rights of Nobles,* 155.

71. Anonymous petition in A.N. DIII 373. Of the more than 100 petitions from widows, at least 20 mention their daughters' inability to pass on nobility to children. To some extent, these widows, as well as certain male petitioners, actually reproduced the logic of the decree for their daughters. While lamenting the parental despotism that forced them to marry nobles, they stressed their role as parents in marrying their daughters to *sans-culottes*.

72. A.N. DIII 373.

73. A.N. DIII 238, pièce 82. Subsequent quotations for this case are from the same petition; the pages are not numbered.

74. Dossiers for Cumelle, Giraud, and Gamaches in A.N. DIII 373 and 375.

75. For more detail, see Goodheart, "Adoption."

76. There were occasional exceptions, like that of Madeline Beauvollier, a noble-born girl adopted by a sans-culotte family who was allowed to stay and help her ailing parents; A.N. AF II 61, vol. 450, document 48.

77. Florence Bellivier and Laurence Boudouard, "Des droits par les bâtards: L'enfant naturel dans les débats révolutionnaires," in Théry et Biet, *La famille, la loi, l'état,* 122–146.

78. A.N. DIII 377.

79. A.N. DIII 375.

80. A.N. DIII 376, 375.

81. Hufton, *Women and the Limits of Citizenship,* 55–58.

82. A.N. DIII 376.

83. A.N. DIII 361, pièce 70.

84. A.N. DIII 361, pièce 121, Epoux Emigres, Observations sur la loi du 20 7bre 1792 relative au divorce.

85. A.N. DIII 373. The petition is signed by "Moreau commis marchand à la raffinerie de sucre à villeneuve la Montagne Dept. de Seine et Oise," but the cover sheet identifies it as an anonymous petition, and it is filed accordingly.

86. Anonymous petition in A.N. DIII 373.

87. A.N. DIII 377. For Dumontier, see A.N. DIII 374. Similarly the widow Houguet, who had married in 1793, claimed that she did not know her husband was noble until after his death; A.N. DIII 240.

88. A.N. DIII 373.

89. Ibid.

90. Dossiers for Gras, Couchu, Lepine, and Gamaches in A.N. DIII 373, 374, 375, and 376. A woman's social status was usually indicated by either her own profession or that of her father. Many were simply referred to as *roturière* or *sans-culotte*. The most common of such mixed marriages involved people on social borders, usually men who had used the title of *écuyer* at some point and women associated with the arts, such as painters and actresses.

91. Dossier Laroque in A.N. DIII 376.

Part II. Toward a Nation of Families

1. See especially Bronislaw Baczko, *Ending the Terror: The French Revolution after Robespierre* (Cambridge, 1994).

2. Legislators first repealed general measures like the infamous Law of 22 Prairial, which had precipitated the Great Terror of June and July 1794, and began to release prisoners. They

were slower to relax policing measures against foreigners, in part because of the context of continuing war. The Germinal law was enforced until its revocation. See Rapport, *Nationality and Citizenship.*

3. Among others, see Gainot, *1799;* Livesey, *Making Democracy;* Howard Brown and Judith Miller, eds., *Taking Liberties: Problems of a New Order from the French Revolution to Napoleon* (Manchester, 2002).

4. On the insurrections as a last push for women's rights, see Hufton, *Women and the Limits of Citizenship;* Godineau, *Women of Paris;* and especially the section "Women's Final Political Efforts, July 1794–May 1795," in Gay, Applewhite, and Johnson, *Women in Revolutionary Paris.*

5. Quoted in Xavier Martin, "Fonction paternelle et Code Napoléon," *Annales historiques de la révolution française,* no. 305 (1996): 468; Hunt, *The Family Romance,* 163.

6. For one typical example, see J. G. G. Chappe, *Discours . . . près l'administration municipale du 7è arrondissement, prononcé à la fête des époux, au temple du Commerce, le 10 floréal an VI* (Paris, n.d.).

Chapter 3. Fathers and Foreigners

1. *Procès-verbaux des séances la Convention Nationale,* 65 vols. (Paris, 1792–1795), 48: 236.

2. Ibid., 110.

3. A.N. DIII 136.

4. Charles Toussaint Guiraudet, *De la famille considérée comme l'élément des sociétés* (Paris, 1797), 9.

5. Ibid., 197, 200.

6. Thierry Lentz, *Roederer, 1754–1835* (Metz, 1989).

7. *Journal d'économie publique de morale et de politique,* Year V, 350–351.

8. See especially his 1788 piece titled "De la députation aux Etats Généraux," and his reflections on defining the *droit de cité* and the *titre de citoyen* in 1793; Pierre-Louis Roederer, *Oeuvres,* 8 vols. (Paris, 1853–59), 7: 552, 6: 95–96. I am indebted to Anne Verjus for bringing Roederer's works to my attention.

9. Hunt, *The Family Romance,* 161; Martin, "Fonction paternelle et Code Napoléon," 467–468.

10. Desan, "Reconstituting the Social."

11. Irène Théry, *Le démariage: Justice et vie privée* (Paris, 1993), 65.

12. Xavier Martin, *Human Nature and French Revolution: From the Enlightenment to the Napoleonic Code,* trans. Patrick Corcoran (New York, 1994), 142.

13. Michel Troper, "La notion de citoyen sous la révolution française," in *Etudes en l'honneur de Georges Dupuis, droit public* (Paris, 1997), 302–322.

14. Titre II, Art. 1, "Tout homme né . . . est citoyen français"; Art. 10, "Un étranger devient citoyen français"; and Art. 12, "L'exercice des droits de citoyen se perd," all in *La nationalité française,* 54.

15. As with earlier constitutions, there is considerable debate about how contemporaries understood the articles. Weil, *Qu'est-ce qu'un Français?,* argues that they were clear on the differences between French and citizen. Sahlins contends that the acquisition of citizenship was tantamount to the acquisition of political rights in 1795 and that jurists and politicians did not seek to distinguish citizens systematically from French nationals; *Unnaturally French,* 291. Others suggest that the 1795 Constitution was an important step in separating legal nationality from citizenship, but still see real confusion; I find this view the most persuasive. See Troper, "La notion de citoyen," 315; and Hincker, "La citoyenneté révolutionnaire," 18.

16. Rapport, *Nationality and Citizenship,* chap. 5.

17. *La nationalité française,* 54.

18. Rapport, *Nationality and Citizenship,* 265.

19. See especially Emmanuel Pastoret, *Rapport . . . sur l'exercice du droit de cité pour les descendants des religionnaires fugitifs, rentrant en France* (Paris, Year V); and Théophile

Berlier, *Opinion . . . sur la question de savoir si l'on peut dispenser les descendans des religionnaires fugitifs de la résidence septennale prescrite par la Constitution pour l'exercice des droits politiques* (Paris, 1797).

20. A.N. DIII 237, pièce 80.

21. *AP*1, 95: 160–161.

22. Aberdam, "L'élargissement du droit de vote," 825.

23. Godineau, *Women of Paris*, 344–346.

24. Aberdam, "L'élargissement du droit de vote," 825–826.

25. Marcel Gauchet, *La révolution des droits de l'homme* (Paris, 1989), 279.

26. Roederer and Corancez, "Aux auteurs du Journal de Paris," *Journal de Paris*, no. 19 (June 1796).

27. The legitimacy of a couple's marriage was often the central issue. For example, one much-publicized *affaire* concerned a marriage between a French general and an Egyptian woman soon after Napoleon's 1798 campaigns in Egypt. The general's heirs contended that since the woman had been a slave in her home country, the marriage should not be considered valid. Maurice Méjan, *Recueil des causes célèbres et des arrêts qui les ont décidées*, 19 vols. (Paris, 1807–1813), 2: 295–323.

28. For an overview of the case, see Aristide Douarche, *Les tribunaux civils de Paris pendant la Révolution, 1791–1800: Documents inédits recueillis avant l'incendie du Palais de Justice de 1871*, 2 vols. (Paris, 1905–1907), 1: clxxi–clxxiii and 2: 357–359.

29. See Douarche, *Les tribunaux civils*. Crowds filled the courtroom at each stage of the trial, and columnists for almost all the contemporary newspapers covered the case.

30. Portalis et al., *Consultation pour M. Hoppé contre la citoyenne Lange, sur une question d'éducation* (Paris, Year V [1797]). Cambacérès presented three versions of a civil code, in 1793, 1794, and 1796, while Portalis was one of the principal artisans of the Napoleonic Code.

31. Duveyrier, *Réponse*. The author appears to be Honoré Marie-Nicholas Duveyrier, a deputy to the National Assembly and later a tribune involved in the creation of the Napoleonic Civil Code.

32. The speaker in question was Simeon, intervening in a legislative debate about divorces based on mutual incompatibility. For more on this debate, see Desan, "Marriage, Religion, and Moral Order."

33. He referred to Cambacérès's third project for a civil code, which had been proposed on 16 Prairial Year IV (June 4, 1796).

34. Duveyrier, *Réponse*, 1.

35. Portalis et al., *Consultation pour M. Hoppé*, 16.

36. Duveyrier, *Réponse*, 50.

37. For Roman law, see Yan Thomas, "À Rome, pères citoyens et cité des pères (IIe siècle avant J.-C.–II siècle après J.-C.)," in *Histoire de la famille*, ed. Christiane Klapish-Zuber, André Burguière, Martine Segalen, and Françoise Zonabend (Paris, 1986), 195–239. For French law on this point, see Marguerite Vanel, *Evolution historique de la notion de français d'origine du XVI siècle au code civil* (Paris, 1944), 34.

38. On fathers of children born out of wedlock and the reasons for their limited authority during the Old Regime, see Jacques Mulliez, "Révolutionnaires, nouveaux pères? Forcement nouveaux pères! Le droit révolutionnaire de la paternité," in *La révolution et l'ordre juridique privé: Rationalité ou scandale? Actes du colloque d'Orléans* (Paris, 1988), 373–398; and idem, "Pater is est . . . la source juridique de la puissance paternelle du droit révolutionnaire au Code Civil."

39. The Law of 12 Brumaire Year II allowed illegitimate children to claim their share of inheritances retroactively. The possibility of retroactive demands was removed on 15 Thermidor Year IV (August 1, 1796).

40. For example, on 26 Germinal Year II (April 15, 1794), the Parisian civil courts had ruled that the *citoyenne* Jacquemin should have custody of her illegitimate child. Douarche, *Les tribunaux civils*, 1: clxxx–clxxxi, 702–703.

41. Portalis et al., *Consultation pour M. Hoppé*, 16, 20, 18.

42. Duveyrier, *Réponse*, 54–55.

43. *Messager du Soir ou Gazette générale de l'Europe*, no. 89 (29 Frimaire Year V [December 19, 1796]): 2–3. For almost identical commentary, see the *Journal de Paris* of the same date, 357.

44. Portalis et al., *Consultation pour M. Hoppé,* 19.

45. On the involvement and perceived involvement of women in the polity in 1793–1795, see Godineau, "Femmes en citoyenneté."

46. Duveyrier, *Réponse,* 53; Guiraudet, *De la famille,* 197.

47. Duveyrier, *Réponse,* 54.

48. Innovative analyses of *causes célèbres* range from the melodramas of the prerevolution to murder trials of the twentieth century. See especially Sarah Maza, *Private Lives and Public Affairs: The Causes Célèbres of Prerevolutionary France* (Berkeley, 1993). On law and family relations during the Directory, see Colwill, "Transforming Women's Empire and the Sovereignty of Man"; and especially Desan, *The Family on Trial.*

49. Goodheart, "Adoption," 267–323; and idem, "The Lepeletier Affair of Year VI: National Adoption of the Revolutionary Idea," in *Symbols, Myths and Images of the French Revolution: Essays in Honour of James A. Leith,* ed. Ian Germani and Robin Swales (Regina, Sask., 1998), 199–210. For narrative details, see the early twentieth-century accounts: Dejob, *Le rétablissement de l'adoption;* and M. P. Dally, *Suzanne Lepeletier, fille de la nation, et son oncle Félix Lepeletier* (Paris, 1912).

50. On Lepeletier as a "martyr of liberty," see Antoine de Baecque, "Le corps meurtri de la Révolution: Le discours politique et les blessures des martyrs (1792–1794)," *Annales historiques de la révolution française* 59, no. 267 (1987): 17–42; idem, *The Body Politic: Corporeal Metaphor in Revolutionary France, 1770–1800,* trans. Charlotte Mandell (Stanford, 1997).

51. Dally, *Suzanne Lepeletier;* and Laurence Constant, *Félix Lepeletier de St. Fargeau: Un itinéraire de la Révolution à la monarchie de Juillet* (Paris, 1995). Félix was acquitted because of lack of evidence.

52. She was emancipated on 13 Pluviôse Year VI (February 1, 1798). For an explanation of *tutelle* and emancipation, see Marcel Garaud and Romuald Szramkiewicz, *La révolution française et la famille* (Paris, 1978).

53. The legislature debated Suzanne's case on several occasions between 22 Frimaire Year VI (December 12, 1797) and 23 Pluviôse Year VI (February 11, 1798). Since the press was heavily censored in wake of the coup of 18 Fructidor Year V (September 7, 1797), many newspapers simply summarized or transcribed speeches in the assembly without substantial additional commentary.

54. Chazal, for example, sat with the Girondins in 1792; though sent on mission during the Terror, he was recalled because of his lack of fervor and subsequently went into hiding. Similarly, Poullain de Grandprey, another member of the commission opposed to the Lepeletier brothers, had been associated with the Girondins and a moderate during the king's trial. For the political histories of most of the participants, see Jean-François Robinet, Adolphe Robert, and J. Le Chaplain, eds., *Dictionnaire historique et biographique de la révolution et de l'empire,* 2 vols. (Paris, 1975).

55. Françoise Fortuent, "Le rétablissement de l'adoption: Une entrée par effraction?," 196–203; and F. Hughes Fulchrion, "Nature, fiction et politique, l'adoption dans les débats révolutionnaires," both in Théry and Biet, *La famille, la loi, l'état,* 204–222.

56. Mulliez, "Pater is." See also Desan, "Reconstituting the Social."

57. Jean-Pierre Chazal, *Rapport . . . au nom d'une Commission spéciale composée des représentans du peuple Poullain-Grandprey, Laujac et Chazal, sur les effets de l'adoption et l'affaire particulière de la citoyenne Lepeletier, adoptée au nom du peuple français* (Paris, Year VI), 4–5.

58. Rey, *Observations sur l'adoption,* 9.

59. Bernard Laujacq, *Opinion . . . sur le Message du Directoire exécutif relatif à la citoyenne Lepeletier* (Paris, n.d.), 15.

60. See Mulliez, "Pater is," 415.

61. Goodheart, "Adoption," 282.

62. P. A. Laloy, *Opinion . . . sur l'adoption nationale et ses effets* (Paris, Year VI). The claims that families should be separate from the state and that paternal authority was based on the protection of property were compatible but not identical. Laloy did not address the basis of paternal authority, and, as Goodheart points out, he saw the Convention's earlier inaction toward Suzanne as evidence that it did not follow its own decrees, not as the absence of a legislative mandate to care for the *enfants de la patrie;* "Adoption," 309.

63. Laujacq, *Opinion*, 24.

64. Julien Souhait, *Opinion . . . sur l'adoption publique* (Paris, Year VI), 3, 5.

65. Félix Lepeletier and Amédée Lepeletier, *Au Conseil des Cinq-Cents ou Mémoire sur l'affaire de S. Lepeletier, première fille adoptive du peuple français* (Paris, n.d.), 21.

66. If the Netherlands had been officially annexed by France—as Belgium was—rather than defined as a sister republic, De Witt would have been considered French.

67. In the brothers' words, "la fille de celui qui mourut pour tous devienne étrangère par un mariage qui l'expatrie et la dénationalise"; Lepeletier and Lepeletier, *Au Conseil des Cinq-Cents ou Mémoire*, 41.

68. As Chazal pointed out, the possibility that Suzanne would be seduced into marrying a foreigner and transporting her fortune out of France ranked among Félix and Amédée's most serious objections, objections amplified in many newspapers; Chazal, *Rapport*, 28.

69. Félix Lepeletier and Amédée Lepeletier, *Au Conseil des Cinq-Cents ou nouvelles observations sur l'adoption publique et l'affaire de S. Lepeletier* (Paris, n.d.), 4.

70. For examples of such rhetoric, see ibid., 5 and 10; and Lepeletier and Lepeletier, *Au Conseil des Cinq-Cents ou Mémoire*, 41.

71. On the seventeenth-century Jean de Witt, see J. F. Michaud, ed., *Biographie universelle, ancienne et moderne*, 45 vols. (Graz, 1966–1970), 44: 736–740. The Lepeletier brothers contested Jean-François's heritage, arguing that the last descendent of Jean de Witt had died seven years previously; Lepeletier and Lepeletier, *Au Conseil des Cinq-Cents ou Mémoire*, 41.

72. Susanne Le Peletier de Saint Fargeau, *Observations pour Susanne-Louise Lepeletier, fille unique et héritière de Michel Lepeletier, représentant du peuple à la Convention Nationale* (Paris, n.d.), 1.

73. Chazal, for example, proclaimed that de Witt was also a descendant of liberty because he was a Batavian; *Rapport*, 29. See also F. J. Febvre, *Opinion . . . sur le message du Directoire exécutif, relatif à la citoyenne Lepeletier et sur l'adoption publique* (Paris, Year VI).

74. Chazal, *Rapport*, 30.

75. Rey, *Observations sur l'adoption*, 11.

76. Bernard Laujacq, *Nouvelle rédaction des projets de résolution et d'arrêté . . . sur l'adoption nationale et l'affaire particulière de la citoyenne Lepeletier* (Paris, n.d.), 4.

77. Testimony reproduced in Chazal, *Rapport*, 30.

78. Lepeletier and Lepeletier, *Au Conseil des Cinq-Cents ou Mémoire*, 5–6. For other examples, see ibid., 4; and Lepeletier and Lepeletier, *Au Conseil des Cinq-Cents ou nouvelles observations*, 4.

79. On the tropes of dissimulation and transparency in the Revolution, see Hunt, *The Family Romance*, 96–97.

80. Farge and Foucault, *Le désordre des familles;* and Arlette Farge, "The Honor and Secrecy of Families," in *A History of Private Life,* ed. Roger Chartier (Cambridge, Mass., 1989), 571–607.

81. A law of August 16, 1790, substituted *tribunaux des familles* as a mechanism for resolving familial conflicts, but the tribunals themselves were accused of exercising arbitrary authority, following the forced arbitration provisions of the statutes passed during the Terror, especially the law on succession passed on 17 Nivôse Year II (January 6, 1794).

82. Chazal, *Rapport*, 15.

83. Laujacq, *Opinion* and *Nouvelle rédaction*.

84. Febvre, *Opinion*, 3.

85. For more on legal formalism, see Goodheart, "Adoption," 320.

86. Rey, *Observations sur l'adoption*, 9–10.

87. Amédée Le Peletier, *Réponse à l'Opinion du Représentant du Peuple B. Laujacq dans l'affaire de la mineure Lepeletier* (Paris, n.d.), 11–12.

88. For the relevant debates, see especially the *Gazette nationale ou le Moniteur universel,* Year V, issues 320 (20 Thermidor Year V/6 août 1797) and 334 (4 Fructidor Year V/21 août 1797) and Year VI, issue 4 (4 Vendémiaire Year VI/25 septembre 1797).

89. Guillaume Robert, *Rapport . . . sur le mariage des mineurs orphelins. Séance du 27 frimaire an 6* (Paris, Year VI), 6.

90. Dally, *Suzanne Lepeletier*, 18.

Chapter 4. Gender and Emigration Reconsidered

1. One exception was for children of either sex (*les enfants de l'un et l'autre sexe*), who were allowed to return to France if they were under fourteen years old; Ragon, *La législation sur les émigrés,* 225.

2. Article 373, titre XIV.

3. For these laws, as well as petitions seeking to clarify their interpretation, see A.N. AD XII 5 Parents et héritiers des émigrés, 1792–an X. André Morellet, author of seven works published from 1795 to 1797 defending the rights of the parents of émigrés, also provides a clear overview of the timing of the debates and the major speeches, proposals, and laws, as well as his responses. Morellet, *Mémoires . . . sur le dix-huitième siècle et sur la Révolution,* introduction and notes by Jeane Pierre Guicciardi (Paris, 1988).

4. It was repealed on 1 Messidor Year III (June 28, 1795), shortly before the institution of the Constitution of Year III.

5. 20 Floréal Year IV (May 9, 1796).

6. The Law of 3 Brumaire was repealed on 9 Messidor Year V (June 27, 1797).

7. Pierre-Jean Audouin, *Rapport . . . sur les pères et mères d'émigrés. Séance du 28 ventôse an IV* (Paris, Year IV), 18; and idem, *Discours sur les pères et mères des émigrés . . . le 19 nivôse, l'an IV* (Paris, Year IV), 2.

8. Jacques-Antoine Creuzé-Latouche, *Rapport fait par . . . au nom d'une commission chargée d'examiner la résolution concernant les pères et mères des émigrés. Séance du 18 nivôse an VI* (Paris, Year VI), 7.

9. André Castaldo, "La révolution et les émigrés: Les partages de présuccession," *Revue historique de droit français et étranger* 71, no. 3 (1993): 383. For a typical example of similar arguments for émigrés during the Terror, see the petition for Serandez in A.N. DIII 236.

10. A.N. DIII 236, dossier C, pièce 35, Pétition de la citoyenne veuve Chastillon 2 floréal an III; A.N. AD XII 5, pièce 27, Réclamation des pères et mères d'émigrés à la Convention Nationale, 13 prairial an III.

11. A.N. DIII 238, pièce 82.

12. A.N. AD XVIIic 411, pièce 21, Les pères de famille soussignés au corps législatif, daté d'Arras le 20 vendémiaire an V.

13. The registers of the Comité de la Législation give some indication of how often such widows petitioned to be released from responsibility for their children's emigration. See especially A.N. *DIII 4, 5, and 6, which cover the period from January 4, 1793, through 13 Floréal Year II.

14. A.N. DIII 236, dossier L, Petition de la veuve Longchamp, 12 Germinal an III.

15. André Morellet, *La cause des pères, ou discussions d'un projet de décret relatif aux pères et mères, aïeuls et aïeules des émigrés, par l'auteur du cri des familles* (Paris, Year III), 72–73.

16. A.N. ADXII 5, pièce 31, Les pères et mères des émigrés du département de la Meurthe, p. 9.

17. A.N. DIII 237, pièce 80, Mémoire à la convention nationale pour les pères, les mères, et ayeux des émigrés.

18. André Morellet, *Discussion du rapport de P. J. Audouin sur les pères et mères d'émigrés. Lu au conseil des Cinq-Cents, le 28 ventôse de l'an IV* (Paris, Year IV), 44.

19. The first quotation is from a manuscript petition by Pierre-André Despommerais in A.N. C560; the second comes from idem, *Pétition . . . aux représentants du peuple composant le Conseil des Anciens* (Paris, 1797).

20. Ragon, *La législation sur les émigrés,* 275.

21. Taillandier and Mongalvy, *Recueil général des lois et des arrêts,* 1: 372.

22. The departments of Haut and especially Bas Rhin had some of the highest incidences of emigration in France, particularly from the lower classes; Greer, *The Incidence of the Emigration.*

23. Trophime-Gérard de Lally-Tolendal, *Défense des émigrés français, adressée au peuple français* (Paris, 1797). Page references are to the Libraires et Marchands edition.

24. Ibid., 28.

25. *Défense des femmes, des enfans et des vieillards émigrés, pour faire suite à l'ouvrage de M. de Lally-Tolendal* (Paris, 1797), 77.

26. Ibid., 8.

27. Lally-Tolendal, *Défense des émigrés*, 28.

28. *Défense des femmes*, 74.

29. Ibid., 8, 54.

30. Lally-Tolendal, *Défense des émigrés*, 29, 7.

31. Jean-Jacques Leuliette, *Des émigrés français, ou réponse à M de Lally-Tolendal* (Paris, 1797), 19, 20. The last name was spelled variously Leuliette, Leuliete, and Leuliète.

32. *Défense des femmes*, 62.

33. Leuliette, *Des émigrés français*, 20, 23.

34. *Les émigrés justifiés ou réfutation de la Réponse de M. Leuiliete à M. Lally-Tolendal, sur sa défense des émigrés. Par F. T.-D.* (Paris, [1797]), 41 and 42.

35. Howard Brown, "Mythes et massacres: Reconsidérer la Terreur directoriale," *Annales historiques de la révolution française*, no. 325 (2001): 23–52.

36. The Bureau was also known as the Conseil du Ministère de la Police and the Comité des Lois; its name changed several times during its history. For simplicity's sake, I refer to it as the Bureau des Lois.

37. Ange Elisabeth Louis Antoine Bonnier d'Alco, *Recherches sur l'ordre de Malte et examen d'une question relative aux français par ci-devant membres de cet ordre par le citoyen Merlin* (Paris, Year VI); Pierre Antoine Laloy, *Derniers réflexions de P. A. Laloy. Séance du 19 brumaire an 6* (Paris, Year VI); and the relevant judgments of the Bureau des Lois in A.N. F7 4323.

38. The measure was officially made law on November 29, 1797.

39. On passports for ex-nobles, see A.N. F7 4323, 2nd series, dossier 189; and F7 4324, 3rd series, dossiers 84 and 97.

40. Higonnet, *Class, Ideology and Rights of Nobles*; Brown, "Mythes et massacres," 33, 36.

41. A.N. F7 4323, 3rd series, dossier 34. The child lived with her aunt; her mother was not in the picture. There were compelling practical reasons for reuniting the girl and her father. François Le Roux was more likely to have the resources to raise and educate Aglée than her aunt. The Bureau acknowledged that the aunt opposed the move, but suspected that she feared losing the money she was given for Aglée's upkeep. However, it ultimately refused to allow the thirteen-year-old to leave France and join her émigré father.

42. Souhait, *Opinion*, 3, 5.

43. Philippe-Laurent Pons de Verdun, *Rapport et projet de résolution sur la suspension de la loi du 12 floréal, concernant les pères et mères d'émigrés* (Paris, Year VI), 4.

44. A.N. F7 4323, 3rd series, dossier 34.

45. A.N. F7 4323, 2nd series, dossier 197.

46. This was only a tentative judgment. The case was postponed until the government had decided on the appropriate means for clearing those who were inscribed as émigrés but were not actually guilty of leaving their country. However, the issue of Marie Montbéliard's "foreignness" was peripheral to the next stage of the case. For the original judgment, see A.N. F7 4323, 2nd series, dossier 197; for the continuation of her case, A.N. F7 4324, 3rd series, dossier 112.

47. A.N. F7 4324, 3rd series, dossier 93.

48. Ibid. Nineteenth-century jurists around the world would use similar language; in 1879 one American court described a foreign woman's decision to marry a citizen man as linking "her destiny with the country by the strongest of ties," implying that for women, marriage was a stronger bond than naturalization. Augustine-Adams, "'With Notice of the Consequences,'" 11.

49. A.N. F7 4323, 2nd series, dossier 226.

50. A.N. F7 4324, 3rd series, dossier 148.

51. Ibid., dossier 92.

52. Article 12, "L'exercice des droits de citoyen se perd . . . 3 par l'acceptation de fonctions ou de pensions offertes par un gouvernement étranger"; *La nationalité française*, 55. Article 13, which suspended such rights, more clearly referred to political citizenship.

53. A.N. F7 4324, 3rd series, dossier 148.

54. Greer, *The Incidence of the Emigration*, 103. See also A.N. BB30 155.

55. Ragon, *La législation sur les émigrés*, 286–292.

56. Joseph Fouché, *Rapport du ministre de la police générale et arrête des consuls, concernant les individus sur la liste des émigrés depuis 1789* (Paris, Year 9). Article 6 also authorized children under sixteen to return.·

57. A.N. BB30 155. Unfortunately, the amount and kind of information provided for each woman vary greatly, so it is difficult to draw statistical conclusions about their marital status and social position. Certainly, there were more women affected by this clause than members of any other group singled out for specific status. One table lists more than 12,000 women granted amnesty, while only 50 émigrés who had left before 1789, 74 granted special status because they were from Malta, 1,031 deported priests, and 6 children were allowed to return.

58. Ragon, *La législation sur les émigrés*, 292.

59. Louis Eugène Poirier, *Sur l'importante question du mariage des prévenus d'émigration, suivie de la décision affirmative du ministre de l'intérieur* (Paris, Year IX [1801]), 13, 4.

60. The Catalogue BN-Opale-Plus of the Bibliothèque Nationale lists three editions published in Year IX/1801.

61. Poirier, *Sur l'importante question*, 11.

Part III. The Napoleonic Solution and Its Limits

1. See the fifty articles collected in Théry and Biet, *La famille, la loi, l'état*. See also Martin, "Fonction paternelle et Code Napoléon"; H. D. Lewis, "The Legal Status of Women in Nineteenth-Century France," *Journal of European Studies* 10 (1980): 178–188; and Claire Goldberg Moses, *French Feminism in the Nineteenth Century* (Albany, N.Y., 1984).

2. Brubaker, *Citizenship and Nationhood*; and Noiriel, *The French Melting Pot*. See also Bruschi, "Droit de la nationalité"; and Jean-Michel Belorgey, "Le droit de la nationalité: Evolution historique et enjeux," 61–80, in *Questions de nationalité: Histoire et enjeux d'un code*, ed. Smain Laacher (Paris, 1987).

3. Key works on the creation and content of the Code include Halperin, *L'impossible code civil*; François Ewald, ed., *Naissance du Code civil: La raison du législateur* (Paris, 1989); and Jean-Michel Poughon, *Le code civil* (Paris, 1992).

Chapter 5. Tethering Cain's Wife

1. The Tribunate temporarily closed discussion on 11 Nivôse Year X (January 1, 1802). On the workings of the Tribunate and the Conseil d'Etat, see Ewald, *Naissance du Code civil*; Halperin, *L'impossible code civil*; and Martyn Lyons, *Napoleon Bonaparte and the Legacy of the French Revolution* (New York, 1994), chap. 8.

2. The most useful collection of documents on the making of the Civil Code is Fenet, *Recueil complet*. The *Procès-verbaux du Conseil d'état contenant la discussion du Code Napoleon*, 2nd ed. (Paris, 1808), has a detailed subject index that complements Fenet. Most of the pertinent speeches are also in A.N. AD II 34, Droits civils, naturalisation (1790–1814).

3. Halperin, *L'impossible code civil*, 263–286; Desan, *Family on Trial*, 287–288.

4. There were inherent contradictions in Napoleon's vision: he wanted a maximum of subjects, but also wanted to control access to citizenship. Weil, *Qu'est-ce qu'un Français?*, 27–35.

5. Brubaker, *Citizenship and Nationhood*, 88–91; Sahlins, *Unnaturally French*, 292–294; and Weil, *Qu'est-ce qu'un Français?*, 27–35. The original debates are in Fenet, *Recueil complet*, vol. 7; and Ewald, *Naissance du code civil*.

6. Christian Bruschi compares this shift to evolutions in classical Rome. Emancipation of a slave was originally a public affair, necessitating formal intervention by the magistrate or popular assembly. It became a matter of private law, although it continued to grant citizenship rights to emancipated slaves. Bruschi, "Le droit de cité dans l'antiquité: Un questionnement pour la citoyenneté aujourd'hui," in *La citoyenneté et les changements de structures*

sociales et nationales de la population française, ed. Catherine Wihtol de Wenden (Paris, 1988), 126–153.

7. *La nationalité française,* 55.

8. Weil, *Qu'est-ce qu'un Français?,* 27.

9. The Conseil d'Etat discussed *admission à domicile* on 18–20 Prairial Year XI. For changes in its consequences, see Bruschi, "Droit de la nationalité," 35.

10. Verjus, *Le cens de la famille,* 84–87.

11. Jean-Baptiste Duvergier, ed., *La collection complète des lois, décrets, ordonnances, règlements, et avis du conseil d'état . . . de 1788 à 1824,* 45 vols. (Paris, 1834–1845), 13: 291. See also Jennifer Heuer and Anne Verjus, "L'invention de la sphère domestique au sortir de la révolution," *Annales historiques de la révolution française,* no. 327 (2002): 20.

12. On the timing of this trend, see Pierre Lascoumes, "L'émergence de la famille comme intérêt protégé par le droit pénal, 1791–1810," in Théry and Biet, *La famille, la loi et l'état,* 340–350. See also Hunt, *The Family Romance,* 66–67.

13. Art. 212: "Married persons owe to each other fidelity, succor, assistance"; art. 213: "The husband owes protection to his wife, the wife obedience to her husband." Adrien Siramy, *Etude sur les origines et les caractères de l'autorisation maritale dans l'histoire du droit français* (Paris, 1901); and Jean Gay, "Capacité de la femme mariée et puissance maritale dans l'élaboration du code civil," *Revue de l'Institut Napoléon,* no. 161 (1993): 33–65.

14. Lewis, "The Legal Status of Women"; and Traer, *Marriage and the Family.* For the ideological underpinnings of these changes, see Ewald, *Naissance du code civil,* especially chap. 9, "Le traitement des inégalités"; and Irène Théry and Christian Biet, "Portalis, ou l'esprit des siècles, la rhétorique du mariage dans le discours préliminaire au projet de Code civil," in Théry and Biet, *La famille, la loi, l'état,* 104–121.

15. Desan, *Family on Trial,* 298–299; Théry et Biet, "Portalis, ou l'esprit des siècles, la rhétorique du mariage dans le discours préliminaire au projet de code civil," in Théry and Biet, *La famille, la loi, l'état,* 104–121.

16. Divorce by mutual consent was refused to minors and forbidden before two years and after twenty years of marriage, as well as for women aged over forty-five; Poughon, *Le code civil,* 34. Desan, *Family on Trial,* 302–303.

17. Bonnecase, *La philosophie du Code Napoléon,* 160. Article 1388 stated explicitly that "married persons cannot derogate from the rights which result from the power of the husband over the persons of his wife and of his children, or which belong to the husband as head, nor from the rights conferred on the survivor of the married parties by the title 'Of the Paternal Power,' and by the title 'Of Minority, Guardianship, and Emancipation,' nor from the prohibitory regulations of the present code." I am indebted to Anne Verjus for the analysis of these articles of the Code. See Heuer and Verjus, "L'invention de la sphère domestique," 24–25.

18. Throughout the nineteenth century, jurists and administrators debated the precise circumstances in which a child's national citizenship could, or should, be treated separately from his or her father's. It was possible that if a father naturalized or lost citizenship rights after a child's birth, the child could have a different national status from his or her father; children born out of wedlock could also have a different status.

19. Réal observed that the original draft of the article limited the obligation to metropolitan France and its colonies, "le sol continental ou colonial de la République," but that the tribunals had asked for the suppression of these words. Ewald, *Naissance du Code civil,* 368.

20. Art. II; Ewald, *Naissance du Code civil,* 368.

21. Ibid., 368, 369.

22. The relevant discussion of the Conseil d'Etat is reprinted in Ewald, *Naissance du Code civil.* On interpretations of article 214, see Charles Demolombe, *Cours de Code Napoléon,* 32 vols. (Paris, 1869–1896), 4: 108–109.

23. A.N. DIII 361, pièce 64; and [Gaspart-Gilbert Delamalle], *Réplique du Citoyen Delamalle, pour Térence Mac-Mahon; contre Madame Mac-Mahon; recueillie par le sténographe en la 3e section du Tribunal d'appel du département de la Seine . . . Audience du 18 pluviôse an 12 [8 février 1804]* (Paris, Year XII–1804), 48.

24. Merlin, *Répertoire universel,* 19: 359–361.

25. On Old Regime law, see Richer, *Traité de la mort civile.* The Conseil d'Etat addressed the relationship between religion and civil death when debating the opening articles of the

Civil Code. See "Procès-verbal du 16 Thermidor an IX–4 août 1801," in Fenet, *Recueil complet*, 7: 42–64.

26. A.N. F7 3330.

27. Jean Grenier, "Opinion . . . pour le projet (29 frimaire an X)," in Fenet, *Recueil complet*, 7: 251.

28. Jean-Pierre Chazal, "Opinion . . . contre le projet (3 nivôse an X)," in ibid., 345.

29. Théodore François Huguet, "Opinion . . . pour le projet (9 nivôse an X)," in ibid., 458.

30. Louis Julien Roujoux, "Opinion . . . pour le projet (1 nivôse an X)," in ibid., 293.

31. Chazal, "Opinion . . . contre le projet (3 nivôse an X)," 354.

32. Louis Joseph Faure, "Opinion . . . contre le projet (9 nivôse an X)," in Fenet, *Recueil complet*, 7: 439.

33. Jean François Curée, "Opinion . . . pour le projet (5 nivôse an X)," in ibid., 422.

34. Halperin, *L'impossible code civil*, 274.

35. Titre 1, chap. 2, sec. 2, art. 25: "Il est incapable de contracter un mariage qui produise aucun effet civil. Le mariage qu'il avait contracté précédemment, est dissous, quant à tous ses effets civils. Son époux est ses héritiers peuvent exercer respectivement les droits et les actions auxquels sa mort naturelle donnerait ouverture." The fact that civil death dissolved marriage was reiterated in Titre CV, chap. VII, art. 227, De la Dissolution du Mariage: "Le mariage se dissout 1. Par la mort de l'un des époux; 2. Par le divorce légalement prononcé; 3. Par la condamnation devenue définitive de l'un des époux, à une peine emportant mort civile."

36. Thomas Laurent Mouricault, "Opinion . . . pour le projet (11 nivôse an X)," in Fenet, *Recueil complet*, 7: 557.

37. Alexandre Gaspard Gary, "Discussion devant le Corps Législatif (17 ventôse an XI)," in ibid., 660.

38. On the *droit d'aubaine* during the Old Regime, see Wells, *Law and Citizenship*; Danjou, *La condition civile de l'étranger*; and Zosa Szajkowski, "The Jewish Status in the Eighteenth Century and the 'Droit d'aubaine,'" in *Jews and the French Revolutions of 1789, 1830, and 1848* (New York, 1970), 220–234.

39. On the principle that "les enfants régnicoles valent à l'aubain des lettres de naturalité," see Danjou, *La condition civile de l'étranger*, 39.

40. On the importance of the *paterfamilias* in antiquity, see Thomas, "À Rome, pères citoyens"; and Bruschi, "Le droit de cité dans l'antiquité."

41. Chazal, "Opinion . . . contre le projet (3 nivôse an X)," 349.

42. J. P. Mathieu, "Opinion . . . sur l'article 13 du deuxième projet du Code Civil. Séance du 11 nivôse an 10," in Fenet, *Recueil complet*, 7: 586.

43. Martin, *Maintenez les propriétés mais n'en disposez pas ou Mémoire sur l'usage barbare des confiscations, en faveur des héritiers de parens proscrits* (Paris, 1797), 11.

44. Art. XXVIIII: "Il n'est point dérogé par les dispositions ci-dessus sur les lois relatives aux émigrés."

45. Mathieu, "Opinion . . . sur l'article 13," 7: 578–579.

46. Alexandre Gaspard Gary, "Communication Officielle au Tribunat, 14 ventôse an 11," in Fenet, *Recueil complet*, 7: 641.

47. It was abolished on July 14, 1819. The prevailing rationale was one of economic liberalism; M. C. Sapey, *Les étrangers en France sous l'ancien et le nouveau droit* (Paris, 1843); and Charles Demangeat, *Histoire de la condition civile des étrangers en France dans l'ancien et dans le nouveau droit* (Paris, 1844). See also Rapport, "'A Languishing Branch'"; and Sahlins, *Unnaturally French*.

48. Louis Barnabé Cotèle, *Notice sur la justice et l'intérêt de la France, comme des autres états de l'Europe, d'abolir le droit d'aubaine* (Orléans, 1814), 20.

49. Ibid., 7.

50. Goodheart, "Adoption," 330–350.

51. The Law of June 19, 1923, granted foreigners the right to adopt in France; Bruschi, "Le droit de la nationalité," 37.

52. Jean-Simon Loiseau, *Traité des enfans naturels, adultérins, incestueux et abandonnés* (Paris, 1811).

53. Virginia Sapiro, "Women, Citizenship, and Nationality: Immigration and Naturalization Policies in the United States," *Politics and Society* 13, no. 1 (1984): 23.

Chapter 6. Looking Backward

1. The courts ruled that it was impossible for an Englishman to legitimate French-born children unless both he and his children were naturalized French; similarly, a foreign child had to become legally French before he could be adopted by a Frenchman. Children of polygamous Egyptians in France were declared not to be the product of adultery. Loiseau, *Traité des enfans naturels*.

2. Etienne Gosse, *Les femmes politiques, Comédie en trois actes et en vers, par le citoyen Gosse, représentée la première fois sur le théâtre des victoires, le 30 fructidor an 7* (Paris, Year VIII), 4–5. According to the ARTFL database, the play ran from September 15 through November 7, 1799, and had twenty-seven showings. Although the play was obviously intended as a comedy, it resonates with a more widespread wariness of women's consumption of political journals, perhaps most clearly epitomized in Sylvan Maréchal's 1801 *Projet d'une loi portant défense d'apprendre à lire aux femmes*. See Geneviève Fraisse, *Reason's Muse: Sexual Difference and the Birth of Democracy* (Chicago, 1994).

3. Taillandier and Mongalvy, *Recueil général des lois et des arrêts*, 1: 222. The case in question, decided on 12 Fructidor Year 12 (August 29, 1803), was that of Rohan-Guémenée-Rohan Rochefort.

4. Ibid., 2: 254. For an overview of the case, see Merlin, *Répertoire universel*, 10: 156–158.

5. The case was decided on 24 Floréal Year 13 (May 13, 1804); Taillandier and Mongalvy, *Recueil général des lois et des arrêts*, 2: 112.

6. Merlin, *Répertoire universel*, 2: 206.

7. Taillandier and Mongalvy, *Recueil général des lois et des arrêts*, 2: 254; *Bulletin des arrêts de la cour de cassation rendus en matière civile*, 144 vols. (Paris, 1804–1942), 8: 215–217.

8. Ragon, *La législation sur les émigrés*, 133.

9. The Conseil insisted that even cohabitation after the divorce did not negate it; men and women who wished to be legally considered a couple had to remarry.

10. The case went before the Cour d'Appel de Paris on 9 Ventôse Year 12 (February 27, 1804) and then to the Cour de Cassation, where it was judged on 30 Pluviôse Year 13 (February 18, 1805). It was appealed again and judged by the Cour d'Appel d'Orléans on 11 Thermidor Year 13 (July 29, 1805) and was decided conclusively by the Cour de Cassation on March 23, 1806.

11. In practice, the government often decreed that petitioners were covered by the amnesty, rather than acknowledging that they had been falsely inscribed on the list of émigrés; Robin, *Le séquestre des biens ennemis*, 283.

12. Courol, *Mémoire et consultation pour Madame Caroline Latour–Saint Igest contre Monsieur MacMahon* (Paris, n.d.), 209.

13. *Consultation signée Poirier, Ferey, Siméon, Jolly, David Portalis, Desèze; Chaveau-Lagarde, le 7 ventôse an XII–27 février 1804* (n.p.: n.d.), xxviij.

14. Kif Augustine-Adams, "'She Consents Implicitly': Women's Citizenship, Marriage, and Liberal Political Thought in Late-Nineteenth- and Early-Twentieth-Century Argentina," *Journal of Women's History* 13, no. 4 (2002): 8–30; and idem, "'With Notice of the Consequences.'"

15. [Delamalle], *Réplique du Citoyen Delamalle, . . . Audience du 18 pluviôse*, 48.

16. Merlin, *Répertoire universel*, 18: 189–190.

17. Ibid., 203.

18. Bureau du Colombier et al., *Consultation pour Dame Caroline Elisabeth-Humbline de Latour Saint Igest, contre le Sieur Térence MacMahon* (Orléans, 1805), 40.

19. Gaspart-Gilbert Delamalle, *Plaidoyers choisis et oeuvres diverses de M. Delamalle* (Paris, 1827), 95.

20. [Delamalle], *Réplique du Citoyen Delamalle, . . . Audience du 2 ventôse an 12*, 26.

21. Delamalle, *Plaidoyers choisis*, 55.

22. [Delamalle], *Réplique du Citoyen Delamalle, . . . Audience du 2 ventôse an 12*, 3.

23. *Consultation signée Poirier*, vi.

24. Patrick Weil refers to Merlin's judgment on the trial to establish that the 1790 Constitution automatically made foreigners who met the conditions of the law into French nationals; *Qu'est-ce qu'un Français?*, 23 and 280–281.

25. Weil acknowledges that the court did not use Merlin's logic to validate the divorce. But later jurisprudence tended to follow Merlin's interpretation of revolutionary law.

26. Arrêt de la Cour de Cassation, Rendu toutes les sections réunies, le 23 mars 1806, quoted in Delamalle, *Plaidoyers choisis,* 120.

27. The *senatus consulte* of 26 Vendémiaire Year XI (September 4, 1802) was in effect for five years. After it had expired, a second *senatus consulte* was proclaimed on February 19, 1808. For the rationale behind the *senatus consultes,* see *Motifs du projet de senatus-consulte organique sur la naturalisation des étrangers, présenté au Sénat dans la séance du 16 vendémiaire an XI par les conseillers d'état Regnault et de Saint-Jean-d'Angely et Bigot-Préameau, orateurs du gouvernement* (n.p., n.d.); and the 1808 "Rapport présenté aux consuls de la République par le Ministre de l'Intérieur," A.N. F2 I 436.

28. Rapport, "'A Languishing Branch,'" 35.

29. Brian Jenkins, *Nationalism in France: Class and Nation since 1789* (Savage, Md., 1990), 36.

30. Marie-Hélène Varnier and Karin Dietrich-Chénel, "Intégration des étrangers par naturalisation ou admission à domicile de 1790/1814 au 10 mai 1871," 8 vols. (Thèse de doctorat, Université Aix-Marseille I, 1994), 1: 22.

31. A.N. BB11 3.

32. A.N. BB11 94.

33. An 1809 decree established that French men, even those who had been naturalized foreigners, could be tried by special courts and military tribunals if they were accused of taking arms against France. If found guilty, they could have their property confiscated or face the death penalty. See Gabriel Lepointe, "Le statut des étrangers dans la France du XIXe siècle," in *L'étranger foreigner* (Paris, 1984), 553–574.

34. Méjan, *Recueil des causes célèbres,* 5: 217, 218.

35. Jean Simon Loiseau, *Plaidoyer pour L. R. A. Voyneau, Fils, Dragon au 15e régiment, contre L. A. F. Voyneau, son père, par M. Loiseau, docteur en droit et avocat à la Cour de cassation* (Paris, 1808); and Méjan, *Recueil des causes célèbres,* 4: 249–316.

36. Loiseau, *Plaidoyer,* 34–35.

37. Ibid., 33.

38. Ibid., 36.

39. Ibid., 21.

40. Gary, "Discussion devant le Corps Législatif (17 ventôse an XI)," in Fenet, *Recueil complet,* 7: 660.

41. Louiseau, *Plaidoyer,* 29.

42. Ibid., 30; the speech is also reproduced in Méjan, *Recueil des causes célèbres,* 4: 304. Loiseau reproduced a speech made earlier in the trial by Joseph-Charles Bera, omitting Bera's comment that "we know only one adoption of this nature, but it was done with a formal and particular decree, that in favor of the daughter of Lepelletier de Saint-Fargeau." Bera, *Choix de plaidoyers prononcés sur des questions d'état et des difficultés intéressantes élevées en interprétation du Code Napoléon et du code de procédure civile* (Paris, 1812), 314.

43. Taillandier and Mongalvy, *Recueil général des lois et des arrêts,* 2: 210; *Bulletin des arrêts de la cour de cassation,* 10: 339–340.

44. Méjan, *Recueil des causes célèbres,* 4: 310.

45. Ibid., 10: 302–410.

Chapter 7. Looking Forward

1. Varnier and Dietrich-Chénel contend that only 278 of 22,954 acts granting foreigners naturalization or civil rights in France from 1790 to May 10, 1871, directly concerned women. Of these, only 72 took place before March 1848. Varnier and Dietrich-Chénel, "Intégration des étrangers," 1: 38. These statistics are incomplete, particularly for the revolutionary period. I have discovered numerous cases of *admission à domicile* in Alsace before the Civil Code that were not formally recorded in the *Bulletin des lois;* there are likely to have been similar acts in other frontier areas. However, the numbers can be taken as reasonably

accurate for the postrevolutionary period, when the procedure for recording such acts was more standardized.

2. The others were for the American Joel Barlow on February 17, 1793; the Italian Philippe Buonnarroti on May 27, 1793; and the Belgian Pierre Blouvier on June 10, 1793.

3. Weil, *Qu'est-ce qu'un Français?*, 20–25 and 212.

4. Guérard, *Mémoire à la Convention Nationale pour Jean Pratbernon et Susanne Néau.*

5. Art. 12: "L'étrangère qui aura épousé un Français suivra la condition de son mari"; art. 19: "Une femme française qui épousera un étranger, suivra la condition de son mari"; and art. 214: "La femme est obligée d'habiter avec le mari, et de le suivre partout, où il juge à propos de résider."

6. Anne McClintock, *Imperial Leather: Race, Gender, and Sexuality in the Colonial Contest* (New York, 1995), 358.

7. *La nationalité française.* See also Merlin, *Répertoire universel*, 12: 357–358.

8. For a sense of the full range of people affected by the law, see the catalogue for A.N. BB11 9–76[1], Autorisations à des Français d'entrer ou de rester au service des puissances étrangères, and specific dossiers within this series.

9. *La nationalité française*, 57.

10. B. J. Legat, *Code des étrangers ou traité de la législation française concernant les étrangers* (Paris, 1832), 55. As we have seen, article 214 did not specify whether a wife was constrained to follow her husband to a foreign country, and could thus be read as obliging women to follow their husbands everywhere; Legat's reading of the article was unusual in the 1830s. See also Demolombe, *Cours de Code Napoléon*, 4: 108–109.

11. A.N. BB11 4.

12. A.N. BB11 95.

13. A.N. BB11 75, 14.

14. A.N. BB11 14.

15. A.N. BB11 75.

16. Decision of the Conseil d'Etat on January 14, 1812; Merlin, *Répertoire universel*, 12: 358.

17. A.N. BB11 95.

18. A.N. BB11 4.

19. *Bulletin des lois* (Paris, 1812). See also Legat, *Code des étrangers*, 75–76.

20. For example, see the letter from the minister of justice to the minister of foreign relations, telling him to remove the names of seven women from the list of twenty-nine petitioners from Würtzburg who were concerned about the edict; A.N. BB11 75.

21. On Napoleon's war machine, see Geoffrey Ellis, *The Napoleonic Empire* (London, 1991); Charles Esdaile, *The Wars of Napoleon* (London, 1995); and Stuart Woolf, *Napoleon's Integration of Europe* (London, 1991).

22. A.N. BB11 4.

23. The Constitution of Year VIII still regulated the loss of "French citizenship," except where it had been explicitly superseded, and stipulated that "le qualité de citoyen français se perd . . . par l'acception des fonctions ou des pensions offertes par un Gouvernement étranger."

24. Taillandier and Mongalvy, *Recueil général des lois et de des arrêts*, 3: 531.

25. A.N. F7 4323.

26. Alauzet, *De la qualité de français*, 173.

27. The article "Naturalisation," in Merlin, *Répertoire universal*, 21: 92–95, provides a particularly clear overview of laws on naturalization from the Revolution through the late Restoration.

28. "L'étranger qui aura été autorisé par le gouvernement à établir son domicile en France y jouira de tous les droits civils, tant qu'il continuera d'y résider."

29. The Conseil d'Etat discussed *admission à domicile* on 18–20 Prairial Year XI. For changes in the consequences of *admission à domicile*, see Bruschi, "Droit de la nationalité," 35.

30. Varnier and Dietrich-Chénel, "Intégration des étrangers," 1: 21; Patrick Weil, *La France et ses étrangers: L'aventure d'une politique d'immigration, 1938–1991* (Paris, 1991), 297. For the text of the decree, see *La nationalité française*, and for the original discussions of

the 1809 decree, particularly the arguments over what branch of government would control naturalization, A.N. F7 4283.

31. For individual petitions based on the *senatus consulte,* see especially A.N. F2 I 437–441 and BB11 3, 94, and 95.

32. For Canaliolly's dossier, see A.N. F2 I 437; for Schmerz's, A.N. F2 I 441; and for Hollingsworth, A.N. BB11 3.

33. Among others, see the dossiers for Jacques Hodson, Jean Stott, and Daniel MacFee, in A.N. BB11 4.

34. For Dowling's dossier, see A.N. F2 I 438; for Jordan's, A.N. F2 I 439.

35. A.N. F2 I 439.

36. See the dubious reception accorded to Joseph Molas, a native Spaniard who taught Spanish, Italian, and Latin in Marseille; A.N. F2 I 439.

37. A.N. F2 I 437.

38. A.N. F2 I 437.

39. A.N. BB11 3.

40. A.N. BB11 94.

41. Ibid. On Theobold Wolfe Tone, Mathilde's husband, see Marianne Elliott, *Wolfe Tone: Prophet of Irish Independence* (New Haven, 1989).

42. Varnier and Dietrich-Chénel compiled charts of the women who naturalized or obtained civil rights between 1790 and 1870; these can found in the appendixes devoted to each nationality in their joint thesis, "Integration des étrangers." Their lists show no records of women who naturalized during the Napoleonic era or women granted civil rights in the period. Some cases of women *admises à domicile* during the Napoleonic period were not formally recorded in the *Bulletin des lois.* There may have been similar cases of naturalization; however, I have yet to find any.

43. About a quarter of immigrants *admis à domicile* can be identified as German; Italians and Belgians respectively form the next-largest groups. The majority of such admissions took place in the departments of Bas Rhin (21 percent), followed by Haut Rhin (13 percent); Seine comes in third (about 13 percent). Varnier and Dietrich, "Integration des étrangers," 1: 86.

44. Strasbourg was besieged during the end of the Napoleonic Wars, and again during the Hundred Days. Georges Weill, *L'Alsace française de 1789 à 1870* (Paris, 1916) and, for a day-to-day narrative of events, the mayor's *arrêts* in A.C. Strasbourg, Administration 12.

45. A.C. Strasbourg, Police 48. He was opposed to such lists in general, precisely because they would "confondre tous les étrangers dans un seul classe de suspicion ou d'évacuation."

46. A.C. Strasbourg, Police 281. Women accounted for 30 percent of names in the census for the northern quarter of the city (146 of 493 names), 16 percent in the southern quarter (91 of 569), 18 percent in the east (64 of 365), and roughly 26 percent in the western quarter. The statistics for the western case are uncertain, as I am missing a page of names; I have located 83 women out of 321 names so far.

47. A.C. Strasbourg, Police 281.

48. For traditional patterns of popular migration, see Olwen Hufton, *The Poor of Eighteenth-Century France, 1750–1789* (Oxford, 1974).

49. Sylvie Dawaele, "Guide des sources archivistes sur les étrangers dans le Haut-Rhin de 1800–1870 aux Archives Départementales du Haut Rhin et aux Archives Municipales de Mulhouse" (Mémoire de maîtrise ME. Ca. D.O.C.T.E. Archivistique, Mulhouse, 1991), especially chap. 4, "Les étapes de l'intégration en France." Dawaele does not examine changes in procedures for women, a shift that may not have happened, or happened as clearly, in the department of Haut Rhin as in that of Bas Rhin. However, she provides a clear description of the general procedures of *admission à domicile* and naturalization in Alsace throughout the nineteenth century.

50. A.N. F7 4327, dossier 16.

51. "Intention d'acquérir les droits de citoyen français," desire that petitioners "acquérir les droits de cité après le terme prescrit par la constitution," or request to be allowed to establish domicile in France "pour y jouir de tous les droits civils et de ceux politiques après le stage de dix ans"; A.N. F7 4327, A.D. Bas Rhin 8M 25 and 38.

52. Marie Josèphe Sculère's petition noted that "elle s'est promise en mariage avec un habitant de cette ville intentionnée de s'y établir et de devenir Française," while Anne Marie

Wanndeutsch similarly proclaimed that "elle est intentionnée de rester en France et de devenir française." A.N. F7 4327, dossier 16.

53. "Intentionnée de s'établir en cette ville et d'acquérir la qualité de citoyen français"; A.N. BB11 80.

54. "Un étranger devient citoyen français, après avoir atteint 21 ans, déclaré son intention de se fixer en France, réside pendant 10 ans consécutives." On the relationship between the Civil Code and the Constitution of Year VIII, see Vanel, *Evolution historique,* 101. Vanel notes that the Constitution was not modified by the Napoleonic Code and argues that the Constitution pertained to citizenship, while the Code regulated nationality or the *qualité de français,* not citizenship.

55. A.D. Bas Rhin 8M 25. The prefect's *arrêt* of 5 Thermidor Year 11 (August 2, 1803) outlined general procedures.

56. A.D. Bas Rhin 8M 25.

57. A.N. F2 I 437.

58. A.D. Bas Rhin 8M 25. "Civils" was added in the margin after "effets."

59. See the registers in A.D. Bas Rhin 8M 30 (1818–1825) and 31 (1825–1838). For Dorothée Branckehaffer, see also the registers of the *Conseil municipal procès-verbaux des séances, années 1821–1830,* vol. 24. The Municipal Council at first dismissed the widow because of her age, lack of funds, and recent arrival in France. They rapidly revised their assessment once they discovered that she had spent her childhood in Strasbourg, still had family in the area, and, perhaps most important, was introducing the manufacture of bone buttons, which otherwise had to be imported at great cost.

60. There were 11 women of some 2,868 acts, 3 of which concerned naturalizations. See Varnier and Dietrich, "Intégration d'étrangers en France," 1: 104 and 2: 139. The list of German immigrants encompasses immigrants in all of France; the department registers for Bas Rhin list primarily German immigrants but also include Swiss and other nationalities.

61. The majority of the debates are reproduced in vol. 12 of AP2. They resulted in the law of October 14, 1814, which laid out the procedures by which natives of the "departments reunited to France since 1791" could become, or continue to be, legally French.

62. See Varnier and Dietrich, "Intégration des étrangers," for a statistical study of these cases. After 1814 the *Bulletin des lois,* which officially recorded naturalizations and *admissions à domicile,* regularly described petitioners' birthplaces in terms of "anciens départements," rather than their post-Napoleonic place names, emphasizing both petitioners' eligibility for naturalization under the October 1814 law and their connections to France.

63. On the June decree and its repercussions for "grande naturalisation," see Varnier and Dietrich, "Intégration des étrangers," 1: 23 and Adolphe L'Esprit, *Situation des étrangers en France au point de vue du recrutement. Petit manuel théorique et pratique d'extranéité à l'usage des Mairies* (Paris, 1888), 3.

64. Rosanvallon, *Le sacre du citoyen.*

65. Varnier and Dietrich, "Integration des étrangers," 3: 93, 118, 132; 5:66.

66. See A.N. BB30 772.

67. Varnier and Dietrich do not systematically note whether the women in question were widows, but the age of women who naturalized suggests strongly that they were; two of the seven women mentioned above were in their thirties; the other five ranged from forty-eight to seventy-three. Varnier and Dietrich, "Integration des étrangers."

68. A.D. Moselle 212 M 210.

Chapter 8. Immigration, Marriage, and Citizenship in the Restoration

1. Jacquinot Pampelune, *Opinion . . . sur la résolution de la Chambre des Pairs, relative à l'abolition des droits d'aubaine et de détraction* (Paris, n.d.), 58.

2. Vogler, "La vie économique," 187–250. The status of *manant* did not exist in the "interior" of France; the categories of *manant* and bourgeois were originally sharply distinguished, but became more similar after the creation of a new category, *manants temporaires,* in 1728.

3. A.C. Strasbourg, Police 294. The Strasbourg municipal council described prerevolutionary practices in detail in order to protest a decree of the National Assembly, which limited

active citizenship rights to those who had been born French or formally naturalized as French citizens. This address was contemporaneous with the better-known anti-Semitic address by the inhabitants of Strasbourg protesting the extension of French citizenship to Alsatian Jews.

4. Vogler, "La vie économique," 200.

5. Isser Woloch, "Corporate Reorganization and the Professions," in *The French Revolutionary Research Collection*, ed. Colin Lucas, 12 vols. (New York, 1990–1995), 9: 1–4; and Michel Sibalis, "Corporatism after the Corporation: The Debate on Restoring the Guilds under Napoleon and the Restoration," *French Historical Studies* 15, no. 4 (1988): 718–730.

6. A.C. Strasbourg, Police 90, *arrêt* of 17 Messidor Year VIII (July 5, 1800), repeating an earlier decree of 1 Brumaire Year VII (October 23, 1798).

7. Paula Hyman, *The Emancipation of the Jews in Alsace: Acculturation and Tradition in the Nineteenth Century* (New Haven, 1991); and Michael Burns, "Emancipation and Reaction: The Rural Exodus of Alsatian Jews, 1791–1848," in *Living with Antisemitism: Modern Jewish Responses*, ed. Jehuda Reinharz (Hanover, NH, 1987), 19–41.

8. See also Simon Schwarzfuchs, *Du juif à l'israélite: Histoire d'une mutation, 1770–1970* (Paris, 1989). The 1808 decree was nominally nationwide, but Gironde, Seine, and various other departments were excluded.

9. Among other cases, see the opposition of metalcasters and scissorsmakers to André Ahr's establishment in Strasbourg in Year X (1801), in A.D. Bas Rhin 8M 32; and the 1807 opposition by master brushmakers of Francbourg to a young Bavarian immigrant; A.D. Bas Rhin 8M 26.

10. Conseil des Prudhommes, 16 janv. 1815, in A.D. Bas Rhin 13M 52.

11. Marriage did become a more common means of access to the bourgeoisie during the eighteenth century, from 39 percent of new admissions in 1700 to 68 percent in 1786. At the beginning of the century, more male immigrants married Strasbourg women—59 percent of men received individually married a widow or a daughter of a bourgeois of Strasbourg, while only 39 percent of women married a bourgeois—but by 1786 the proportions reversed, and the quasi-totality of women received as bourgeois married a bourgeois themselves. Vogler, "La vie économique," 190–191.

12. Ronsin, *Le contrat sentimental*.

13. J. P. Chrestien de Poly, *Essai sur la puissance paternelle* (Paris, 1820); Antoine-Toussaint Desquiron de Saint-Agnan, *La puissance paternelle en France, mise en rapport avec les intérêts de la société, essai sur l'adultère considéré dans ses rapports avec nos lois et avec nos moeurs* (Paris, 1821); Jo Burr Margadant, "The Duchesse de Berry and Royalist Political Culture in Postrevolutionary France," *History Workshop*, no. 43 (1997): 23–52.

14. On the founding of the Conseil de Prud'hommes in 1813 and its purpose and social composition, see A.C. Strasbourg, Administration 12 and Police 182. The Conseil had jurisdiction over all workers in Strasbourg.

15. Report from the police commissionaire of the second arrondisement to the mayor on February 7, 1809, in A.C. Strasbourg, Police 48.

16. A.D. Bas Rhin 8M 26. The conseiller d'état responded by claiming that the solution was obvious: the central government's approval of requests for *admission à domicile* and full citizenship would be given only on the advice of local authorities. Unfortunately, the situation was not as easily resolved as he believed.

17. *Mémoire sur les inconvéniens et les abus résultant du système actuel des patentes. Par le Conseil des prud'hommes de Strasbourg* (Strasbourg, 1815); in A.D. Bas Rhin 13M 52.

18. A.D. Bas Rhin 8M 26, "Rapport fait au maire de la ville de Strasbourg par l'adjoint du maire, délégué à la division de police, ce 2 février 1815."

19. A.D. Bas Rhin 8M 26.

20. Ibid.

21. Ibid. Proposed measures however, exempted foreigners who had adequate fortunes, brought new industry, or whose skills were rare and did not threaten local labor markets.

22. A.D. Bas Rhin 13M 52.

23. A.C. Strasbourg, Police 48.

24. Ibid.

25. Ibid.

26. A.D. Bas Rhin 8M 29, Enregistrement des actes d'admission à domicile et de naturalisation (an IX–1818). These numbers may not be completely accurate, given the frequent

delays in processing applications and potential gaps in the registers, but the general shift is undeniable.

27. A.C. Strasbourg, Police 281.

28. Ibid. On the 1816–17 famine in Alsace and Strasbourg's economic troubles throughout the early Restoration, see Paul Leuilliot, *L'Alsace au début de XIX siècle. Essais d'histoire politique, économique et religieux, 1815–1830*, 3 vols. (Paris, 1959); and André Jardin and André Jean-Tudesq, *Restoration and Reaction, 1815–1848* (Cambridge, 1983).

29. The Conseil was explicit about which occupations were overcrowded, but see also the comparative table of professions exercised in Strasbourg in 1784 and 1816 presented by Jean Frédéric Herman, mayor of Strasbourg from Year IX to 1814; *Notices historiques, statistiques et littéraires sur la ville de Strasbourg*, 2 vols. (Strasbourg, 1817–1819).

30. A.C. Strasbourg, Police 281.

31. For example, the joiner François Xavier Putz, whom they recommended for admission, was a native of Prussia; A.D. Bas Rhin 8M 29.

32. A.C. Strasbourg, Police 281.

33. Ibid.

34. Ibid.

35. The registers of those *admis à domicile* are in A.D. Bas Rhin 8M 29–31. They cover the department as a whole, but the majority of immigrants in Bas Rhin settled in Strasbourg. The registers do not usually mention whether immigrants were married; on this point, they are best supplemented by the *Procès-verbaux des séances du conseil municipal* in A.C. Strasbourg.

36. A.D. Bas Rhin 13M 52.

37. A.D. Bas Rhin 8M 28.

38. Ibid.

39. Ibid.

40. Ibid.

41. Katherine Lynch, *Family, Class, and Ideology in Early Industrial France: Social Policy and the Working-Class Family, 1825–1848* (Madison, 1988). See also Dawaele, "Guide des sources archivistes sur les étrangers."

42. There were over 11,000 foreigners by 1826; Leuilliot, *L'Alsace au début de XIX siècle*, 2: 12. Two reports vividly demonstrate changing administrative attitudes toward foreign workers in Haut Rhin. In 1808 the prefect Deporte claimed that immigrants posed no threat to public order; in contrast, Puymaigre, the prefect in 1821, attempted to prove that more crimes were committed by foreigners than by native French men and women, requesting that the *procureur général* compile a list of arrests and highlight those committed by Germans and Swiss. A.D. Haut Rhin 4M 140, 1 Z 237, and 4M 148.

43. A.N. F7 4327.

44. On the importance of honor and scandal during the Restoration, see William Reddy, *The Invisible Code: Honor and Sentiment in Post-Revolutionary France, 1814–1848* (Berkeley, 1997); Raymond Deniel, *Une image de la famille et de la société sous la Restauration (1815–1830): Etude de la presse catholique* (Paris, 1965); and Caroline Ford, "Private Lives and Public Order in Restoration France: The Seduction of Emily Loveday," *American Historical Review* 90, no. 1 (1994): 21–43.

45. A.D. Haut Rhin 1Z 237.

46. Lynch vividly describes the campaign against concubinage in Mulhouse in the 1820s and 1830s in *Family, Class, and Ideology*, and analyzes the extent to which concubinage was associated both with foreign immigration and the experience of industrialization. See also individual dossiers in A.D. Haut Rhin 4M 144–158 and A.D. Haut Rhin 1 Z 237 and 1Z 238, "Surveillance de la conduite des étrangers, plaintes contre des étrangers, arrestation et expulsions d'étrangers, plaintes d'étrangers contre la xénophobie de maires 1804–1828."

47. A.D. Haut Rhin 4M 148.

48. There were occasional complaints in 1820s; see A.D. Haut Rhin 1Z 237. But there were generally few indigenous artisans; indeed, in 1808, the prefect declared, although the claim was subsequently crossed out, that the departments' workshops would be empty without foreigners. A.D. Haut Rhin 4M 140.

49. A.N. BB30 772 contains a lengthy exchange between local and central authorities about the movement to limit *avantages communaux* to naturalized foreigners in

Moselle—and to make non-naturalized foreigners apply for naturalization status—and briefer exchanges pertaining to the departments of Meuse and Ain.

50. A.N. DIII 361, pièce 257, Abolition indirecte et modifiée du célibat, motifs général.

51. A.N. F3 II Haut Rhin.

52. A.D. Haut Rhin 4M 140 and 1 Z 235, and A.N. F3 (II) Haut Rhin and F2(I) 106/34.

53. A.D. Haut Rhin 4M 148, document 377.

54. A.D. Haut Rhin 6M 384.

55. A.D. Haut Rhin 4M 148, document 418.

56. Ibid., document 419.

57. Ibid., document 347.

58. A.N. F7 9313.

59. Authorities often sought pretexts for expelling workers. For example, the prefect of Haut Rhin wrote to the subprefect in 1821, noting that he shared his subordinate's belief that foreign riffraff were responsible for public disorder, but added that it was insufficient to claim that an immigrant had a bad reputation to justify an expulsion; he needed to cite specific facts. A.D. Haut Rhin 1 Z 237.

60. A.D. Haut Rhin 1 Z 387.

61. A.D. Haut Rhin 1 Z 237.

62. A.N. F7 9313.

Conclusion

1. Emmanuel de Waresquiel and Benoît Yvert, *Histoire de la restauration, 1814–1830: Naissance de la France moderne* (Paris, 1996), 68. On the Bourbon self-presentation as a benevolent patriarchy, see Margadant, "The Duchesse de Berry."

2. G. de Bertier de Sauvigny, *La Restauration* (Paris, 1955), 244.

3. The deputy Clausel, for example, proclaimed that such people should be considered French, since it was "fitting that they have a bond of gratitude to the common father of the French"; *AP2*, 12: 748.

4. J. V. Melle, *Lettre d'un Belge à Sa Majesté Louis XVIII* (n.p., 1814). Petitions to Napoleon during the Hundred Days also referred to the great family of the nation. For example, an anonymous petition written, or supposedly written, by Belgians proclaimed: "we have been French for twenty years; do not allow us to be separated from the *grande famille* for which we have sacrificed everything"; *Les plaintes et le voeu des départements toujours français composant l'ancienne Belgique, adressés à S. M. l'empereur Napoléon* (Paris, 1815), 15–16.

5. A.N. F2 I 438.

6. On the June decree, especially its repercussions for "grande naturalisation," see L'Esprit, *La situation des étrangers*, 3.

7. Danjou, *La condition civile de l'étranger*, 14.

8. Varnier and Dietrich-Chénel, "Intégration des étrangers," 1: 34.

9. Deniel, *Une image de la famille*; Ford, "Private Lives and Public Order"; Ronsin, *Le contrat sentimental*; and Michelle Perrot, "The Family Triumphant," in *A History of Private Life*, ed. Michelle Perrot (Cambridge, Mass., 1990), 99–165.

10. Reddy, *The Invisible Code*.

11. The term first appeared in the early nineteenth century. Restoration writers rarely used it, but historians and propagandists seized upon it during the early 1830s. Noiriel, "Socio-histoire d'un concept."

12. *AP2*, vol. 12. See also *Observations sur le projet de loi sur les naturalisations* (Paris, 1814) in A.N. F2 I 436; selected petitions in A.N. series C 2026–2226, *Pétitions à la Chambre des députés*; and Sahlins, *Unnaturally French*, 310–311.

13. Légat, *Le code des étrangers*, 53.

14. For example, see the dossier for Bouvet in A.N. C2028.

15. Nicolas de Bonneville, *Le nouveau code conjugal, établi sur les bases de la constitution et d'après les principes de la loi qui a préparé ce nouveau code* (Paris, 1792), 15; Ewald, *Naissance du Code civil*, 169.

16. Bonneville, *Le nouveau code*, 15, 31–32.

17. Most notably, local governments continued to try to limit *avantages communaux* to those who were legally French; see the 1846 proposal from Meuse, in A.N. F3(I) 3, or the 1850 petition for Wabnitz in A.D. Bas Rhin 8M 72. On conscription and the extension of *jus soli*, see Brubaker, *Citizenship and Nationhood*.

18. Lynch, *Family, Class, and Ideology*.

19. Bruschi, "Droit de la nationalité." On intermediary stages of citizenship specific to the colonies, see Damien Deschamps, "Une citoyenneté différée: Cens civique et assimilation des indigènes dans les établissements français de l'Inde," *Revue française de sciences politiques* 47, no. 1 (1997): 49–69; Alice Conklin, "Redefining Frenchness: Citizenship, Imperial Motherhood, and Race Regeneration in French West Africa, 1890–1940," in *Domesticating the Empire: Languages of Gender, Race and Family Life in French and Dutch Colonialism*, ed. Julia Clancy-Smith and Frances Gouda (Charlottesville, 1998), 65–83; and Ruth Dickens, "Defining French Citizenship Policy in West Africa, 1895–1956" (Ph.D. diss., Emory University, 2001).

20. Restrictions on such relationships were particularly common when European supremacy appeared vulnerable. On changing policies toward regulating sexual relationships and marriages, see Ann Laura Stoler, *Carnal Knowledge and Imperial Power: Race and the Intimate in Colonial Rule* (Berkeley, 2002).

21. Michael Crowder, *Senegal: A Study of French Assimilation Policy* (London, 1967).

22. Stoler, *Carnal Knowledge and Imperial Power*.

23. There are numerous legal briefs and reports for the case; one of the best introductions is Daniel de Folleville, *Un mot sur le cas de Mme la Princesse de Bauffremont aujourd'hui Princesse Bibesco: De la naturalisation en pays étranger des femmes séparées de corps en France* (Paris, 1876).

24. See especially Alauzet, *De la qualité de français*.

25. Pierre Guillaume, "L'accession à la nationalité: Le grand débat, 1882–1932," in *Citoyenneté et nationalité: perspectives en France et au Québec*, ed. Dominique Colas, Claude Emeri, and Jacques Zylberberg (Paris, 1991), 137–148; and Weil, *La France et ses étrangers*.

26. See Moses, *French Feminism*; Steven Hause, *Women's Suffrage and Social Politics in the French Third Republic* (Princeton, 1984); and James McMillan, *France and Women, 1789–1914: Gender, Society and Politics* (London, 2000).

27. The 1855 law established that an American-born woman who married an alien would be considered a foreigner; Candice Bredbenner, *A Nationality of Her Own: Women, Marriage, and the Law of Citizenship* (Berkeley, 1998); and Nancy Cott, "Marriage and Women's Citizenship in the United States, 1830–1934," *American Historical Review* 103, no. 5 (1998): 1440–1474.

28. Schafer, *Children in Moral Danger*.

29. A. Chastel Saint-Bonnet, *De l'influence du changement de nationalité d'un chef de famille sur la condition et les droits de la femme et des enfants mineurs* (Paris, 1887), 77.

30. Those born in France of a French-born mother and a foreign-born father could choose whether or not to be French; Bruschi, "Droit de la nationalité," 49.

31. Elisa Camiscioli, "Intermarriage, Independent Nationality, and the Individual Rights of French Women: The Law of 10 August 1927," *French Politics, Culture, and Society* 17, nos. 3–4 (1999): 52–74.

Select Bibliography

Abbreviations

A.N.	Archives Nationales
A.D. Bas Rhin	Archives Départementales, Bas Rhin
A.D. Haut Rhin	Archives Départementales, Haut Rhin
A.D. Moselle	Archives Départementales, Moselle
A.C. Strasbourg	Archives Communales, Strasbourg
AP1	*Archives Parlementaires*, Série 1
AP2	*Archives Parlementaires*, Série 2

Archival Sources

Archives Nationales, Paris, series

ADI   Revolutionary laws and police measures concerning foreigners.

ADII   Laws and debates on naturalization and on the rights of illegitimate children; includes the Hoppé-Lange case.

ADXII   Pamphlets, petitions, and police reports pertaining to émigrés and their relatives.

C   Petitions sent to the Restoration Chamber of Deputies.

DIII   Petitions from alleged nobles and foreigners affected by the law of 27 Germinal Year II; men and women accused of emigration and their families; foreigners throughout the Revolution.

F2 I   Naturalization records from the Napoleonic era; administrative correspondence about naturalization and *avantages communaux* in the 1820s.

F3   Police and administrative exchanges on *avantages communaux*, and the policing of foreigners in the Haut Rhin.

F7   Reports on émigrés and their families, judgments of the Bureau des Lois, and general police records.

AFII   Reports on nobles and foreigners affected by the law of 27 Germinal Year II.

BB11   Dossiers of men and women requesting naturalization or civil rights in France or seeking permission to serve a foreign sovereign, receive a pension from a foreign government, or be "reintegrated" as French.

BB30   Documents on the amnesty granted to émigrés; memoirs and reports on "civil matters," particularly marriage.

Archives Départementales, Bas Rhin, Strasbourg, series

8M   Instructions and administrative correspondence pertaining to *admission à domicile* and naturalization, registers of those granted citizenship rights, and individual dossiers. Includes complaints against immigrants and testimony supporting them.

13M   Industrial legislation and conflicts, especially concerning the Conseil des Prud'hommes.

Archives Communales, Strasbourg, series

Admin.   Decrees from the mayor, laws and decisions concerning foreigners, correspondence and decisions concerning the *patente* and labor conflicts.

Police   Dossiers on individual foreigners, records of *admission à domicile*, etc.

Procès-verbaux des séances du Conseil municipal.

Archives Départementales, Haut Rhin, Colmar, series

4M   Instructions and administrative correspondence pertaining to *admission à domicile* and naturalization, registers of those granted citizenship rights, individual petitions, and dossiers.

6M   Dossiers on individual immigrants and workers.

1Z   Surveillance and complaints about foreigners, particularly at the level of the *sous-préfecture*. Includes expulsions, arrests, and petitions.

Archives Départementales, Moselle, Metz, series

212M   Naturalizations

Newspapers

Gazette des tribunaux
Gazette nationale ou le Moniteur universel
Journal d'économie publique du morale et politique
Journal de Paris
Messager du soir ou Gazette générale de l'Europe

Printed Primary Sources

Archives Parlementaires de 1787 à 1860. Recueil complet des débats législatifs et politiques des chambres françaises (première série, 1787 à 1799). 100 vols. to date. Paris, 1867–.

Archives Parlementaires de 1787 à 1860. Recueil complet des débats législatifs et politiques des chambres françaises (deuxième série, 1800 à 1860). 127 vols. to date. Paris, 1867–.

Audouin, Pierre-Jean. *Discours sur les pères et mères des émigrés . . . le 19 nivôse, l'an IV.* Paris, Year IV.

——. *Rapport . . . sur les pères et mères d'émigrés. Séance du 28 ventôse an IV.* Paris, Year IV.

Azéma, Michel. *Rapport et projet de loi sur l'adoption, présenté à la Convention Nationale, au nom du comité de législation.* Paris, [1793].

Badinter, Elisabeth, ed., *Paroles d'hommes, 1790–1793.* Paris, 1989.

Bera, Joseph-Charles. *Choix de plaidoyers prononcés sur des questions d'état et des difficultés intéressantes élevées en interprétation du Code Napoléon et du code de procédure civile.* Paris, 1812.

Berlier, Théophile. *Exposé sommaire des motifs qui ont déterminé les bases qui renferme le projet du Code civil sur l'adoption.* Paris, 1793.

——. *Opinion . . . sur la question de savoir si l'on peut dispenser les descendans des religionnaires fugitifs de la résidence septennale prescrite par la Constitution pour l'exercice des droits politiques.* Paris, 1797.

Bonneville, Nicolas de. *Le nouveau code conjugal, établi sur les bases de la constitution et d'après les principes de la loi qui a préparé ce nouveau code.* Paris, 1792.

Bonnier d'Alco, Ange Elisabeth Louis Antoine. *Recherches sur l'ordre de Malte et examen d'une question relative aux français ci-devant membres de cet ordre par le citoyen Merlin.* Paris, Year 6.

Bulletin des arrêts de la cour de cassation rendus en matière civile. 144 vols. Paris, 1804–1942.

Bureau-du-Colombier, Percheron, Jullien, Johanet, and Filliatre. *Consultation pour Dame Caroline Elisabeth-Humbline de Latour Saint Igest, contre le Sieur Térence MacMahon.* Orléans, 1805.

Chappe, J. G. G. *Discours . . . près l'administration municipale du 7è arrondissement, prononcé à la fête des époux, au temple du Commerce, le 10 floréal an VI.* Paris, n.d.

Chastel Saint-Bonnet, A. *De l'influence du changement de nationalité d'un chef de famille sur la condition et les droits de la femme et des enfants mineurs.* Paris, 1887.

Chazal, Jean-Pierre. *Rapport . . . au nom d'une Commission spéciale composée des représentans du peuple Poullain-Grandprey, Laujacq, et Chazal, sur les effets de l'adoption et l'affaire particulière de la citoyenne Lepeletier, adoptée au nom du peuple français.* Paris, Year 6.

Chrestien de Poly, J. P. *Essai sur la puissance paternelle.* Paris, 1820.

Consultation signée Poirier, Ferey, Siméon, Jolly, David Portalis, Desèze; Chaveau-Lagarde, le 7 ventôse an XII–27 février 1804. N.p., n.d.

Cotèle, Louis Barnabé. *Notice sur la justice et l'intérêt de la France, comme des autres états de l'Europe, d'abolir le droit d'aubaine.* Orléans, 1814.

Cournol. *Mémoire à consulter et consultation pour Madame Caroline Latour-Saint Igest contre Monsieur MacMahon.* Paris, n.d.

Creuzé-Latouche, Jacques-Antoine. *Rapport fait par . . . au nom d'une commission chargée d'examiner la résolution concernant les pères et mères des émigrés. Séance du 18 nivôse an VI.* Paris, Year VI.

Déclaration du roy, portant commutation de la peine de mort en celle des galère, contre ceux qui s'habituent dans les pays étrangers, sans permission du Roy. Registrée en Parlement le 14 aoust 1685. Paris, 1685.

Défense des femmes, des enfans et des vieillards émigrés, pour faire suite à l'ouvrage de M. de Lally-Tolendal. Paris, 1797.

Delamalle, Gaspart-Gilbert. *Plaidoyers choisis et oeuvres diverses de M. Delamalle.* Paris, 1827.

——. *Réplique du Citoyen Delamalle, pour Térence Mac-Mahon; contre Madame Mac-Mahon; . . . Audience du 18 pluviôse an 12 (8 février 1804).* Paris, Year XII–1804.

——. *Réplique du Citoyen Delamalle, pour Térence MacMahon; contre Madame MacMahon; . . . Audience du 2 ventôse an 12 (22 février 1804).* Paris, Year XII–1804.

Despommerais, Pierre–André. *Pétition de . . . aux représentants du peuple composant le Conseil des Anciens.* Paris, 1797.

Desquiron de Saint-Agnan, Antoine Touissant. *La puissance paternelle en France, mise en rapport avec les intérêts de la société, essai sur l'adultère considéré dans ses rapports avec nos lois et avec nos moeurs.* Paris, 1821.

——. *Traité de la mort civile en France.* Paris, 1822.

Dillon. *Pétition de la citoyenne veuve Dillon à la convention nationale.* Paris, Year II.

Douarche, Aristide. *Les tribunaux civils de Paris pendant la Révolution, 1791–1800.* 2 vols. Paris, 1905–1907.

Ducanel, Charles-Pierre. *Justice, humanité, Les femmes absentes et les enfans appelans de la Convention nationale à elle-même.* Paris, n.d.

Duvergier, Jean-Baptiste. *La collection complète des lois, décrets, ordonnances, règlements, et avis du Conseil d'Etat . . . de 1788 à 1824.* 45 vols. Paris, 1834–1845.

Duveyrier, H. *Réponse à la consultation faite par M. Hoppé hambourgeois, et signée Portalis, Tronson du Coudray, Muraire, et Cambacérès.* Paris, n.d.

Edict du Roy, pour empescher les sujets de sa Majesté, de s'habituer dans les pays étrangers, et faire retourner en France ceux qui y sont établis. Paris, 1669.

Les émigrés justifiés ou réfutation de la réponse de M. Leuiliete à M. Lally-Tolendal, sur sa défense des émigrés. Par F. T.-D. Paris, [1797].

Febvre, François Joseph. *Opinion . . . sur le message du Directoire exécutif, relatif à la citoyenne Lepeletier et sur l'adoption publique.* Paris, Year 6.

Fenet, Pierre-Antoine. *Recueil complet des travaux préparatoires du Code civil.* 15 vols. Paris, 1827.

France (Ministère de Justice). *La nationalité française: Textes et documents.* Paris, 1985.

France (Parlement de Metz). *Arrêt du parlement qui a jugé que Me. Luc de Craye.* Metz, 1685.

Fresne, Jean du. *Journal des principales audiences du Parlement, depuis l'année mil six cens vingt-trois jusques à present, avec les arrests intervenus en icelles.* Paris, 1646.

Gosse, Etienne. *Les femmes politiques, Comédie en trois actes et en vers, par le citoyen Gosse, représentée la première fois sur la théâtre des victoires, le 30 fructidor an 7.* Paris, Year VIII.

Guérard. *Mémoire à la Convention Nationale pour Jean Pratbernon et Susanne Néau, son épouse, contre Nicolas Costard.* Paris, 1795.

Guiraudet, Charles-Philippe-Toussaint. *De la famille considérée comme l'élément des sociétés.* Paris, 1797.

Hennet, Albert Joseph. *Du divorce.* Paris, 1789.

Hermann, Jean Frédéric. *Notices historiques, statistiques et littéraires sur la ville de Strasbourg.* 2 vols. Strasbourg, 1817–1819.

Isambert, François André, Athanase-Jean-Léger Jourdan, and M. Decrusy. *Recueil des anciennes lois françaises depuis l'an 420 jusqu'à la révolution de 1789.* 29 vols. Paris, 1829–1833.

Jourdain, Yves Claude. *Table générale-alphabétique des matières contenus dans les décrets rendus par les assemblées nationales de France, depuis 1789 jusqu'au 18 Brumaire an 8.* Paris, Year X.

Lally-Tolendal, Trophime-Gérard de. *Défense des émigrés français, adressée au peuple français.* Paris, 1797.

Laloy, Pierre Antoine. *Derniers réflexions de P. A. Laloy. Séance du 19 brumaire an 6.* Paris, Year VI.

——. *Opinion . . . sur l'adoption nationale et ses effets.* Paris, Year VI.

Laujacq, Bernard. *Nouvelle rédaction des projets de résolution et d'arrêté . . . sur l'adoption nationale et l'affaire particulière de la citoyenne Lepeletier.* Paris, n.d.
——. *Opinion . . . sur le Message du Directoire exécutif relatif à la citoyenne Lepeletier.* Paris, n.d.
Le Peletier, Amédée. *Réponse à l'Opinion du Représentant du Peuple B. Laujacq dans l'affaire de la mineure Lepeletier.* Paris, n.d.
Lepeletier, Félix, and Amédée Lepeletier. *Au Conseil des Cinq-Cents ou Mémoire sur l'affaire de S. Lepeletier, première fille adoptive du peuple français.* Paris, n.d.
——. *Au Conseil des Cinq-Cents ou nouvelles observations sur l'adoption publique et l'affaire de S. Lepeletier.* Paris, n.d.
Le Peletier de Saint Fargeau, Susanne. *Observations pour Susanne-Louise Lepeletier, fille unique et héritière de Michel Lepeletier, représentant du peuple à la Convention Nationale.* Paris, n.d.
Leuliette, Jean-Jacques. *Des émigrés français, ou réponse à M de Lally-Tolendal.* Paris, 1797.
Loiseau, Jean Simon. *Dictionnaire des arrêts modernes.* Paris, 1809.
——. *Plaidoyer pour L. R. A. Voyneau, Fils, Dragon au 15e régiment, contre L. A. F. Voyneau, son père, par M. Loiseau, docteur en droit et avocat à la Cour de cassation.* Paris, 1808.
——. *Traité des enfans naturels, adultérins, incestueux et abandonnés.* Paris, 1811.
Martin. *Maintenez les propriétés mais n'en disposez pas ou Mémoire sur l'usage barbare des confiscations, en faveur des héritiers de parens proscrits.* Paris, 1797.
Méjan, Maurice. *Recueil des causes célèbres et des arrêts qui les ont décidées.* 19 vols. Paris, 1807–1813.
Mémoire pour Marguerite Doucet, veuve et donataire par son contrat de mariage de Barthélemy Tourton. Paris, 1733.
Mémoire sur le partage pour Marie Anne de James, veuve de Phillipes Tourton, mère et héritière de Claude Tourton. Paris, 1733.
Merlin, Philippe-Antoine. *Répertoire universel et raisonné de jurisprudence.* 5th ed. 36 vols. Brussels, 1825–1828.
Morellet, André. *Discussion du rapport de P. J. Audouin sur les pères et mères d'émi-grés. Lu au conseil des Cinq-Cents, le 28 ventôse de l'an IV.* Paris, Year IV.
——. *La cause des pères, ou discussions d'un projet de décret relatif aux pères et mères, aïeuls et aïeules des émigrés, par l'auteur du cri des familles.* Paris, Year III.
——. *Mémoires . . . sur le dix-huitième siècle et sur la Révolution.* Introduction and notes by Jean-Pierre Guicciardi. Paris, 1988.
Motifs du projet de senatus-consulte organique sur la naturalisation des étrangers, présenté au Sénat dans la séance du 16 vendémiaire an XI par les conseillers d'état Regnault et de Saint-Jean-d'Angely et Bigot-Préameau, orateurs du gouvernement. N.p, n.d.
Nougarède, André. *Essai sur l'histoire de la puissance paternelle.* Paris, Year IX.
Observations d'une femme sur la loi contre les émigrés. Paris, n.d.
Observations sur les exceptions à faire à la qualification d'émigrés. Paris, n.d.
Oudot, Charles-François. *Rapport et projets d'articles additionnels sur le divorce, présentés au nom du Comité de législation, le 27 germinal, l'an II de la République.* Paris, Year II.
Pampelune, Jacquinot. *Opinion . . . sur la résolution de la Chambre des Pairs, relative à l'abolition des droits d'aubaine et de détraction.* [Paris], n.d.
Pastoret, Emmanuel. *Rapport . . . sur l'exercice du droit de cité pour les descendans des religionnaires fugitifs rentrant en France.* Paris, Year V.
Les plaintes et le voeu des départements toujours français composant l'ancienne Belgique, adressés à S. M. l'empereur Napoléon. Paris, 1815.
Poirier, Louis Eugène. *Sur l'importante question du mariage des prévenus d'émigration, suivie de la décision affirmative du ministre de l'intérieur.* Paris, Year 9.

Pons de Verdun, Philippe-Laurent. *Rapport et projet de résolution sur la suspension de la loi du 12 floréal, concernant les pères et mères d'émigrés.* Paris, Year VI.

Portalis, Jean-Etienne-Marie et al. *Consultation pour M. Hoppé contre la citoyenne Lange, sur une question d'éducation.* Paris, Year 5.

Procès-verbaux du Conseil d'état contenant la discussion du Code Napoléon, 2nd ed. Paris, 1808.

Procès-verbaux des séances de la Convention Nationale, 65 vols. Paris, 1792–1795.

Proudhon. *Cours de législation et jurisprudence françaises.* 2 vols. Besançon, 1799.

Ragu. *Conclusions motivées pour Dame Caroline Elisabeth Humbline de Latour Saint Igest, contre le Sieur Térence MacMahon.* Orléans, n.d.

Rapport du ministre de la police générale et arrêté des consuls concernant les individus sur la liste des émigrés depuis 1789. Paris, Year 9.

Réclamations pour l'interprétation de la loi du 12 novembre concernant les émigrés. [Paris], n.d.

Réflexions faites par une infortunée, femme d'émigré, divorcée, pour elle et ses co-infortunées. N.p., [1796].

Rey. *Observations sur l'adoption.* Paris, n.d.

Richer, François. *Traité de la mort civile: Tant que celle qui résulte des condamnations pour cause de crime que celle qui résulte des vœux en religion.* Paris, 1755.

Robert, Guillaume. *Rapport . . . sur le mariage des mineurs orphelins. Séance du 27 frimaire an 6.* Paris, Year VI.

Roederer, Pierre-Louis. *Oeuvres.* 8 vols. Paris, 1853–1859.

Rondonneau, Louis. *Table générale par ordre alphabétique de matières des lois, Sénatus consultes, décrets, arrêtés, avis du Conseil d'état etc.* Paris, 1816.

Souhait, Julien. *Opinion . . . sur l'adoption publique.* Paris, Year VI.

Taillandier, Alphonse-Honoré, and Sylvian-Charles Théodore Mongalvy. *Recueil général des lois et des arrêts concernant les émigrés, déportés, condamnés, leurs héritiers, créanciers et ayants-cause, depuis 1791 jusqu'en 1825.* 2 vols. Paris, 1825.

Secondary Works

Aberdam, Serge. "L'élargissement du droit de vote entre 1792 et 1795 au travers du dénombrement du Comité de division et des votes populaires sur les Constitutions de 1793 et 1795." Thèse de doctorat, Université de Paris 1 Panthéon-Sorbonne, UFR d'Histoire, Paris, 2001.

Alauzet, Isadore. *De la qualité de français, de naturalisation et du statut personnel des étrangers.* 2nd ed. Paris, 1880.

Augustine-Adams, Kif. "'She Consents Implicitly': Women's Citizenship, Marriage, and Liberal Political Thought in Late-Nineteenth- and Early-Twentieth-Century Argentina." *Journal of Women's History* 13, no. 4 (2002): 8–30.

——. "'With Notice of the Consequences': Liberal Political Theory, Marriage, and Women's Citizenship in the United States." *Citizenship Studies* 6, no. 1 (2002): 5–20.

Baczko, Bronislaw. *Ending the Terror: The French Revolution after Robespierre.* Cambridge, 1994.

Badinter, Robert. *Libres et égaux: L'émancipation des Juifs, 1789–1791.* Paris, 1989.

Baecque, Antoine de. *The Body Politic: Corporeal Metaphor in Revolutionary France, 1770–1800.* Translated by Charlotte Mandell. Stanford, 1997.

——. "Le corps meurtri de la révolution: Le discours politique et les blessures des martyrs (1792–1794)." *Annales historiques de la révolution française* 59, no. 267 (1987): 17–42.

Baker, Keith, ed. *The French Revolution and the Creation of Modern Political Culture.* Vol. 4: *The Terror.* Oxford, 1994.

Bart, Jean. "Les entraves à la liberté de se marier à la fin de l'Ancien Régime." In *Les droits de l'homme et la conquête des libertés, des Lumières aux révolutions de 1848. Actes du Colloque de Grenoble-Vizille 1986,* 15–21. Grenoble-Vizille, 1988.

——. "L'individu et ses droits." In Théry and Biet, 351–362.

Bayard, Françoise. "Naturalization in Lyon during the Ancien Regime." *French History* 4, no. 3 (1990): 277–316.

Bell, David. *The Cult of the Nation in France: Inventing Nationalism, 1680–1800.* Cambridge, Mass., 2001.

Bellivier, Florence et Laurence Boudouard, "Des droits par les bâtards: L'enfant naturel dan les débats révolutionnaires." In Théry and Biet, 122–146.

Belorgey, Jean-Michel. "Le droit de la nationalité: Evolution historique et enjeux." In *Questions de nationalité: Histoire et enjeux d'un code,* ed. Smain Laacher, 61–80. Paris, 1987.

Benot, Yves. *La révolution française et la fin des colonies.* Paris, 1988.

Bertier de Sauvigny, Guillaume de. *La Restauration.* Paris, 1955.

Bien, David. "Manufacturing Nobles: The Chancelleries in France until 1789." *Journal of Modern History* 61, no. 3 (1989): 445–486.

Boizet, Jacques. *Les lettres de naturalité sous l'Ancien Régime.* Paris, 1943.

Bonnecase, Julien. *La philosophie du Code Napoléon appliqué au droit de la famille: Ses destinées dans le droit civil contemporain.* Paris, 1928.

Bordeaux, Michèle. "L'universalisme juridique ou l'impasse de l'égalité." In *Les femmes et la Révolution française,* 3 vols. ed. Marie-France Brive, 1: 426–440. Toulouse, 1989–1991.

Borgetto, Michel. "Métaphore de la famille et idéologies." In *Le droit non civil de la famille,* ed. Michel Borgetto et al., 1–21. Paris, 1983.

Boroumand, Ladan. "Emigration and the Rights of Man: French Revolutionaries Equivocate." *Journal of Modern History* 72, no. 1 (2000): 67–108.

Bossenga, Gail. "Rights and Citizens in the Old Regime." *French Historical Studies* 29, no. 2 (1997): 217–243.

Bouamama, Saïd. "Petite histoire d'une grande idée." In *La citoyenneté dans tous ses états: de l'immigration à la nouvelle citoyenneté,* ed. Saïd Bouamama, Albano Cordeiro, and Michel Roux, 31–44. Paris, 1992.

Bouland, Joseph. *Douze femmes d'émigrés divorcées à Limoges sous la Terreur, 1793–1794.* Limoges, 1913.

Bourguet, Marie-Noëlle. *Déchiffrer la France: La statistique départementale à l'époque napoléonienne.* Paris, 1988.

Bredbenner, Candice. *A Nationality of Her Own: Women, Marriage, and the Law of Citizenship.* Berkeley, 1998.

Brinton, Crane. *French Revolutionary Legislation on Illegitimacy, 1789–1804.* Cambridge, 1936.

Broers, Michael. *Europe under Napoleon, 1799–1815.* London, 1996.

Brown, Howard. "Mythes et massacres: Reconsidérer la Terreur directoriale." *Annales historiques de la révolution française,* no. 325 (2001): 23–52.

Brown, Howard, and Judith Miller, eds. *Taking Liberties: Problems of a New Order from the French Revolution to Napoleon.* Manchester, 2002.

Brown, Stephanie A. "Women on Trial: The Revolutionary Tribunal and Gender." Ph.D. diss., Stanford University, 1996.

Brubaker, Rogers. *Citizenship and Nationhood in France and Germany.* Cambridge, 1992.

——. "The French Revolution and the Invention of Citizenship." *French Politics and Society* 7 (1989): 30–49.

Brunelle, Gayle. "Dangerous Liaisons: Mésalliance and Early Modern French Noblewomen." *French Historical Studies* 19, no. 1 (1995): 75–104.

Bruschi, Christian. "Le droit de cité dans l'antiquité: Un questionnement pour la citoyenneté aujourd'hui." In *La citoyenneté et les changements de structures sociales et nationales de la population française*, ed. Catherine Wihtol de Wenden, 126–153. Paris, 1988.

——. "Droit de la nationalité et égalité des droits de 1789 à la fin du XIXe siècle." In *Questions de nationalité: Histoire et enjeux d'un code*, ed. Smain Laacher, 21–59. Paris, 1987.

——. "Essai sur un jeu de miroir: Famille/Etat dans l'histoire des idées politiques." In *L'état, la révolution française et l'Italie. Actes du colloque de Milan (14–15–16 septembre 1989)*, ed. Association Française des Historiens des Idées Politiques, 49–65. Aix-en-Provence, 1990.

Burguière, André. "Demande d'état et aspirations individualistes. Les attentes contradictoires des familles à la veille de la révolution." In *L'enfant, la famille et la révolution française*, ed. Marie-Françoise Lévy, 25–32. Paris, 1990.

Burns, Michael. "Emancipation and Reaction: The Rural Exodus of Alsatian Jews, 1791–1848." In *Living with Antisemitism: Modern Jewish Responses*, ed. Jehuda Reinharz, 19–41. Hanover, N.H., 1987.

Camiscioli, Elisa. "Intermarriage, Independent Nationality, and the Individual Rights of French Women: The Law of 10 August 1927." *French Politics, Culture, and Society* 17, nos. 3–4 (1999): 52–74.

Carbonnier, Jean. "Le statut de l'enfant en droit civil pendant la révolution." In *L'enfant, la famille et la révolution française*, ed. Marie Françoise Lévy, 297–305. Paris, 1990.

Castaldo, André. "La révolution et les émigrés: Les partages de présuccession." *Revue historique de droit français et étranger* 71, no. 3 (1993): 371–403.

Certeau, Michel de, Dominique Julia, and Jacques Revel, eds. *Une politique de la langue: La révolution française et les patois: L'enquête de Grégoire*. Paris, 1975.

Chaussinand-Nogaret, Guy. *The French Nobility in the Eighteenth Century: From Feudalism to Enlightenment*. Cambridge, 1985.

Clère, Jean-Jacques. "L'émigration dans les débats de l'assemblée nationale constituante." In *Les droits de l'homme et la conquête des libertés, des Lumières aux révolutions de 1848. Actes du Colloque de Grenoble-Vizille 1986*, 156–162. Grenoble-Vizille, 1988.

Colas, Dominique, Claude Emeri, and Jacques Zylberberg, eds. *Citoyenneté et nationalité: Perspectives en France et au Québec*. Paris, 1991.

Colwill, Elizabeth. "Transforming Women's Empire and the Sovereignty of Man in *La Décade Philosophique*, 1794–1807." *Eighteenth-Century Studies* 29, no. 3 (1996): 265–285.

Conklin, Alice. "Redefining Frenchness: Citizenship, Imperial Motherhood, and Race Regeneration in French West Africa, 1890–1940." In *Domesticating the Empire: Languages of Gender, Race, and Family Life in French and Dutch Colonialism*, ed. Julia Clancy-Smith and Frances Gouda, 65–83. Charlottesville, 1998.

Constant, Laurence. *Félix Lepeletier de St. Fargeau: Un itinéraire de la révolution à la monarchie de juillet*. Paris, 1995.

Cott, Nancy. "Marriage and Women's Citizenship in the United States, 1830–1934." *American Historical Review* 103, no. 5 (1998): 1440–1474.

Dally, M. P. *Suzanne Lepeletier, fille de la nation, et son oncle Félix Lepeletier*. Paris, 1912.

Danjou, Colette Joutard. *La condition civile de l'étranger dans les trois derniers siècles de la monarchie.* Paris, 1939.

Darrow, Margaret. *Revolution in the House: Family, Class, and Inheritance in Southern France.* Princeton, 1989.

David, Marcel. *Fraternité et la révolution française, 1789–1799.* Paris, 1987.

Davis, Natalie Zemon. *Fiction in the Archives: Pardon Tales and Tellers in Sixteenth-Century France.* Stanford 1987.

Dawaele, Sylvie. "Guide des sources archivistes sur les étrangers dans le Haut-Rhin de 1800–1870 aux Archives Départementales du Haut Rhin et aux Archives Municipales de Mulhouse." Mémoire de maîtrise ME. Ca. D.O.C.T.E. Archivistique, Mulhouse, 1991.

Dejob, Lucien. *Le rétablissement de l'adoption en France.* Paris, 1911.

Demangeat, Charles. *Histoire de la condition civile des étrangers en France dans l'ancien et dans le nouveau droit.* Paris, 1844.

Demolombe, Charles. *Cours de Code Napoléon.* 32 vols. Paris, 1869–1896.

Deniel, Raymond. *Une image de la famille et de la société sous la Restauration (1815–1830): Etude de la presse catholique.* Paris, 1965.

Desan, Suzanne. *The Family on Trial in Revolutionary France.* Berkeley, 2004.

——. "Marriage, Religion, and Moral Order: The Catholic Critique of Divorce during the Directory." In *The French Revolution and the Meaning of Citizenship,* ed. Renée Waldinger, Philip Dawson, and Isser Woloch, 201–210. Westport, Conn., 1993.

——. "Reconstituting the Social after the Terror: Family, Property, and the Law in Popular Politics." *Past and Present,* no. 164 (1999): 81–121.

——. "'War between Brothers and Sisters': Inheritance Law and Gender Politics in Revolutionary France." *French Historical Studies* 20, no. 4 (1997): 597–635.

Deschamps, Damien. "Une citoyenneté différée: Cens civique et assimilation des indigènes dans les établissements français de l'Inde." *Revue française de sciences politiques* 47, no. 1 (1997): 49–69.

Dessertine, Dominique. *Divorcer à Lyon sous la Révolution et l'Empire.* Lyon, 1981.

Dickens, Ruth. "Defining French Citizenship Policy in West Africa, 1895–1956." Ph.D. diss., Emory University, 2001.

Dubost, Jean-François, and Peter Sahlins. *Et si on faisait payer les étrangers? Louis XIV, les immigrés, et quelques autres.* Paris, 1999.

Elliott, Marianne. *Wolfe Tone: Prophet of Irish Independence.* New Haven, 1989.

Ellis, Geoffrey. *The Napoleonic Empire.* London, 1991.

Esdaile, Charles. "The Napoleonic Period: Some Thoughts on Recent Historiography." *European History Quarterly* 23 (1993): 415–432.

——. *The Wars of Napoleon.* London, 1995.

Ewald, François, ed. *Naissance du Code civil: La raison du législateur.* Paris, 1989.

Farge, Arlette. "The Honor and Secrecy of Families." In *A History of Private Life,* ed. Roger Chartier, 571–607. Cambridge, Mass., 1989.

Farge, Arlette, and Michel Foucault. *Le désordre des familles: Lettres de cachet des Archives de la Bastille au XVIIIe siècle.* Paris, 1982.

Fauré, Christine. *Democracy without Women: Feminism and the Rise of Individualism in France.* Bloomington, 1991.

Fehrenbach, Elisabeth. "Nation." In *Handbuch politisch-sozialer Grundbegriffe in Frankreich, 1680–1820,* ed. Rolf Reichardt and Hans-Jürgen Lüsebrink, 75–107. Munich, 1986.

Folleville, Daniel de. *Un mot sur le cas de Mme la Princesse de Bauffremont aujourd'hui Princesse Bibesco: De la naturalisation en pays étranger des femmes séparées de corps en France.* Paris, 1876.

Ford, Caroline. "Private Lives and Public Order in Restoration France: The Seduction of Emily Loveday." *American Historical Review* 90, no. 1 (1994): 21–43.

——. "Which Nation? Language, Identity, and Republican Politics in Post-Revolutionary France." *History of European Ideas* 17, no. 1 (1993): 31–46.

Fortuent, Françoise. "Le rétablissement de l'adoption: Une entrée par effraction?" In Théry and Biet, 196–203.

Fraisse, Geneviève. *Reason's Muse: Sexual Difference and the Birth of Democracy.* Chicago, 1994.

——. "Rupture révolutionnaire et l'histoire des femmes." In *Femmes et pouvoirs sous l'ancien régime,* ed. Danielle Haase-Dubosc and Eliane Viennot, 291–305. Paris, 1991.

Fulchiron, Hughes. "Nature, fiction et politique, l'adoption dans les débats révolutionnaires." In Théry and Biet, 204–221.

Gager, Kristin Elizabeth. *Blood Ties and Fictive Ties: Adoption and Family Life in Early Modern France.* Princeton, 1996.

Gainot, Bernard. *1799, un nouveau Jacobinisme? La démocratie représentative, une alternative à brumaire.* Paris, 2001.

Garaud, Marcel, and Romuald Szramkiewicz. *La révolution française et la famille.* Paris, 1978.

Garnier, Sylvie. "Les conduites politiques en l'an II: compte rendu et récit de vie révolutionnaires." *Annales historiques de la révolution française,* no. 295 (1994): 19–38.

Gauchet, Marcel. *La révolution des droits de l'homme.* Paris, 1989.

Gay, Jean. "Capacité de la femme mariée et puissance maritale dans l'élaboration du code civil." *Revue de l'Institut Napoléon,* no. 161 (1993): 33–65.

Geffroy, Annie. "Citoyen/citoyenne (1753–1829)." In *Dictionnaire des usages socio-politiques, 1770–1815,* 63–86. Paris, 1989.

Godechot, Jaques. *Les institutions de la France sous la révolution et l'empire.* Paris, 1951.

——. "The New Concept of the Nation and Its Diffusion in Europe." In *Nationalism in the Age of the French Revolution,* ed. Otton Dann and John Dinwiddy, 13–26. London, 1988.

Godineau, Dominique. "Autour du mot citoyenne." *Mots, languages/langue de la révolution française* 16 (1988): 91–110.

——. "Femmes en citoyenneté: Pratique et politique." *Annales historiques de la révolution française* no. 300 (1995): 197–207.

——. "Masculine and Feminine Political Practice during the French Revolution, 1793-Year III." In *Women and Politics in the Age of Democratic Revolution,* ed. Harriet Applewhite and Darline G. Levy, 61–81. Ann Arbor, 1990.

——. "Qu'y a-t-il de commun entre vous et nous? Enjeux et discours opposés de la différence des sexes pendant la révolution française (1789–1793)." In Théry and Biet, 72–81.

——. *The Women of Paris and Their French Revolution.* Translated by Katherine Streip. Berkeley, 1998.

Goodheart, Eric Andrew. "Adoption in the Discourses of the French Revolution." Ph.D. diss., Harvard University, 1997.

——. "The Lepeletier Affair of Year VI: National Adoption of the Revolutionary Idea." In *Symbols, Myths and Images of the French Revolution: Essays in Honour of James A. Leith,* ed. Ian Germani and Robin Swales, 199–210. Regina, Sask., 1998.

Goy, Joseph. "La révolution française et la famille." In *Histoire de la population française,* ed. Jacques Dupaquier, Alfred Sauvy, and Emmanuel Le Roy Ladurie, 84–115. Paris, 1988.

Grandmaison, Olivier Le Cour. *Les citoyennetés en révolution, 1789–1794.* Paris, 1992.

Greer, Donald. *The Incidence of the Emigration during the French Revolution.* Cambridge, 1951.

Guillaume, Pierre. "L'accession à la nationalité: Le grand débat 1882–1932." In *Citoyenneté et nationalité: perspectives en France et au Québec,* ed. Dominique Colas, Claude Emeri, and Jacques Zylberberg. Paris, 1991, 137–148.

Gundersen, Joan. "Independence, Citizenship, and the American Revolution." *Signs* 13, no. 1 (1987): 59–77.

Gutton, Jean-Pierre. *Histoire de l'adoption en France.* Paris, 1993.

Hafter, Daryl. "Female Masters in the Ribbonmaking Guild of Eighteenth-Century Rouen." *French Historical Studies* 20, no. 1 (1997): 1–14.

Halperin, Jean-Louis. *L'impossible code civil.* Paris, 1992.

Hampson, Norman. "The Idea of the Nation in Revolutionary France." In *Reshaping France: Town, Country and Region during the French Revolution,* ed. Alan Forrest and Peter Jones, 13–25. Manchester, 1991.

Hanley, Sarah. "Engendering the State: Family Formation and State Building in Early Modern France." *French Historical Studies* 16, no. 1 (1989): 4–27.

——. "Family and State in Early Modern France: The Marriage Pact." In *Connecting Spheres: Women in the Western World from 1550 to the Present,* ed. Marilyn Boxer and Jean Quataert, 53–63. New York, 1987.

Hause, Steven. *Women's Suffrage and Social Politics in the French Third Republic.* Princeton, 1984.

Herzog, Tamar. *Defining Nations: Immigrants and Citizens in Early Modern Spain and Spanish America.* New Haven, 2003.

Hesse, Carla. *The Other Enlightenment: How French Women Became Modern.* Princeton, 2001.

Heuer, Jennifer. "Adopted Daughter of the French People: Suzanne Lepeletier and Her Father, the National Assembly." *French Politics, Culture, and Society* 17, nos. 3–4 (1999): 31–51.

——. "'Afin d'obtenir le droit de citoyen . . . en tout ce qui peut concerner une personne de son sexe': Devenir ou cesser d'être femme française à l'époque napoléonienne." *Clio: Histoire, femmes et sociétés,* no. 12 (2000): 15–32.

——. "Family Bonds and Female Citizenship: Emigré Women under the Directory." In *Taking Liberties: Problems of a New Order from the French Revolution to Napoleon,* ed. Howard Brown and Judith Miller, 51–69. Manchester, 2002.

Heuer, Jennifer, and Anne Verjus. "L'invention de la sphère domestique au sortir de la révolution." *Annales historiques de la révolution française,* no. 327 (2002): 1–28.

Higonnet, Patrice. *Class, Ideology and the Rights of Nobles during the French Revolution.* Oxford, 1981.

——. *Goodness beyond Virtue: Jacobins during the French Revolution.* Cambridge, Mass., 1998.

Hincker, François. "La citoyenneté révolutionnaire saisie à travers ses exclus." In *Le citoyen fou,* ed. Nathalie Robatel, 7–28. Paris, 1991.

Hufton, Olwen. *The Poor of Eighteenth-Century France, 1750–1789.* Oxford, 1974.

——. *Women and the Limits of Citizenship in the French Revolution.* Toronto, 1992.

Hunt, Lynn. *The Family Romance of the French Revolution.* Berkeley, 1992.

——. *The French Revolution and Human Rights: A Brief Documentary History.* New York, 1996.

——. "Male Virtue and Republican Motherhood." In *The French Revolution and the Creation of Modern Political Culture,* ed. Keith Baker, 195–210. Oxford, 1994.

Hyman, Paula. *The Emancipation of the Jews in Alsace: Acculturation and Tradition in the Nineteenth Century.* New Haven, 1991.

Jardin, André, and André Jean-Tudesq. *Restoration and Reaction, 1815–1848.* Cambridge, 1983.

Jenkins, Brian. *Nationalism in France: Class and Nation since 1789.* Savage, Md., 1990.

Kates, Gary. "'The Powers of Husband and Wife Must Be Equal and Separate': The Cercle Social and the Rights of Women, 1790–91." In *Women and Politics in the Age of Democratic Revolution*, ed. Harriet Applewhite and Darline G. Levy, 221–233. Ann Arbor, 1990.

——. "Jews into Frenchmen: Nationality and Representation in Revolutionary France." In *The French Revolution and the Birth of Modernity*, ed. Ferenc Feher. Berkeley, 1990.

Kerber, Linda. *No Constitutional Right to Be Ladies: Women and the Obligations of Citizenship*. New York, 1998.

——. "The Paradox of Women's Citizenship in the Early Republic: The Case of Martin vs. Massachusetts, 1805." *American Historical Review* 97, no. 2 (1992): 349–378.

——. *Women of the Republic: Intellect and Ideology in Revolutionary America*. New York, 1980.

Kettner, James. *The Development of American Citizenship, 1608–1870*. Chapel Hill, 1978.

Kley, Dale Van, ed. *The French Idea of Freedom: The Old Regime and the Declaration of Rights of 1789*. Stanford, 1994.

Kroen, Sheryl. *Politics and Theater: The Crisis of Legitimacy in Restoration France, 1815–1830*. Berkeley, 2000.

Landes, Joan. *Women and the Public Sphere in the Age of the French Revolution*. Ithaca, 1988.

Lascoumes, Pierre. "L'émergence de la famille comme intérêt protégé par le droit pénal, 1791–1810." In Théry and Biet, 340–350.

Leca, Jean. "La citoyenneté entre la nation et la société civile." In *Citoyenneté et nationalité: Perspectives en France et au Québec*, ed. Dominique Colas, Claude Emeri, and Jacques Zylberberg, 479–505. Paris, 1991.

Legat, B. J. *Code des étrangers ou traité de la législation française concernant les étrangers*. Paris, 1832.

Lentz, Thierry. *Roederer, 1754–1835*. Metz, 1989.

Lepointe, Gabriel. "Le statut des étrangers dans la France du XIXe siècle." In *L'étranger foreigner*, Receuils de la societé Jean-Bodin pour l'histoire comparative des institutions, 553–574. Paris, 1984.

Lequin, Yves, ed. *Histoire des étrangers et de l'immigration en France*. Paris, 1992.

L'Esprit, Adolphe. *Situation des étrangers en France au point de vue du recrutement. Petit manuel théorique et pratique d'extranéité à l'usage des Mairies*. Paris, 1888.

Leuilliot, Paul. *L'Alsace au début de XIX siècle. Essais d'histoire politique, économique et religieux, 1815–1830*. 3 vols. Paris, 1959.

Levy, Darline Gay, and Harriet Applewhite. "A Political Revolution for Women? The Case of Paris." In *Becoming Visible: Women in European History*, ed. Renate Bridenthal, Susan Mosher Stuard, and Merry Wiesner, 265–294. Boston, 1998.

——. Women and Militant Citizenship in Revolutionary Paris." In *Rebel Daughters: Women and the French Revolution*, ed. Sara Melzer and Leslie Rabine, 79–101. Oxford, 1992.

Levy, Darline Gay, Harriet Branson Applewhite, and Mary Durham Johnson. *Women in Revolutionary Paris, 1789–1795*. Urbana, 1980.

Lévy, Marie Françoise, ed. *L'enfant, la famille et la révolution française*. Paris, 1990.

Lewis, H. D. "The Legal Status of Women in Nineteenth-Century France." *Journal of European Studies* 10 (1980): 178–188.

Lhote, Jean. "Les divorces d'émigrés et de suspects à Metz sous la révolution." In *Les femmes et la révolution française: Modes d'action et d'expression nouveaux droits—nouveaux devoirs*, ed. Marie-Françoise Brive, 191–195. Toulouse, 1989.

Livesey, James. *Making Democracy in the French Revolution.* Cambridge, Mass., 2001.

Livret, Georges, and Francis Rapp, eds. *Histoire de Strasbourg des origines à nos jours.* 4 vols. Strasbourg, 1980–1982.

Lochak, Danièle. *Etrangers: de quel droit?* Paris, 1985.

———. "Etrangers et citoyens au regard du droit." In *La citoyenneté et les changements de structures sociales et nationales de la population française,* ed. Catherine Wihtol de Wenden, 73–86. Paris, 1988.

Lottes, Gunther. "Le débat sur le divorce et la formation de l'idéologie contre-révolutionnaire." In *La révolution et l'ordre juridique privé: Rationalité ou scandale,* actes du colloque d'Orléans, 317–333. Paris, 1988.

Lucas, Colin. *The Structure of the Terror: The Example of Javogues and the Loire.* Oxford, 1975.

Lynch, Katherine. *Family, Class, and Ideology in Early Industrial France: Social Policy and the Working-Class Family, 1825–1848.* Madison, 1988.

Lyons, Martyn. *France under the Directory.* Cambridge, 1975.

———. *Napoleon Bonaparte and the Legacy of the French Revolution.* New York, 1994.

Malino, Frances. *A Jew in the French Revolution: The Life of Zalkind Hourwitz.* Oxford, 1996.

Margadant, Jo Burr. "The Duchesse de Berry and Royalist Political Culture in Postrevolutionary France." *History Workshop,* no. 43 (1997): 23–52.

Martin, Xavier. "Fonction paternelle et Code Napoléon." *Annales historiques de la révolution française,* no. 305 (1996): 465–475.

———. *Human Nature and the French Revolution: From the Enlightenment to the Napoleonic Code.* Translated by Patrick Corcoran. New York, 2001.

Mathiez, Albert. *La révolution et les étrangers: Cosmopolitisme et défense nationale.* Paris, 1918.

Mathorez, Jules Henri. *Les étrangers en France sous l'Ancien Régime.* 2 vols. Paris, 1919–1921.

Maza, Sarah. *Private Lives and Public Affairs: The Causes Célèbres of Prerevolutionary France.* Berkeley, 1993.

———. *Servants and Masters in Eighteenth-Century France: The Uses of Loyalty.* Princeton, 1983.

McClintock, Anne. *Imperial Leather: Race, Gender, and Sexuality in the Colonial Contest.* New York, 1995.

McCoy, Rebecca. "Alsatians into Frenchmen: The Construction of National Identities at Sainte-Marie-aux-Mines, 1815–1870." *French History* 12, no. 4 (1998): 429–451.

McMillan, James. *France and Women, 1789–1914: Gender, Society and Politics.* London, 2000.

Merrick, Jeffrey. "Fathers and Kings: Patriarchalism and Absolutism in Eighteenth-Century French politics." *Studies on Voltaire and the Eighteenth Century* 308 (1993): 281–303.

———. "Patriarchalism and Constitutionalism in Eighteenth-Century Parlementary Discourse." *Studies in Eighteenth-Century Culture* 20 (1990): 317–330.

Michaud, J. F., ed. *Biographie universelle, ancienne et moderne.* 45 vols. Graz, 1966–1970.

Moses, Claire Goldberg. *French Feminism in the Nineteenth Century.* Albany, N.Y., 1984.

Mulliez, Jacques. "Droit et moral conjugale: Essai sur l'histoire des relations personnelles entre époux." *Revue historique* 278 (1987): 35–106.

———. "Pater is est . . . la source juridique de la puissance paternelle du droit révolutionnaire au code civil." In Théry and Biet, 412–431.

——. Révolutionnaires, nouveaux pères? Forcement nouveaux pères! Le droit révolutionnaire de la paternité." In *La révolution et l'ordre juridique privé: Rationalité ou scandale*, actes du colloque d'Orléans, 373–398. Paris, 1988.

Murat, Pierre. "La puissance paternelle et la révolution française: Essai de régénération de l'autorité des pères." In Théry and Biet, 390–411.

Noiriel, Gérard. "French and Foreigners." In *Rethinking the French Past: Realms of Memory*, ed. Pierre Nora, 145–179. New York, 1996.

——. *The French Melting Pot: Immigration, Citizenship, and National Identity.* Minneapolis, 1996.

——. "Socio-histoire d'un concept: Les usages du mot nationalité au XIX siècle." *Genèses* 20 (1995): 4–23.

——. *La tyrannie du national: Le droit d'asile en Europe, 1793–1993.* Paris, 1991.

Nora, Pierre. "Nation." In *A Critical Dictionary of the French Revolution*, ed. François Furet and Mona Ozouf, 781–791. Cambridge, Mass., 1989.

Offen, Karen. "The New Sexual Politics of French Revolutionary Historiography." *French Historical Studies* 16, no. 4 (1990): 909–922.

——. "Women, Citizenship and Suffrage with a French Twist, 1789–1993." In *Suffrage and Beyond: International Feminist Perspectives*, ed. Caroline Daley and Melanie Nolan, 151–170. New York, 1994.

Ozouf-Marignier, Marie-Vic. *La formation des départements: La représentation du territoire française à la fin du 18e siècle.* Paris, 1989.

Pateman, Carol. *The Sexual Contract.* Stanford, 1988.

Peabody, Sue. "Colonialism's Challenge to French and English Marriage and Citizenship Law: The Case of Mary Anne Raworth." *Eighteenth-Century Life* 18 (1994): 64–91.

Perrot, Michelle. "The Family Triumphant." In *A History of Private Life*, ed. Michelle Perrot, 99–165. Cambridge, Mass., 1990.

Petiteau, Natalie, ed. *Voies nouvelles pour l'histoire du premier empire: Territoires, pouvoirs, identités.* Paris, 2003.

Phillips, Roderick. "The Attack on Celibacy in Eighteenth-Century France." *Proceedings of the Annual Meeting of the Western Society for French History* 17 (1990): 165–171.

——. "Family and Political Ideology in Eighteenth-Century France." *Proceedings of the Annual Meeting of the Western Society for French History* (1989): 361–368.

——. *Family Breakdown in Late Eighteenth-Century France: Divorces in Rouen, 1792–1803.* Oxford, 1981.

——. "Remaking the Family: The Reception of Family Law and Policy during the French Revolution." In *The French Revolution: Paris and the Provinces*, ed. Clarke Garrett et al., 64–89. Arlington, Tex., 1992.

Poovey, Mary. *Uneven Developments: The Ideological Work of Gender in Mid-Victorian England.* Chicago, 1988.

Portemer, Jean. "L'étranger dans le droit de la révolution française." In *L'étranger-foreigner*, Recueils de la Societé Jean-Bodin pour l'histoire comparative des institutions, 533–552. Paris, 1984.

Poughon, Jean-Michel. *Le code civil.* Paris, 1992.

Poussou, J. P., and F. Malino. "De la grande nation au grand empire." In *Histoire des étrangers et de l'immigration en France*, ed. Yves Lequin, 287–307. Paris, 1992.

Proctor, Candice. *Women, Equality, and the French Revolution.* New York, 1990.

Ragon, Marcel. *La législation sur les émigrés, 1789–1825.* Paris, 1904.

Rapport, Michael. "'A Languishing Branch of the Old Tree of Feudalism': The Death, Resurrection, and Final Burial of the Droit d'Aubaine in France." *French History* 14, no. 1 (2000): 13–40.

——. *Nationality and Citizenship in Revolutionary France: The Treatment of Foreigners, 1789–1799.* Oxford, 2000.
——. "Robespierre and the Universal Rights of Man, 1789–1794." *French Historical Studies* 10, no. 3 (1996): 303–333.
Reddy, William. *The Invisible Code: Honor and Sentiment in Post-Revolutionary France, 1814–1848.* Berkeley, 1997.
——. "Marriage, Honor, and the Public Sphere in Post-Revolutionary France: Separations de Corps, 1815–1848." *Journal of Modern History* 65 (1993): 437–472.
Rétat, Pierre. "Citoyen-Sujet, Civisme." In *Handbuch politisch-sozialer Grundbegriffe in Frankreich, 1680–1820,* ed. Rolf Reichardt and Hans-Jürgen Lüsebrink, 75–105. Munich, 1988.
Robin, Pierre. *Le séquestre des biens ennemis sous la révolution française.* Paris, 1929.
Robinet, Jean-François, Adolphe Robert, and J. Le Chaplain, eds. *Dictionnaire historique et biographique de la Révolution et de l'Empire.* 2 vols. Paris, 1975.
Ronsin, Francis. *Le contrat sentimental: Débats sur le mariage, le divorce de l'Ancien Régime à la Restauration.* Paris, 1990.
Ronzeaud, Pierre. *Peuple et représentations sous le règne de Louis XIV: Les représentations dans la littérature politique en France sous le règne de Louis XIV.* Aix en Provence, 1988.
Rosa, Annette. *Citoyennes: Les femmes et la révolution française.* Paris, 1988.
Rosanvallon, Pierre. *Le sacre du citoyen: Histoire du suffrage universel en France.* Paris, 1992.
Sahlins, Peter. *Boundaries: The Making of France and Spain in the Pyrenees.* Berkeley, 1989.
——. "Fictions of a Catholic France: The Naturalization of Foreigners, 1685–1787." *Representations* 47 (1994): 85–110.
——. "La nationalité avant la lettre: Les pratiques de naturalisation en France sous l'ancien régime." *Annales: Histoire, Sciences Sociales,* no. 5 (2000): 1081–1108.
——. *Unnaturally French: Foreign Citizens in the Old Regime and After.* Ithaca, 2004.
Salmon, Marylynn. "'Life, Liberty, and Dower': The Legal Status of Women after the American Revolution." In *Women, War and Revolution,* ed. Carol Ruth Berkin and Clara Lovett, 85–106. New York, 1980.
——. *Women and the Law of Property in Early America.* Chapel Hill, 1986.
Sapey, M. C. *Les étrangers en France sous l'ancien et le nouveau droit.* Paris, 1843.
Sapiro, Virginia. "Women, Citizenship, and Nationality: Immigration and Naturalization Policies in the United States." *Politics and Society* 13, no. 1 (1984): 1–23.
Schafer, Sylvia. *Children in Moral Danger and the Problem of Government in Third Republic France.* Princeton, 1997.
Schnapper, Bernard. "L'autorité domestique et les hommes politiques de la Révolution." In Théry and Biet, 221–236.
——. "Liberté, égalité, autorité: La famille devant les assemblées révolutionnaires, 1790–1800." In *L'enfant, la famille et la révolution française,* ed. Marie Françoise Lévy, 325–340. Paris, 1990.
——. "La naturalisation française au XIXe siècle: Les variations d'une politique." In *La condition juridique de l'étranger, hier et aujourd'hui. Actes du colloque organisé à Nimègue, les 9–11 mai 1988,* 209–221. Nijmegan, 1988.
Schwarzfuchs, Simon. *Du juif à l'israélite: Histoire d'une mutation, 1770–1970.* Paris, 1989.
Scott, Joan. *Only Paradoxes to Offer: French Feminists and the Rights of Man.* Cambridge, Mass., 1996.

Sewell, William. "Le citoyen/la citoyenne: Activity, Passivity, and the Revolutionary Concept of Citizenship." In *The French Revolution and the Creation of Modern Political Culture*, ed. Colin Lucas, 105–123. Oxford, 1987.

——. "Ideologies and Social Revolutions: Reflections on the French Case." *Journal of Modern History* 57 (1985): 57–96.

——. *A Rhetoric of Bourgeois Revolution: The Abbe Sieyes and What Is the Third Estate?* Durham, N.C., 1994.

——. *Work and Revolution in France: The Language of Labor from the Old Regime to 1848.* Cambridge, 1980.

Sibalis, Michel David. "Corporatism after the Corporation: The Debate on Restoring the Guilds under Napoleon and the Restoration." *French Historical Studies* 15, no. 4 (1988): 718–730.

Singham, Shanti Marie. "Betwixt Cattle and Men: Jews, Blacks, and Women and the Declaration of the Rights of Man." In *The French Idea of Freedom: The Old Regime and the Declaration of Rights of 1789*, ed. Dale Van Kley, 114–150. Stanford, 1994.

Siramy, Adrien. *Etude sur les origines et les caractères de l'autorisation maritale dans l'histoire du droit français.* Paris, 1901.

Sledziewski, Elisabeth. "Individualité et modernité: Regards sur une civilisation de l'individu." In Théry and Biet, 363–371.

——. *Révolutions du sujet.* Paris, 1989.

Smith, Jay Michael. *The Culture of Merit: Nobility, Royal Service, and the Making of Absolute Monarchy in France, 1600–1789.* Ann Arbor, 1996.

Sonenscher, Michael. *Work and Wages: Natural Law, Politics and the Eighteenth-Century French Trades.* Cambridge, 1989.

Soprani, Anne. *La Révolution et les femmes de 1789 à 1796.* Paris, 1988.

Stoler, Ann Laura. *Carnal Knowledge and Imperial Power: Race and the Intimate in Colonial Rule.* Berkeley, 2002.

Szajkowski, Zosa. "The Jewish Status in the Eighteenth Century and the 'Droit d'aubaine.'" In *Jews and the French Revolutions of 1789, 1830, and 1848*, 220–234. New York, 1970.

Texier, Alain. "Le régime politique applicable aux nobles pendant la révolution ou la dialectique de l'égalité et de la répression." In *Noblesse et révolution*, IRENA: Institut de recherches européennes sur les noblesses et aristocraties, 107–119. Les Eyzies, 1991.

Thao, Trinh Dinh. *De l'influence du mariage sur la nationalité de la femme.* Aix-en-Provence, 1929.

Théry, Irène. *Le démariage: Justice et vie privée.* Paris, 1993.

Théry, Irène, and Christian Biet, eds. *La famille, la loi, l'état de la révolution au code civil.* Paris, 1989.

Théry, Irène, and Christian Biet. "Portalis, ou l'esprit des siècles, la rhétorique du mariage dans le discours préliminaire au projet de code civil." In Théry and Biet, 221–236.

Thomas, Yan. "À Rome, pères citoyens et cité des pères, IIe siècle avant J.-C.-II siècle après J.-C." In *Histoire de la famille*, ed. Christiane Klapish-Zuber, André Burguière, Martine Segalen, and Françoise Zonabend, 195–239. Paris, 1986.

Tilly, Charles. "The Emergence of Citizenship in France and Elsewhere." *International Review of Social History* 40 (suppl. 3) (1995): 223–236.

Traer, James. "The French Family Court." *History: The Journal of the Historical Association* 59 (1974): 211–225.

——. *Marriage and the Family in Eighteenth-Century France.* Ithaca, 1980.

Troper, Michel. "La notion de citoyen sous la révolution française." In *Etudes en l'honneur de Georges Dupuis, droit public*, 302–322. Paris, 1997.

Vanel, Marguerite. *Evolution historique de la notion de français d'origine du XVI siècle au code civil*. Paris, 1944.

Varnier, Marie-Hélène, and Karin Dietrich-Chénel. "Intégration des étrangers par natu-ralisation ou admission à domicile de 1790/1814 au 10 mai 1871." 8 vols. Thèse de doctorat, Université Aix-Marseille I, 1994.

Verjus, Anne. *Le cens de la famille: Le sexe des individus politiques de la révolution de 1789 à celle de 1848*. Paris, 2002.

——. Les femmes dans les lois électorales de la Restauration (1817 et 1820)." In *La démocratie à la française ou les femmes indésirables (1793–1993)*, ed. Eliane Viennot. Paris, 1996, 167–180.

——. "Vote familialiste et vote familial: Contribution à l'étude du processus d'individu-alisation des femmes dans la première partie du XIXe siècle." *Genèses* 31 (1998): 29–47.

Vidalenc, Jean. *Les émigrés français, 1789–1825*. Caen, 1963.

Villers, Robert. "La condition des étrangers en France dans les trois derniers siècles de la monarchie." In *L'étranger-foreigner*, Recueils de la Société Jean-Bodin pour l'his-toire comparative des institutions, 139–150. Paris, 1984.

Vogler, Bernard. "La vie économique et les hiérarchies sociales." In *Histoire de Stras-bourg des origines à nos jours*. Vol. 3: *Strasbourg de la Guerre de Trente ans à Napoléon*, ed. Georges Livet and Francis Rapp, 187–250. Strasbourg, 1980–1982.

Wahnich, Sophie. *L'impossible citoyen: L'étranger dans le discours de la révolution française*. Paris, 1997.

Waldinger, Renée, Philip Dawson, and Isser Woloch, eds. *The French Revolution and the Meaning of Citizenship*. Westport, Conn., 1993.

Waltz, Waldo Emerson. *The Nationality of Married Women*. Urbana, 1937.

Waresquiel, Emmanuel de, and Benoît Yvert. *Histoire de la restauration, 1814–1830: Naissance de la France moderne*. Paris, 1996.

Weber, Eugen. *Peasants into Frenchmen: The Modernization of Rural France, 1870–1914*. Stanford, 1976.

Weil, Georges. *L'Alsace française de 1789 à 1870*. Paris, 1916.

Weil, Patrick. *La France et ses étrangers: L'aventure d'une politique d'immigration, 1938–1991*. Paris, 1991.

——. *Qu'est-ce qu'un Français? Histoire de la nationalité française depuis la Révolu-tion*. Paris, 2002.

Wells, Charlotte. *Law and Citizenship in Early Modern France*. Baltimore, 1995.

Wildenthal, Lora. "Race, Gender, and Citizenship in the German Colonial Empire." In *Tensions of Empire: Colonial Cultures in a Bourgeois World*, ed. Frederick Cooper and Ann Laura Stoler, 263–283. Berkeley, 1997.

Woloch, Isser. "Corporate Reorganization and the Professions." In *The French Revolu-tionary Research Collection*, 12 vols. ed. Colin Lucas, 9: 1–4. New York, 1990–1995.

——. *The New Regime: Transformations of the French Civic Order, 1789–1820s*. New York, 1994.

Woolf, Stuart. "French Civilization and Ethnicity in the Napoleonic Empire." *Past and Present*, no. 124 (1989): 96–120.

——. *Napoleon's Integration of Europe*. London, 1991.

Index